Civilization

The Age of Masked Gods and Disguised Kings

Abdullah Öcalan

Civilization

The Age of Masked Gods and Disguised Kings

Manifesto for a Democratic Civilization

Volume I

International Initiative Edition

new-compass.net

Civilization: The Age of Masked Gods and Disguised Kings
Manifesto for a Democratic Civilization: Volume I
2015 © International Initiative Edition
Second Printing, 2015

ISBN 978-82-93064-42-8
ISBN 978-82-93064-43-5 (ebook)
ISBN 978-82-93064-37-4 (hardcover)

Original title: *Uygarlık: Maskeli Tanrılar ve Örtük Krallar Çağı,*
Demokratik Uygarlık Manifestosu, Birinci Kitap
Translation: Havin Guneser
Edited by: Riekie Harm and Arjen Harm

Published by New Compass Press
Grenmarsvegen 12
N–3912 Porsgrunn
Norway
new-compass.net

And:
International Initiative Edition
"Freedom for Abdullah Öcalan—Peace in Kurdistan"
P.O.Box 100 511
D-50445 Cologne
Germany
freedom-for-ocalan.com
info@freedom-for-ocalan.com

Design and layout by Eirik Eiglad
Cover Artwork: Ayşe Kazcı, "Unnamed," detail.

Contents

Volume I

Editorial Note by International Initiative   7

Preface by David Graeber   11

Introduction   21

Section 1: **On Method and the Regime of Truth**   32

Section 2: **The Main Sources of Civilization**   70

The Contribution of the Taurus-Zagros Arc to Humanity   71
Problems Associated with the Expansion of Aryan Culture and Language   73
Interpreting the Evolution of Social Structures in the Fertile Crescent   80
At the Skirts of the Mountains   89

Section 3: **Urban Civilized Society**   94

An Analysis of Sumerian Society   95
An Analysis of Civilized Society   109
Problems Associated with the Expansion of Civilized Society   129
Stages of Civilized Society and Problems Associated with Resistance   165
Final Remarks   197

Notes   199
Index   208

Publications by Abdullah Öcalan in English

Manifesto for a Democratic Civilization
II: *Capitalism: The Age of Unmasked Gods and Naked Kings* (New Compass, 2017)
I: *Civilization: The Age of Masked Gods and Disguised Kings* (New Compass, 2015)

Prison Writings:
III: *The Road Map to Negotiations* (Mesopotamien, 2011)
II: *The PKK and the Kurdish Question in the 21st Century* (Pluto Press and Transmedia, 2011)
I: *The Roots of Civilisation* (Pluto Press, 2007)

The Political Thought of Abdullah Öcalan (Pluto Press, 2017)
Declaration on the Democratic Solution of the Kurdish Question (Mesopotamien, 1999)

Pamphlets:
Democratic Nation (2016)
Liberating Life: Woman's Revolution (2013)
Democratic Confederalism (2011)
War and Peace in Kurdistan (2008)
The Third Domain: Reconstructing Liberation (2003)

All of Abdullah Öcalan's English-language books are published with the cooperation of International Initiative Edition. Further information about Öcalan's books can be found at www.ocalan-books.com.

Editorial Note

By International Initiative

We are happy to publish the first of five volumes of what the author describes as his most important work. The publication of this book occurs in a period when hopes for a peaceful resolution to the Kurdish Question have been rekindled.

During the 10 years in which we have published Öcalan's prison writings in English, his publicly acknowledged position has changed considerably. After his death sentence was handed down in 1999, few non-Kurds believed that he would ever again play a significant role in Kurdish politics. We firmly believed, however, as we stated in our founding document, that Öcalan "is still regarded as the undisputed leader by a majority of the Kurdish people," and that "it seems reasonable to assume that the solution of the Kurdish question in Turkey will be closely linked to his fate in the future. Many Kurds see him as a safeguard for peace and democratization."

After his imprisonment, Öcalan intensified his efforts to find a lasting solution to the Kurdish issue, even in those years when the conflict did not make headlines. His perseverance and willingness to search for creative solutions has brought him the deep respect even of his opponents, the officials of the Turkish state that hold him captive. During those years, he emerged as the uncontested leader of negotiations for the Kurdish side in what is called the "solution process." Now he is widely regarded as one of the most important driving forces for peace and democratization in Turkey and Kurdistan.

During these last months, there has been tangible movement in the talks between Öcalan, the PKK, and the Turkish state. The Turkish government is now closer than ever to entering into actual negotiations with Öcalan and the PKK. While the whole process is still tenuous and fragile, hope is again blossoming this spring.

Paradoxically, Öcalan, like the other prisoners on Imrali Island, is still held in solitary confinement. Despite ongoing talks with different government bodies, he has not been allowed to see his lawyers since June 2011. He is still not able to write or receive letters, or to make any phone-calls. The paradox of a negotiation leader in isolation is still not resolved.

The conditions of solitary confinement are harsh for a thinker like Öcalan. At times, isolation meant that he did not even have pen or paper, and that he was not allowed to have any books in the cell. These limitations did not stop him from penning down his thoughts. Öcalan authors his hand-written manuscripts in one go. Afterwards, he does not have the opportunity to revise them or to look at the typed manuscripts. Due to these conditions he is unable to cite his sources. Most of the footnotes to this text have therefore been added by the editors and translator. We have done so to the best of our knowledge, but may have missed some allusions and implicit references. Some comments in the text have also been moved to footnotes where deemed necessary. Most of the difficulties in translating and editing were due to the fact it was impossible to communicate with the author.

Despite these limitations, Öcalan's writings have broad appeal and a huge practical impact. His books reach a wide readership in Kurdistan and elsewhere, and they inspire countless people to struggle for freedom and a better society. Recently—and very visibly—the revolutionary changes in Rojava and the resistance in Kobanê have been spurred by Öcalan's concepts and ideas.

We are confident that the years ahead will see further progress on the road to peace and freedom. In a worldwide signature campaign, activists recently collected 10,328,623 signatures for "Freedom for Abdullah Öcalan and the political prisoners in Turkey." This demand is absolutely necessary for the peace process. As Nelson Mandela famously stated while he was in prison: "Only free men can negotiate. A prisoner cannot enter into contracts." We are certain that the demand for Abdullah Öcalan's freedom will ring ever louder—until it is finally met, and he can join his friends and comrades in the quest to build a truly democratic civilization.

International Initiative
"Freedom for Abdullah Öcalan–Peace in Kurdistan"
Cologne, March 2015

Preface

By David Graeber

Marx believed it was imagination that made us human: unlike bees, architects first imagine the houses they would like to build, and only then set about actually constructing them. In a sense, the great question driving all revolutionary thought is simply this: if we can do this with our houses, why can't we do it with the social order as a whole? Because after all, how many of us, were we to simply imagine a society we would like to live in, would come up with anything remotely like the ones that currently exist? Yet almost every serious effort to proceed like the architect, to simply imagine what a just society should be like, and then set about creating it, seems to lead to frustration or disaster.

One might well argue that this is why we have social theory. The very idea of a social science is born from the ruins of revolutionary projects. We imagine the social equivalents of floating palaces and Tatlin's Towers, we try to build them, and find ourselves watching in dismay as they crash and crumble all around us. Surely, there must be some social equivalents to the laws of physics and gravitation that we were unaware of. As the positivists argued in the wake of the French revolution, or Marx when he wrote Capital in wake of the failed revolutions of 1848, perhaps if we understood those laws, we can also understand how to avoid such pitfalls in the future. Yet every attempt to apply such a scientific approach to human society—whether by right or left, whether it takes the form of neoclassical economics or historical materialism—has proved if anything even more disastrous.

One problem—at least, this is what a lot of revolutionaries around the world began to realize by the 1990s—is that we were working with a decidedly limited notion of imagination. After all, even architects don't build their designs out of nothing, and when they do, most would prefer not to live in the sort of structures they create. And some of most of the most vital, most creative, most imaginative revolutionary movements of the dawn of the new millennium—the Zapatistas of Chiapas are only the most obvious, perhaps—have been those that, simultaneously, root themselves most strongly in a deep traditional past. There was a growing recognition, in revolutionary circles, that freedom, tradition, and the imagination have always been—and presumably, always will be, entangled in one another in ways that we do not completely understand. Our theoretical tools are inadequate.

Perhaps the only thing we can do at this point is to return to the past and start over.

In such circumstances, one might say, the more ambitious the thinker, the further back into the past one is likely to reach. If so, Öcalan's work, over the last fifteen years of his captivity, has been nothing if not ambitious. True, he carefully avoids taking on the role of the prophet. The latter would be easy enough, under the circumstances: to speak ex cathedra in epochal declarations like some latter-day Zarathustra. Clearly he does not wish to do this. At the same time, a radical by temperament, neither does he want to sit at anybody else's feet. He is never quite satisfied even with the thinkers he most admires—Bookchin, Braudel, Foucault; rather, he wishes to speak, as a self-proclaimed amateur, about a history and social science that does not currently exist, but itself, perhaps, can only be imagined. What would a sociology of freedom actually be like? One can only guess. Surely, existing social theory has confined itself above all to those dimensions of social life in which we are not free, in which we can at least imagine that our actions are predetermined by forces beyond our control.

Above all else, Öcalan's intellectual project is driven by a recognition that the revolutionary left's embrace of positivism, the notion that it would even be possible to create this sort of science of society, has been the "disease of modernity," the religion of its technocrats and officials, and, for the revolutionary left, an unmitigated disaster—since it means nothing to those classes that actually create things:

> It is with pain and anger that I have to admit that the noble struggle that has raged for the past one hundred and fifty years was carried out on the basis of a vulgar, materialist positivism doomed to failure. The class struggle underlies this approach. However, the class—contrary to what they believe—is not the workers and laborers resisting enslavement, but the petit bourgeoisie who has long ago surrendered and became part of modernity. Positivism is the ideology that has formed this class's perception and underlies its meaningless reaction against capitalism.

Even worse, such an ideology ensures any revolutionary experiment can only be instantly reincorporated into the logic of capitalist modernity, as past revolutions have invariably done.

How does one begin to go about developing an alternative—one that would do justice to the sense of meaning, mystery, creativity, even divinity, that escapes the calculations of the traders and bureaucrats, but so clearly informs the daily existence of the majority of the laboring classes of this earth? We can only begin by turning back to history, to try to understand how this situation came about to begin with. But this, in turn, means that to a certain extent, we must be dealing in myth. I should hasten to add: here I mean myth not in its (positivist) colloquial sense of "story that isn't true," but rather, in the sense that any historical account that doesn't simply describe events but organizes them in such a way to tell a larger, meaningful story, thus necessarily takes on a mythic character. If your history is not in some sense mythic, then it's meaningless. In this sense, there's obviously nothing wrong with creating myths—it's hard to imagine how an effective political movement could *not* do so. Positivists do it too. The key thing is that one is honest about what one is doing while one is doing it.

Here Öcalan is nothing if not honest. Disarmingly so. His own sense of greater meaning, he explains, traces back into his own well of mythic imagery from his childhood beside the Zagros mountains, once haunts of Dionysus' Maenads, from his lingering guilt at tearing the heads off birds to his first experience of the divine in the children's play of village girls temporarily set free from patriarchal authority. Let us assume, he effectively says, there is something universal here. That such experiences speak to the historical tragedy of a region whose women once made unprecedented contributions to human civilization, but which has ever since been reduced to a bloody plaything of empire:

> Upper Mesopotamia became a region of battle and continuously changed hands between the Roman Empire and the two Persian Iranian Empires of the Parthians and the Sassanids. It thus became a region which was no longer a source of civilisations but a region of destruction. … It is one of the most tragic developments of history that it has always been subjected to incursion, occupation, annexation and exploitation by other forces. It is like the fate suffered by women: although she has achieved the biggest cultural revolution, she has been violated the most.

In a sense, one can say that Öcalan here begins with that sense of outrage that has sparked a thousand patriarchal rebellions through history ("we are being treated like women!") and instead concludes that, if we do not wish to reproduce the same endlessly destructive pattern, we must turn the logic entirely on its head.

How to do so? Well, over the course of the twentieth century, I think it's fair to say that there have been two great civilizational narratives that have managed to capture the popular imagination, and thus, that have had profound political effects.

The first actually traces back to Enlightenment stories about the origins of social inequality. In its contemporary variant, it runs something like this: Once upon a time, human beings lived in happy little egalitarian bands of hunter/gatherers. Innocent of power and dominance, they lacked any real social structure at all. Things began to go downhill with the invention of agriculture, which created the possibility of storable surpluses and invidious distinctions of property, but the real fundamental break came with the emergence of cities, and hence, civilization—that is, "civilization" in the literal sense, which simply means people living in cities. The concentration of population and resources urbanism made possible was held to inevitably also mean the rise of ruling classes capable of seizing control of those surpluses, hence, states, slavery, conquering armies, ecological devastation, but also, at the same time, writing, science, philosophy, and organized religion. Civilization thus came as a package. One could embrace it as inevitable, accept violent inequalities as the price of human progress, or one could dream of someday returning to some new version of the old Edenic state—either by revolutionary transformation, technological progress, or, in some radical versions, by encouraging industrial collapse and returning to being actual hunter/ gatherers again. But civilization itself was a single entity, the inevitable outgrowth of the original sin of domesticating animals and plants, and its essence could not be modified, just embraced, or rejected.

The other story was quite different. Call it the Myth of the Aryan invaders. Here the story begins: once upon a time, there was a matriarchal civilization that stretched across the Fertile Crescent and beyond. In just about all hunter/gatherer societies, women are the experts in plant life; logically, then, it was assumed that women must have invented agriculture, and that this is the reason for the extraordinary emphasis on goddess-figures, and representations of powerful women more generally, during the first five thousand years or so of agrarian life. Here the rise of cities was not considered to be inherently problematic—Minoan Crete, a Bronze-Age urban civilization whose language we cannot read, but whose art lacks any representations of male figures of authority of any kind—was often held out as the peaceful, graceful, artistic culmination of this Neolithic matriarchal order. The real point of rupture came not with the rise of cities but with the incursions of patriarchal, nomadic or semi-nomadic invaders, such as the Semitic tribes who descended on the Tigris and Euphrates from the surrounding deserts, but even more, the Indo-European or Aryan cattle-people who were assumed to have spread out somewhere in what's now Southern Russia to lands as far away as Ireland and the Ganges valley, bringing their languages, their warrior aristocracies, their heroic epics, and sacrificial ritual. Again, one could identify with either side. For many poets, romantics, revolutionaries, and feminists, this was the wistful dream of a lost, pacifistic, collectivist paradise. Imperialists tended to turn the whole story on its head: British colonial officials, for instance, were notorious for trying to identify such "manly warrior races" to favor, over the supposedly passive, "effeminate" peasants they were forced to administer. And as in so many things, the Nazis simply applied colonial logic back to Europe again. Hitler, notoriously, identified entirely with the patriarchal invaders, reframing it as the overcoming of inferior womanly stock by their virile natural overlords.

What Öcalan is doing here is taking the same pieces and putting them together in quite a different way. In doing so, he is taking the lead from the unique situation of his native Kurdistan, in the mountainous northern fringes of that very Fertile Crescent where agriculture seems to have first emerged. Noting that "Ari" in Kurdish means "related to earth, place, field," he argues that the original Indo-Europeans, or "Aryans," were not pastoral invaders at all, but the inventors of agriculture, and of the Neolithic culture which effectively created much of the everyday life we still take for granted, our most basic habits in terms of food, shelter, our sense of spirituality and community. This was a revolutionary transformation of human life and as Öcalan stresses, it was a revolution created above all by women free of patriarchal authority. Such was its obvious appeal that it spread across the world, often taking Indo-European languages with it, not by migration, but by the sheer power of example, and the cosmopolitan flow of individuals and hospitality that this new and largely peaceful agrarian world made possible. The counterforce here is not the nomads, but again, the rise of cities, and particularly the ideological ground laid by the Sumerian priesthood, who managed to introduce the subordination of women, and the seeds of the state, mystifying ideology, the factory system and the brothel, all at the same time. The predatory elites, often of nomadic extraction, only then imposed themselves on a structure that already existed, ensuring that the rest of history would also be marked by endless, spectacular, pointless, wars.

This is what Öcalan calls "civilization"—an order that presents itself as gentility, moderation, legality, and reason, but whose actual essence is rape, terror, treachery, cynicism, and war. Much of the conflict of the last five thousand years has been between the violence of this originally urban system of human exploitation, and the values that still exist in the enduring Neolithic bedrock of our collective existence. Here his analysis of the role of ideology—and particularly, religion—takes a number of surprising turns.

It is precisely—if paradoxically—because of the revolutionary nature of social change that the logic of revealed religions make intuitive sense. Rather than the positivist sensibilities which—for all its disavowals since the crash of Fabian dreams in the First World War—still assumes history is mainly characterized by progress, that social change is normal and relatively incremental and benevolent phenomenon—since it really can't imagine anything else, real history is more typically marked by intense moments of social imagination, the creation of patterns of life that then doggedly remain with us, in relatively the same form, for millennia thereafter. The Neolithic revolution, as Gordon Childe originally dubbed it, involved the invention of patterns of life—everything from techniques of animal husbandry or putting cheese on bread to the habits of sitting on pillows or chairs—that remained, afterwards, fixtures of human existence. The same is true of our basic social categories like domestic life, art, politics, religion: "generally speaking, the social realities created in the Fertile Crescent during the Neolithic are still in existence today." In that sense we are all still living in the Neolithic. What the holy books like the Avesta, the Bible or Koran teach, then—that the truths that underpin our lives were the product of moments of divine revelation long ago— appeal to ordinary farmers, workmen and tradespeople not because they mystify the conditions of their existence, or not primarily so; rather, they make intuitive sense because, in many very real ways, what they are saying is true—or more true than the alternate rationalist theology of the bureaucrats. In a larger sense, religion, ideology, "metaphysics," becomes both the domain in which one can speak truths that cannot be expressed otherwise, but also a battlefield for struggles over meaning whose political implications could not be more profound. What is one to make of the prominence of Mother Goddess figures like Ishtar or Cybele in times of patriarchal domination? Are they not, Öcalan argues, both expressions of, and weapons in, battles over the meaning of gender relations, and the actual power of real-life men and women, whose very existence might otherwise have been entirely lost?

Academics are snobbish creatures, they tend to dismiss anyone infringing on their territory unless they can be reduced to an object of study in their own right. No doubt many will object: how much of this really stands up? Considering the circumstances under which the book was written, I'd say the achievement here is quite impressive. Abdullah Öcalan seems to have done a better job writing with the extremely limited resources allowed him by his jailers than authors like Francis Fukuyama or Jared Diamond did with access to the world's finest research libraries. True, much of the picture defies the current wisdom of professional archeologists, anthropologists, and historians. But often this is a good thing, and anyway, this wisdom is itself in a process of continual transformation. The past is always changing. The one thing we *can* be sure of is that fifty years from now, much that is now accepted without question will have gone by the boards.

Still, in one way, this study does smack up against what has been a particular point of scholarly resistance when it embraces the idea of early matriarchy. Most theories ebb and flow with intellectual fashion; there's a generational pattern where theories once widely embraced (Karl Polanyi or Moses Finley's ideas of the ancient economy are nice examples) come to be universally rejected, then once again revived. In the case of theories of matriarchy, or even ones that granted women a uniquely exalted status in Neolithic societies, this has not happened. To even speak of such matters has become something of a taboo. In part, no doubt, it is because the idea continues to be so eagerly embraced by precisely the tendencies within feminism that academics tend to take least seriously, but even so, resistance is so stubborn it's hard to avoid the conclusion there's some kind of profound patriarchal bias here at play.

(It is a telling sign that the most common objections here make little logical sense. The most common is an appeal to the ethnographic record: while Neolithic and Chalcolithic art, not to mention Minoan art, does seem to represent a social order in which women hold almost all authoritative positions, there is little or no evidence for similar societies in the anthropological literature. True. But the ethnographic record also contains no evidence for democratically organized city-states like ancient Athens, and we know that they existed, indeed, that such city-states were fairly common in the late Iron Age, before largely disappearing around 300 BCE. But even if one does insist on ethnographic parallels, the logic doesn't work. Because another common argument is that the existence of a material culture in which virtually all representations of powerful figures are female demonstrates nothing in itself, since these might simply be mythological scenes, and actual social life might have been organized entirely differently. However, no one has ever managed to produce an example of a patriarchal society in which artistic representations focus nearly exclusively on images of powerful women, mythical or otherwise, either. So either way, we are dealing with something ethnographically unprecedented. The fact that almost all scholars, however, take that to mean we must conclude that men were running things, strikes me as a clear an example of patriarchal bias as it is possible to find.)

Like anthropologists, archeologists and historians have developed the annoying habit of writing only for each other. Most don't even write anything that would be meaningful for scholars in other disciplines, let alone for anyone outside the academy. This is unfortunate, because in recent decades, information has begun to accumulate that could, potentially, throw all our received understandings into disarray. Almost all the key assumptions of the civilizational narrative we have been telling, in one way or another, since the time of Rousseau, appear to be based on false assumptions—ones that are simply factually incorrect. Hunter/gatherers for instance do not live exclusively in tiny bands, and they are not necessarily all that egalitarian (many seem to have had seasonal patterns of creating hierarchies, and then tearing them down again.) Early cities, in contrast, were often startling egalitarian. Before the birth of the ziggurat system to which Öcalan draws attention, there was perhaps a millennium of egalitarian urbanism about which we know very little. But the implications are potentially extraordinary—particularly because, once you know what to look for, egalitarian experiments begin to appear everywhere across human history. "Civilization" or even what we call "the state" are not single entities that come as a package, take it or leave it, but uncomfortable amalgams of elements that may now be in the process of drifting apart. All of these processes of rethinking will have enormous political implications. In some areas I suspect it will soon be evident that we have been asking all the wrong questions. To take just one example: It is almost universally assumed that creating equality or democracy in a small group is relatively easy, but that to operate on a larger scale would create enormous difficulties. It's becoming clear that this simply isn't true. Egalitarian cities, even regional confederacies, are historically commonplace. Egalitarian households are not. It's the small scale, the level of gender relations, household servitude, the kind of relations that contain at once the deepest forms of structural violence and the greatest intimacy, where the most difficult work of creating a free society will have to take place.

In this context, it seems to me that Öcalan is asking precisely the right questions, or many of them, at a moment when doing so could hardly be more important. Let us only hope that as political movements learn the lessons of history, as new social theories are born, as they will inevitably be, and as our knowledge of the past is likewise revolutionized, and that the author of this book will be released from his present captivity and able to participate as a free man.

Introduction

After the betrayal of friendship by the Greek nation-state and her relationship with the Republic of Turkey being added to the equation of interests, I was handed over to the USA (thus, the CIA). When I was first taken to the Imrali Prison, I was met by the then president of the European Committee for the Prevention of Torture (CPT), Silvia Casale. She said, "You will stay in this prison and we shall try to find some kind of solution under the supervision of the Council of Europe." I was thus chained to the rocks of Imrali; doomed to live a destiny more severe than that of the mythological Prometheus.

It is important to discuss how and why I left Syria, as this started the chain of events that eventually led to my abduction. My departure from Syria resulted from the contradiction that arose yet again from the value I put on friendship and Israel's Kurdish policies. After its founding, shortly after World Word II, Israel tried to patronage the Kurdish issue but was so sensitive that she had no tolerance for the alternative solution to the Kurdish issue proposed by our movement that became more influential.

Our proposed alternative did not serve the interest of Israel. I should not, however, deny their efforts; MOSSAD *did* indirectly invite me to work with them on their own solution. But I was not open to, nor desired, this—neither politically nor morally.

On the other hand, the Syrian-Arab government never wished to surpass their tactical alliance with the PKK leadership. An alliance with the PKK had been part of Syria's answer to the threats that had been coming from Turkey since 1958 and Turkey's extreme pro-Israel tendencies.[1] The PKK did not object to such a tactical relationship. (No one wanted to see that this relationship could lead to an alternative Kurdish policy; thus, the efforts of the Turkish administrations were ineffective.) But, seeing that Hafez al-Assad obtained the Syrian leadership due to the power struggle between the USA and the USSR, Syria was in no position to maintain any of its tactical alliances after the disintegration of the Soviet Union.

Even this short reminder shows that, although political pressure by the USA and military pressure by Turkey undoubtedly played a role, the real power that forced me out of Syria was Israel. It should not be forgotten that Israel and Turkey already had clandestine agreements in the 1950s, and with the second "anti-terror" agreement of 1996 the anti-PKK alliance between the USA, Israel and the Turkish Republic was complete.[2]

Another critical factor was the anti-PKK coalition which the Turkish Republic had entered into with the Patriotic Union of Kurdistan (PUK) and the Kurdistan Democratic Party (KDP), both of whom already had relations with the USA and Israel; in other words, with the Kurdish Federal Assembly and its administration established in 1992.

The combination of all these adverse factors led me to leave Syria in 1998. Besides, I knew that it was time to leave. I had already been in Syria too long, lured by the political developments around Kurdistan and the friendship that I had hoped would result in strategic cooperation. I have to admit that high-ranking officials in the Syrian government had warned me about its disadvantages. Yet, I did not want to give up my belief in the power of friendship and cooperation between peoples. For the same reason I left Syria for Greece. I wanted to develop ties of friendship with the Greek people, to learn from its classical culture and its tragic history.

My only alternative was to go off into the mountains of Kurdistan. Two factors made me decide to not do this. First, my presence would attract massive military force. This would lead to serious damage to the civilians in the area and my comrades; it could also lead to the armed struggle becoming the exclusive means of obtaining a solution for the Kurdish question. Second, it was a pressing need to educate the youth joining our organization.

In short, the official and unofficial claims in Turkey of "we have him cornered" and "see the results we have obtained" do not altogether reflect reality. Notwithstanding this, Turkey is still trying to ensnare Iran and Iraq in the same way it did Syria. The outcome of Turkey's alliance with Syria and Iran can also not be predicted. If the antagonisms between the USA, EU, Israel, Iran, Russia and China intensify, will the Turkish Republic be ready for the consequences?

My three-month peregrination between Athens, Moscow and Rome was not without value, though. This adventure led me to understand the essence of capitalist modernity—the basis on which this defense is built—despite its many masks and disguises. If not for this insight, I would either have been a primitive nationalist aspiring for a nation-state, or I would have ended up in a classical left-wing movement. Thus, my change in thought and policy can be ascribed to this forced adventure.

It has now become clear to me: *The real power of capitalist modernity is not its money or its weapons; its real power lies in its ability to suffocate all utopias—including the socialist utopia which is the last and the most powerful of all—with its liberalism.* Unless this power of liberalism is analyzed thoroughly, no ideology will escape being the humble servant of capitalism. There is hardly anyone who analyzed capitalism as comprehensively as Marx did, or focused on the state and revolution as much as Lenin did. However, it has become much clearer today that, despite claiming to be its negation, the Marxist-Leninist tradition's contribution to capitalism in terms of material and meaning was significant.

To help channel humanity into its natural stream, we need to understand the individual and the society brought about by liberalism. (I shall explain this in full detail later.) Moreover, for me to understand my own fate, I need to understand the capitalist modernity behind the representative of the Council of Europe who welcomed me to the Imrali Prison. The whole odyssey was planned by Israel, the USA, EU, and a disintegrated Soviet Russia. The Syrian, Greek and Turkish governments had a secondary role; they only lent a helping, bureaucratic hand.[3] The way I was captured demonstrated that the capitalist modernity, of which the USA is the world leader, is a system with no inhibition to oppress and abuse.

It is not as if I did not understand the way the Turkish state operated. On the contrary. At the time, there existed a death decree for Kurdishness. I had a choice: I was either going to resist—to not give up my honor, my humanness, my Kurdishness—or I was going to deny who I am and vanish into obscure captivity. In the beginning I was alone and very weak, but I resisted. I am not about to enter into a discourse on this; those who have witnessed it will attest that I have struggled well. I do not feel any anger either.

But I *am* angry that I could not transcend the concepts and the ideology underlying the Western capitalist system. The system we are confronted with is supposedly based on human rights. In reality though, it is an elite group manipulating and exploiting the rest of humanity and nature, unleashing war whenever that is in their interest. They are the ones dictating the roles the rest of humanity must play.

Although the society I was born into has not really progressed beyond Neolithic culture, it has readily integrated the negative effects of the different stages of civilization. Capitalist modernity combined with the strictest and most conservative traditions of the Middle East resulted in our society being besieged by the ideal of ethnic nationalism and nation-statehood. This is in fact the dominant ideology in our society and the most difficult to disentangle ourselves from. Combined with the ever-present possibility for violence, this ideal enslaves us all in an opportunity-less life before even being born. Nevertheless, I did not leave Turkey in the cause of "glorious resistance." I was in fact looking for some breathing space for the resolution of the national question to which we were devoted through some dogmatic left-wing analysis. The PKK stood no chance of surviving in the Middle East if it did not take advantage of the vacuums in the system. Still, the fact that the PKK has been able to wage an armed struggle was important because of the implications thereof. For the Kurds it has meant an increased politicization. The fact that the Kurds were able to progressively free themselves from the classic collaborators meant that, for the first time, the alternative of freedom had been felt and understood.

This is exactly why this movement has never been embraced by the so-called "modern" nation-states (states that in reality resemble the despotic regimes of medieval times); why the Kurdish collaborators, the nation-states of the region, and the imperialist world leaders colluded in branding the PKK a "terrorist organization." The fallacy that the conquering ideology of Islam and the nationalist ideology of liberalism had wiped out and excluded the Kurds from history was destroyed by the free Kurd—a free Kurdish individual and a free Kurdish society. In fact, it is not me but this free Kurdishness that serves the sentence of solitary confinement in this single-inmate island prison. That this sentence is not about the individual Abdullah Öcalan is clear from the imprisonment policies implemented daily during the nine years I have been in isolation on Imrali—they are not the policies that are applied in the average Turkish prison.

I came to understand that Turkey cannot decide to either fight or to make peace in its own name. The role that has been assigned to Turkey is to be the vulgar gendarme, the watchdog and the prison guard of all Middle Eastern peoples in order to make them more susceptible to the oppression and exploitation of the capitalist system. Hence, stable Turkish and Anatolian societies—both in and outside Europe—are of critical importance to the system. Turkey's relations with NATO and the EU should be understood in terms of these policies.

The above should suffice to illustrate the impossibility of a meaningful defense before the court without a deep understanding of capitalist modernity. It should also be clear that a meaningful defense couldn't be constructed solely on the basis of law. A superficial political and strategic approach will not expose why the "retrial" judgment of the court was not implemented.[4] Such a retrial would also have had important implications for clarifying what a free Kurdishness-solution would entail.

The Imrali trials were nothing but pretense. I responded to it with my defense speech titled "Declaration on the Democratic Solution of the Kurdish Question" and then later with the comprehensive submissions I made to the European Court of Human Rights titled *Roots of Civilisation*.[5]

My work *In Defense of a People* was in essence an attempt to make true democracy and justice understandable.[6] These defenses, however, aim not only to problematize capitalist modernity and the need to surpass this modernity; they also aim to determine the political system of democratization and its link to freedom as an alternative solution.

Everything about the Imrali trial was a showcase and, to the finest detail, was planned in advance—the date on which the judgment would be announced, the choice of the judge, the duration of the trial and how the media would be used. I was not given the opportunity to defend myself properly. The whole plan was to use me as best as possible in relation to the Kurdish question and all else had to serve this end. The Kenya ordeal was nothing but a violation of European, Kenyan and Turkish law, and the threat of the death penalty was held over me to attain political results. The plan was to scare me. Under these circumstances the only thing I could do was to make as big a political contribution as possible. For this reason my defense rested on political argumentation. Besides, there was a need to search for deep-rooted answers to the mistakes that led to this outcome. This is what I tried to do. This was the only way to have a minimal role in the game of the conspirators and to contribute to the freedom struggle.

I must admit that I expected that the European Court of Human Rights would find my arrest to be unlawful. Only this verdict would have led to a fair trial. But it was not made. The court later had no choice but to determine that it was an unfair trial. After a prolonged wait for a fair trial the Committee of Ministers of the Council of Europe scandalously agreed to close the case, probably in return for important political concessions from the Turkish government. No one questioned the Turkish government's handling of the judgment of the court; in the name of a retrial, Ankara 11th Assize Court and Istanbul 14th Assize Court unilaterally upheld the previous judgment.[7] My defense lawyers have taken this situation back before the European Court of Human Rights. It will be interesting to see the Court's stance towards its own judgment. I had begun to prepare a proper defense for the retrial only to discover that the trial would be nothing but a showcase.

I also came to a better understanding about the degree of communication and cooperation between the USA, EU and Turkish Republic in relation to the PKK, me, and the Kurdish question in general. Turkey, in return for comprehensive economic concessions, was allowed to eliminate the Kurdish question in Turkey and it seems that Turkey will conditionally support the construction of the Kurdish Federal state in Iraq. It is clear that there was much discussion to this end. In fact, concessions and cooperation with the USA were conducted openly in the case of my arrest, the elimination of the Kurdish question in Turkey and the declaration of the PKK as a "terrorist organization." The IMF and the EU's Copenhagen Criteria are nothing more than a pretext for disguising clandestine cooperation.

Frankly, I was not expecting such foul play and questionable attitude on the part of the EU institutions. This outcome led me to deeply question the human rights and democratic norms of the EU. I reached the conclusion that the problems we face are very deeply rooted and thus require equally deep solutions. Undoubtedly, the EU has a progressive approach to human rights and democracy and offers hope to the rest of the world. However, the capitalist modernity at its roots has tied it down so firmly that one becomes pessimistic about its future.

The Russian revolutionaries believed that the victory of their revolution was guaranteed if there would be revolution in at least a part of Europe. But their expectations were not realized. On the contrary, the European liberal counterrevolution caused the disintegration of not only Soviet Russia but of the entire system it led. Europe takes the same approach to the democratic revolutions of today. If we want to prevent a similar fate for them, the European ideal of what constitutes democracy could not be our sole model. In an age where global capital is so highly developed, to pursue global democratization would be more realistic. In a paradigm of global democratization, the democracy, human rights and freedom of Europe would make a more meaningful contribution.

I realized that, without a thorough and detailed analysis of capitalist modernity as a basis for concepts like *democratic republic, society* and *nation,* I would simply end up being superficial. However, I am confident that my subsequent writings will contain the necessary depth. I plan to develop these ideas in several books.

I have broadly outlined why my "re-trial" did not take place, but there is a need for a detailed analysis. In my previous defense, I took great care to uncover the origins of the main issues. Although excessive reductionism can result in serious misinterpretation in our analysis of modernity, we have to run the risks. I have tried to minimize the dangers presented by reductionism by handling main sections in full.

Following on this foreword, is a discourse on method and the regime of truth. Since *method* is the accepted way of analyzing and investigating a specific issue, it should be beneficial to first define the modus operandi employed in the past and the present. Disclosing the underlying reasons for the positive and negative aspects of the various approaches to method can only benefit our analysis. For any serious discourse the issues of "what is truth" and "how can we arrive at truth" need to be resolved. Therefore, I will deal with the issue of "how to best reach the meaning of life" under *the regime of truth*. Here I will try to expose objectivism and subjectivism together with some of the main theorems that have captivated the human mentality.

Later on in the book I will make it clear that the questions involved with the construction of fundamental categories cannot be detached from time and location. The characteristics and formation of society are either envisioned to be a chain of mere "historical events" or some abstract storytelling as if these events have no location. As a result these social perceptions lead to much deceitful rhetoric and demagogy. "Human life" will be more meaningful if we base social realities on the time and space of what is really important. We will also see that many of the notions and theorems are nothing but speculation and deception. More concretely, I will consider the historical and locational development of today's civilization.

In the second volume, *Capitalist Civilization: The Age of Unmasked Gods and Naked Kings*, I will try to display the birth of capitalism and its detrimental impact on society. Although capitalism may look very transparent, I will show how capitalism has used political power and science to construct itself and how it has later subjugated them. I will also show how a hegemonic vicious circle has been established over our mentalities through the creation of ongoing conflict and the employment of the scientism method, notions and theorems. I will try to analyze its capacity to transform a vast variety of opposing movements like social democracy, anarchism, national liberation, and even Marxism into a tool that can be used for its own benefit. How was it possible that commodification and exchange value that were scorned by all societies became the new gods that later commanded society? How was it possible that the limited number of kings who were disguised in colorful clothes and had separate lives later multiplied themselves and could no longer be differentiated from their subjects? If it proclaims that it is a very scientific, powerful and material system then why are societies at the brink of environmental and internal exhaustion? I will try to answer these questions. I will also question the true role of scientific categorization as it relates to nation-states in terms of its economic, social structure and political institutions and how they add meaning to life or make life meaningless. I will also attempt to clarify the role of liberalism, nationalism and individualism.

In volume three, *The Sociology of Freedom*, I will examine how we can achieve a utopian and free lifestyle. I will concentrate on the new mentality necessary to arrive at the much talked about "free life." The capitalist modern forms have made the antagonistic dualism of death and life meaningless and so doing it detaches life from all its magical and poetic aspects and creates an era of perpetual death, similar to judgment day. The alternative of utopian free life is neither a form of production nor a society but a life that can be constructed daily by communities.

In the fourth volume I will concentrate solely on the Middle East in the Age of Capitalism. I will not only evaluate what the fundamental aspects are that make it possible for the Middle East to stay on its two feet despite the two World Wars engineered by capitalism, but also question why it has become one of the most problematic regions in the world. As the location of what could be called the Third World War, what will its probable future be? How can we interpret its resistance against capitalist modernity? Can this region, which was once the cradle of civilization but is now a cemetery, become the region that can make the transition to free utopias? Could this region re-construct its sublime values in order to deliver meaningful, enthralling and poetic "free lifestyles"? Will it at the same time be able to break the material and scientific forms and idols of the capitalist modernity in order to make free life possible? Will the constitution of democratic administration methods, environmentally friendly production groups and meaningful assemblies of wisdom be attained? I will attempt to answer these fundamental questions.[8]

The plight of the Kurds remains tragic. The Kurds can be called a nation that is not a nation. Nowhere will one find another nation, another distinct human community, that has run away from—been made to flee from—its own essential values. One cannot call them a weak nation, a nation lacking the ability to fight: the nature of their land and their hereditary characteristics have made them fierce fighters, and the potential courage of the women and youth is very high. However, they have been turned into such cowards that they have come to fear their own shadows.

The overall situation in the Middle East might one day demand that the USA will have to choose the Kurds as its new strategic ally in the Middle East. Israel has a completely separate Kurdish project of its own.

However, it would be a mistake to see the role of the Kurds in this new period of chaos as one of mere collaboration. The vast majority, who are yearning to live a life of freedom, will find the champions to fulfill this expectation. It has the potential to both leave behind its medieval way of life and to escape the ideal of the nation-state of capitalist modernity—a system that has not given any nation the possibility to live a life of freedom. Given the historical, geographical and hereditary features of Kurdistan and the Kurds, democratic confederalism is the most suitable political format. This form of governance also offers the best possibility for attaining the ideals of freedom and equality. Besides, it will be spared the problems that establishing a new nation-state will bring.

Hence, the Kurdistan Communities Union (Koma Civakên Kurdistan, KCK) will be the entity with the role of resolving the problems with the rigid nation-states that surround it. KCK can be the leading model for a Middle Eastern democratic confederalism that will reunite those whose free lives were destroyed by the nation-state wars imposed on the former mosaic of the Middle Eastern peoples—the Arabs, Iranians, Turks, Kurds, Armenians, Greeks, Jews, Caucasians and all the others who dream of a free life and material comfort.

But should the present situation give rise to a democratic federal republic from the chaos in Iraq, such a form of government can play a leading role too. The "Third World War" of the capitalist modernity is open-ended. The outcome will be determined by the efforts and initiatives of the leading groups, of which the PKK is only one.

We can only surpass this system that feeds on a continuous state of warfare within and outside the society by constituting meaningful centers of resistance and justice against exploitation and power, and by evermore embracing our utopia of freedom. All other paths seem to be nothing but vicious circles.

I am writing under the conditions of total isolation on the island of Imrali. Under these conditions, I was not able to do the research necessary for the customary acknowledgement. But the works of the leaders of humanity, who have contributed to the whole of human society, have been a source of knowledge to me. It is not possible to list them all. I dedicate this defense to those who have been and will be good friends and comrades.

On Method and the Regime of Truth

In our quest to understand and live a meaningful life, humankind throughout the ages has used three basic methods to obtain and interpret knowledge, or "the truth," namely the mythological, the religious, and the scientific methods. In this regard, we can loosely define the concept *method* as a particular approach and related forms of habit that lead to the desired outcome (in this case, to understand and live a meaningful life) in the most economic way. The fact that it has been tried out many times before and is successful in yielding results extends credibility to a method.

The first method, encountered in the depths of history, is the mythological approach. Nature is seen as animate, abundant with spirits.

In the light of recent scientific insights, the mythological approach may seem less naive than once was thought. In my opinion, lifeless and static methodological approaches are far less meaningful than mythology. The mythological approach is environmentally oriented, free of notions of fatalism and determinism and conducive to living life in freedom. Its fundamental approach to life is one of harmony with nature.

This perception exalted and vivified all human groups up until the age of the major religions. Myth, legend, and reverence for the sacred formed the outlook of the Neolithic period in particular.

The fact that mythology seems to contradict objectivity does not mean that meaningful interpretations cannot be deduced from its content. On the contrary, one cannot fully understand history without such interpretations. Seeing that humans had been living according to the dictates of mythology for the greatest part of our history, interpreting mythology is essential for understanding humanity.

What is more, there are indications that many of the current scientific theories that are seen as the antipode of the mythological approach are themselves nothing but mere mythology.

The mythological method should be given back the prestige it lost when it was discredited by monotheistic religious dogma and by the scientific method; methods alleging to bow to absolute laws. These mythologies—related to utopian ideologies—cannot be discarded because the richness of the human psyche cannot be reduced to a mathematical and analytical mind, a mind that would be inconsistent with life itself. With a mind that is nothing more than a calculator, how will we be able to understand and interpret the psyches of the millions of different living beings, the movement of subatomic particles, the immenseness of astronomic sizes? Mathematics by itself is not sufficient to analyze these micro and macro universes.

The intuition of living beings cannot be underestimated. The meaning of life that we are searching for may well be hidden in this intuition. We should not think of intuition as something independent of the macro or the micro universes but as a fundamental characteristic of the universe. It follows that the mythological method cannot be insignificant; it may, indeed, contribute as much to our understanding of the universe as the scientific method.

Occurring for the first time just before or just after the onset of recorded history, the religious perception occupies the second longest period in the history of humanity. The transition from mythological to dogmatic religious perception is closely connected to the transition from an egalitarian, classless society to a hierarchic society and the formation of social classes. The relationship between the newly formed classes of the exploited and the exploiters demanded indisputable dogmas. In order to disguise and legitimize the exploitation and power of hierarchical and class interests, these dogmas were endowed with "indisputable" characteristics such as sacredness, being god's infallible words, and immunity.

The dogmatic religious perception holds that the aim of life and the path to the truth can only be found if one acts in accordance with the Word of God, transcending nature and society. If not, life itself will be slavery and the afterlife hell. In reality, the god is the despot exploiting and dominating society. That this excessive masking of the god is nothing but deception is evident if we consider that, at their onset, the despots had named themselves "god-kings"; later they enforced their word as law, presenting it as the absolute truth. As the oppression and exploitation became deeply rooted, the dogmatic religious approach was constructed as the social reality through which, for a very long time, humanity was submitted to the slavery of the masked despots. In fact, one of the most important aspects of the religious method is its legitimation of slave-like submission and the establishment of the fatalistic perception. Without this method, the terrible exploitative and ferocious wars waged by humanity would not have been possible.

Creeds such as "live in accordance with the holy Word and divine Law!" made it very easy to govern through the religious method. A shepherd-herd dialectic was established. On the one hand, a passive nature and society; on the other, a very active, transcendent ruler who creates and makes all things possible. It is no exaggeration to say that antiquity and the Middle Ages were governed through this method.

One of the most unfavorable aspects of the dogmatic method is that, instead of a living, evolving conception of nature, it brought about the concept of a passive nature, a nature unable to act except under the external command of the Almighty. This concept, in turn, led to the natural acceptance of a similar mentality in the social arena.

The dogmatic religious method reached its peak in the Middle Ages, especially in terms of its transcendent subjectiveness. The physical world was nearly declared incomprehensible and ignored. The world was considered a temporary stop in life, whereas the eternal ideals were postulated as the ultimate form of life. Those who knew the dogmas and clichés best were regarded as scholars and elevated to the highest ranks.

This method, which in essence is anti-mythological, played the leading role in confining life.

The positive aspect of the religious method is its improvement of society's morals. During this period and under this approach, the distinction between good and evil was developed and absolute decrees were imposed. This method revealed the flexibility of, and hence the possibility to mold, the human mind. Without morality, neither socialization nor government is possible. Undoubtedly, morality is a metaphysical perception but this does not annul it or lessen its importance. Humanity without morals either will cause the end of its own species or the end of an inhabitable environment. In fact, it is the considerable decay of morality in the post-religious era that has brought the environment to the brink of disaster.

The prophetic approach of the major religions have employed and developed the dogmatic method, especially in Zoroastrianism where its fundamental philosophy—good and evil—was held akin to light and darkness. These religions are the founders of metaphysical morals. However, the dogmatic method has influenced not only the major religions but also classical Greek thought, where a restricted use of dialectics and objectivity reigned. The idealism of Aristotle and Plato was the strongest anchor of the dogmatic religious method during the Middle Ages. Plato, the greatest philosopher—indeed the creator—of idealism, was revered as a prophet during the Middle Ages. But morality reached its climax with Zoroaster, Confucius, and Socrates. These sages led humanity to great moral advancement.

The concept of *scientific method* has played an important role in capitalism becoming a world system. In this new approach (pioneered by Roger and Francis Bacon, and Descartes) a careful distinction is made between subject and object, whereas in the dogmatic method of the Middle Ages there was no room for such a distinction.

Western Europe emerged with the Renaissance when the way for a new era was paved through the Reformation and Enlightenment. The subjectiveness of the human being and the objectiveness of the world became the two fundamental factors in life. Hence, the dogmatic method based on the Word of God—along with morality—lost its supremacy.

The disguised kings and masked gods were replaced by naked kings and unmasked gods. The underlying urge now is capitalistic exploitation, which is necessary to make profits. The terrible exploitation humanity and nature would encounter in this process demanded a radical change in society's perception. The need for profits is thus the underlying reason for the spread of the new scientific method.

But society did not so easily adopt the new morality—society can only be reconstructed through an enormous change in thought-pattern and mentality. This is where the new methodology comes into play—to find the truth. It is well known that Descartes went through a radical transformation and that his skepticism about everything which led him to arrive at "I think, therefore I am."[1] While Descartes paved the way for the individual to think independently, Roger and Francis Bacon's work on the concept of *objectivity* allowed the "object" to be at the disposal of the individual.

The concept of *objectivity* as employed in the scientific method entails that nature as a whole—that is, animate and inanimate nature including the human body but excluding analytical thought—is defined as an object. This new interpretation plays a key role in capitalism's exploitation and domination of nature and society. The mental transformation needed for the acceptance of this would have been impossible, were the distinction between subject and object not legitimized and widely accepted. The conflict between the church and science should not be seen purely as a contention for "the truth"—mighty social struggles are fought beneath the surface. One way to interpret this is as the contention between the old society, charged with morality, and the nakedly capitalistic society that wishes to strip itself off these moral covers. What we have here is a new, capitalist, social project that wishes to fully expose society to exploitation and domination and the "objective approach" is the key notion in this project.

While *subject* is the most legitimate factor of analytical thought, *object* is the physical element open to contemplation. There is not a single value that "analytical thought" will not tamper with in the name of objectivity. Not only human labor but animate and inanimate nature as a whole can be taken possession of and put through any examination or investigation in order to gain the right to its exploitation and domination. The individual citizen, nation or state becomes the fundamental subject, locked in ongoing struggle against the object of nature and society. These new, unmasked gods have been endowed with unlimited power—from committing genocide to rendering the environment uninhabitable. The Leviathan of old has become mad and there is no object that it will not subjugate. The objective approach cannot be perceived as an innocent notion of the scientific method—such a perception can only lead to enormous disasters, conflicts, and massacres more ruthless than those of the Inquisition.

The alleged scientific method is instrumental for contemporary class division and the main reason for the dysfunction and failure of contemporary social sciences. In my opinion, the objective scientific method played a determining role in the failure of scientific socialism, which I once regarded as the most far-reaching approach of the social sciences.

Scientific socialism collapsed from within and the systems derived from it transformed themselves from state capitalist institutions to private capitalist institutions. This was due to the scientific method and its fundamental concept of objectivity. I shall discuss this later in more detail but let me just say here that I have never for a moment doubted the good intentions, beliefs and efforts of those who contributed to the struggle for socialism.

All scientific structures that regard the distinction between subject and object as fundamental also assert the right to freedom—in some cases even to the extent that they claim not to be bound by any social values. These claims have resulted in enormous distortions by science. The level of integration between science and the ruling system is alarming. The world of science has become the power that constructs, legitimizes, and protects the system's methods and contents. The scientific method of the capitalist age and the sciences based on it thus have provided the power for the profitable functioning of the system. This in turn has caused wars, crises, hunger, unemployment, environmental disasters and population explosion. The innocuous aphorism "knowledge is power" proudly claims this reality.[2] Therefore, if capitalist modernity signals discontinuity in all its parameters, then the biggest blame can be laid on the "scientific method" that it rests upon.

It thus becomes very important that critique of the system is directed against this method and the "scientific disciplines" based on it. The fundamental weakness of all system critique, including socialist critique, is that it uses the very method that the capitalist system rests upon. Any society built on this method will encounter the same consequences. Hence, despite their criticism, all opponents to the system—including scientific socialism—have suffered the same consequences as the capitalist society.

My analysis of the characteristics of class and society is based on the subject-object dichotomy, because these two seemingly innocent concepts are the ontological reasons for the unsustainability of modernity. This notion of *nature* and *subject* is as obsessive as the dogmatic method of the Middle Ages. Despite popular belief, scientific progress cannot be reduced to these two concepts. On the contrary, such a clear-cut subject-object distinction leads to a more material and primitive understanding of life than that of the Middle Ages. While the dogmatic method deprived human life of freedom, capitalist modernity has torn it apart on the basis of this distinction. A deep division in all fields of life is being constructed. Science has torn apart the whole—right down to its smallest unit. Hence, the integrity of social life and its indivisibility with time and location were lost to us. There is nothing worse than a life detached from its essence.

This critique does not entail that I propose a new method, nor does it entail that I propose a total lack of methodology. What I *am* saying is that we should take note of what is signified by this method, and by the laws it claims all life—including human life—and inanimate matter are bound by. Should we persist with the notions and method of the scientific approach, we may deprive ourselves and nature of development and freedom. I do not envisage the existence of universes without method and law. At the same time, I do not believe that the universe rests on the mathematical order of the Cartesian mechanism. I detect striking similarities in attitude between adherents of this theory and the Sumerian priests, and in my opinion they represent the same civilization.

But more important than denouncing a particular method or searching for an alternative is investigating the possible interpretations of the concept of *free life*. If the aim of employing a specific method is to arrive at a meaningful life, then the method should indeed facilitate this. But the enormous industry and state that emerged with the scientific method have brought war and destruction on humanity, not happiness. The big accumulators have always initiated intolerance toward life. Society, on the other hand, has always regarded accumulation with suspicion.

Successfully addressing the question of method requires a proper investigation into the relevant era and civilization. Without a radical critique of the methodology and scientific disciplines that have shaped capitalism, all efforts to reconstruct a science that will foster a meaningful, free life are in vain. I do not wish to contribute to the discussion on modernity and post-modernity. I have much respect for many of the opinions expressed on this topic but I am in agreement with the widely held belief that we are still far from the essence of the problem.

I wish to present my own interpretation under the notion regime of truth. It is not an endeavor for an alternative method but rather an endeavor to find a solution to the problems that a life detached from the values of freedom creates. Undoubtedly, there has always been a quest for truth by humanity; throughout the ages, various options—from mythology to religion, from philosophy to contemporary science—have been hailed as holding the answer. But, although we cannot perceive of a life outside of these fields, we also cannot deny that many of our problems stem from them.

However, contemporary modernity is unique in that it has reached an unsustainable level: the proliferation of nuclear weapons, population explosion, exhaustion of resources, environmental destruction, excessive growth of social rifts, disintegration of moral bonds and a stressful life that has lost its charm and lyricism are but a few examples that demonstrate that our regimes of truth have failed.

To prevent us from falling into a state of silent desperation, we need to remedy the situation. To find a solution, we have to question when and where we have made the enormous mistakes that led to these aberrations. Mighty struggles have been waged against capitalist modernity to no avail—we all know what happened to the systems that claimed they were alternatives. Does this mean that the world we live in is the final and eternal one, precisely as the system proclaims? Is another world not possible? Attempting to answer these questions is my duty to the values of freedom.

I am convinced that capitalist modernity acquires most of its power from erroneous social construction. Our reasoning has been weakened and distorted by the juxtaposing of the dualistic pairs subject-object, idealist-materialist, dialectical-metaphysical, philosophical-scientific and mythological-religious. The intense polarization of these dichotomies constitutes the fundamental methodological error that has led to capitalist modernity.

Though this reasoning has reached its peak in capitalism, rulers and exploiters through the ages have encouraged beliefs and arguments based on these dichotomies because of the fundamental role they have played in legitimizing the continuation of ruling systems. If the human mind were not conditioned to these distinctions, exploitative systems would not have been so successful. The continuation of the intellectual wars they cause leads to the desire for more power and more exploitation. Those in pursuit of the truth will receive acclaim from rulers and exploiters only for success in developing these dichotomies: "Truth is power, power is truth." Such a regime of truth is the strongest possible ally of the political and exploitative regime. The consequence of such an alliance is more oppression and exploitation, which in turn means the loss of a free and meaningful life.

Such a regime of truth should not be tolerated any longer. We need to reject the system's regime of truth on all fronts. In other words, I am not talking about merely opposing the system but about developing an alternative system based on the analysis of the flawed system. By resisting not only the power networks but also the exploitation centers and by developing the ability to build communities, the system can be attacked at its most vulnerable spot. Every social construction is the product of a specific mentality. All important events, all periods of development and their resulting structures have been the work of influential minds and their will. Thus, indeed, the world we live in does not have to be the final and eternal one; another world is possible.

One of the biggest errors of the Marxian method was that the proletariat, who were already under daily oppression and exploitation, were expected to bring about the new societal construction without the necessary mental revolution having been initiated. Marxists failed to see that the proletariat consisted of re-conquered slaves; the Marxists themselves fell for the "free worker" fallacy.

Thus, what is the world-view that needs to be acquired? In order to answer this question clearly we need to have a clear understanding of the present mentality, originating from the subject-object dichotomy.

Firstly, despite claims to this regard, objectivity is not purely an expression of the laws of nature and society. Profound research will show that the so-called "objective laws" are nothing but the modern equivalent of the "Word of God" of antiquity. The voice of the powers that transcend nature and society have always echoed in this objectivity. If we dig deeper, we will find the source of this voice to be the domination of tyrant and exploiter. The objective mind and the orders given by the voice are closely connected to the systems of civilization. It has been disciplined by and made familiar to these systems. Even if new information is extracted from an object, it is immediately adjusted to conform to the system. If resistance is shown, the culprits are punished by the gods of the system, just like Adam and Abraham, Mani and Mansur Al-Hallaj, Saint Paul and Giordano Bruno. If, on the other hand, objectivity is that which we perceive intuitively, objectivity is very valuable—it may even lead to true wisdom when aligned with the values of free life. But in order to achieve this type of objectivity, one has to be as brave as Mansur Al-Hallaj or Giordano Bruno.[3]

We need to be aware that we can reach two sets of conclusions through "objectivity" and that it requires great effort and resistance to understand which represents the established, dominant system and which represents the truth. If objective thought cannot be freed from analytical intelligence, if it cannot be coupled with the momentary, intuitive thought originating from emotional intelligence, then it will play a terrible role in history. The ancient Leviathan has been replaced by the monster that bore the atomic bomb—a monster equipped with the analytic thinking structures of capitalist modernity. Later, when we examine the mask-less new god—the nation-state—the capabilities of objective analytic thought will become clear.

Subjectivism, which positions itself on the opposite side of objectivity, claims that truth is to be attained through insight and contemplation rather than through scrupulous study of the subject matter alone. Subjectivism is another version of Platonism and is in danger of repeating the erroneous and obsessive aspects of the latter, expressed in the dictum: "Truth is only that which can be felt and sensed." This attitude may even lead to existentialism, which considers a human being to be whatever he makes of himself. When it comes to its perception of nature and society, subjectivism is a strong advocate of individualism and has played a significant role in turning modernity's individual into an egoist. Instead of fostering a healthy "I" it brings forth a selfish individual, firmly enchained to the consumptive society. And, as does its opposite, subjectivism does not hesitate to take its place within the system. In fact, the capitalist system owes much to this way of thinking. This attitude has been reflected primarily in the arts, particularly in literature and through the use of the art industry, which has formed a whole new virtual world; it keeps the whole of society under its influence. In this way, it provides the system its much needed legitimacy. Society is continuously bombarded with the sentiments of a virtual world and thus faces losing the possibility of self-reflectivity. The truth is reduced to a world of simulation. It is no longer meaningful to distinguish between the original and the copy. The only positive aspect of subjectivism (as an insight) is its close link with emotional intelligence, due to the fact that feeling and intuition play a major role in subjectivism.

In Sufism and Middle Eastern wisdom an attempt was made to capture the unity of nature and society through the method of contemplation. Much progress was indeed made and it could still be utilized, as it is a substantial source. Eastern subjectivity is superior to Western objectivity when it comes to its moral approach to nature and society. But subjectivity, just as objectivity, has often fallen into the trap of presenting itself as the god's voice. In this respect the two attitudes converge. This very aspect of their inner and transcendental gods, together with their conceptions of nature and society, cannot but end up serving the system's disguised or naked kings, who are the masked or mask-less gods.

Objectivity with all its academic institutions on the one hand, and subjectivism with its various spiritual and religious institutions on the other hand, breed a two-way legitimacy for capitalist modernity. Instead of playing their roles as regimes or methods of truth, they become the system's sycophants. The cadres and institutions that legitimize power and exploitation play a role as vital as that of the institutions of brute force and exploitation. Yet again we encounter the forces of the system that have been unified with the aphorisms "power is truth" and "knowledge is power." Hence, the quest for truth becomes the name of the game played by the triumvirate of capital, science and politics. Any quest for truth outside of this game is the enemy of the system and it must either be annihilated or absorbed into the system.

We are besieged by the most advanced stage of the material world and we face an enormous loss of meaning. How are we to break free from this power circle of capital, science and politics? The answer to this has been searched for by philosophers of freedom such as Nietzsche and Foucault, but there is no ready answer. We should truly understand these philosophers who, when evaluating modernity, proclaimed the death of man and the castration of society. The existence of death camps, atomic bombs, wars of ethnic cleansing, destruction of the environment and increased cancer and AIDS not only confirms these judgments, but necessitates an urgent counter-quest for truth. I must reiterate that social democrats, national liberation movements and even scientific socialism, although seen as the strongest opposition, have long ago abandoned this role and have taken their position as denominations of modernity. It has also been understood that many post-modern quests are indeed modernist thoughts in disguise.

Systems begin to dissolve when they have reached their climax and then start to decline. The 1970s is the period when capitalist modernity began its decline and its chosen method began losing esteem. Ecological consideration, feminist trends and ethno-cultural movements gained prominence. This was possible because criticism of the scientific method had paved the way for alternative schools of thought and independent interpretation. It is important that we understand the value of periods like these—periods that are often called "chaotic"—and appreciate the different intellectual groupings in their own right as centers of resistance. We have to understand that such historical periods are intellectually productive in terms of new and different methods and in terms of construction of truth because this insight will increase the chances of a successful reconstruction of society at the community level.

One of our practical responsibilities today is to see to the materialization of our utopias of freedom and equality by building these ideals into social structures. To obtain this, we need to realize the scientific importance of the chosen path and we need the strength of will to obtain freedom. We have arrived at a time where the love for truth is the only guarantee of free life. Our slogan then becomes "Truth is love; love is free life!" Thus, if we are not filled with love for a free life—which is both the method to obtain truth and the regime of truth—then we can neither attain the necessary knowledge nor build our desired social world.

Let us now examine the leading structures and knowledge in the light of this hypothesis. We start off by rejecting the progenitors of the Bacons and Descartes—taking the human being as our basis may be more appropriate than the subject-object, spirit-body dichotomy. I am not pleading for a human-centric world-view, nor for a humanistic approach. I am referring to the totality of facts that comprises the human being, facts such as:

1. Atoms, the building blocks of matter, have their richest existence and composition—both in terms of number and arrangement—in the human being.
2. The human being has the advantage of representing all the plant and animal structures of the biological world.
3. The human being has realized the most advanced forms of social life.
4. The human being has access to a very elastic and free intellectual world.
5. The human being is capable of metaphysical thought.

Clearly, the human being constitutes a unique source of knowledge, where all these characteristics are intertwined, occurring simultaneously and functioning as a unit. The understanding of this source in its entirety, in its wholeness, is equal to understanding the known material universe (or, at the very least, it is a correct first step in that direction). I will now discuss the five points set out above in more detail.

1. Atoms, the building blocks of matter, have their richest existence and composition—both in terms of number and arrangement—in the human being.

The relationship between the inter- and intra-atomic entities and life forms can best be detected in the human being. In a way, the human being can be perceived as a living alignment of matter. This does not mean that the human being is nothing more than the sum of its matter. Nor does it mean that matter is a structure without living emotions. It is quite difficult to lend meaning to the relationship between matter, which has a living emotion of its own, and the human being, which transcends being the simple sum of its matter. I think the source of metaphysical thought lies in this perception. If we can attain an unlimited flexibility in our perception, we may overcome the dichotomy between matter and meaning. It just may be that the aim of all animate and inanimate forms is to overcome this dichotomy. Thus, the aim of matter is to have meaning and the aim of meaning is to surpass matter. It may be possible to find the faintest breath of love in this dichotomy. Could it be that the action-reaction principle has evolved from the matter-meaning dichotomy? Can this dual antagonism be the origin of the saying "the basis of the universe is love"? This love seems to have situated itself on a strong basis within the human being.

I believe the search for matter within the human being is a method that may bring us closer to the truth. It seems impossible to do so in the isolated laboratories of modernity. In quantum physics, the relationship between the observer and the observed does not allow for measurement. Just as the observer changes, matter—the observed—can escape the attention of the observer under laboratory conditions. Therefore, the human being can best perceive itself through introspection. Democritus was able to discover the atom through this method several millennia ago.[4] Besides, the human being is a more comprehensive laboratory. I am not saying that laboratories are of no use, but that fundamental principles can be determined through human introspection.

We can observe all the laws of chemistry and physics within the human being and attain a better knowledge thereof. We can come to understand the transformation of matter to energy and the rich chemical compounds in the structure of the human being. It is also possible to come to understand the relationship between energy and matter as well as the unity between matter, energy and thought in the human brain. This leads us to the all-important question: Can the unity realized in the human being be a characteristic of the universe as well?

Therefore, our first principle is the potentially rich perception of the human being. It can be held as the main path to knowledge and a sound principle of regime in relation to what the truth is.

2. The human being has the advantage of representing all the plant and animal structures of the biological world.

The human being offers a rich example for observation of the aliveness-lifelessness dichotomy. Aliveness has reached its developmental peak and displays its most advanced characteristics in the human being. Lifeless matter has attained its most advanced level in parallel and in combination with aliveness. The arrangement of matter in the brain and the development of life still holds many mysteries. The link between the matter of the brain and the animate being that has acquired the ability to think abstractly still has to be discovered.

In searching for a hypothesis to explain the relationship between aliveness and lifelessness in the human being, an important assumption should be that matter has the potential to become alive. Without this potential, the collection of matter within the human being would not be able to sustain this advanced form of aliveness, this life form with emotions and thought.

Given this assumption, how can we arrive at an understanding of the potential aliveness of matter through stronger perception?

Firstly, we should make the fundamental principle of action-reaction the cornerstone of our notion of potential aliveness. It may be meaningful to interpret this principle (for every action there is a reaction), which can be observed throughout the entire universe, as potential aliveness.

In the second place, the existence-vacuum dichotomy should be part of our notion of potential aliveness. We cannot conceive of an existence without a vacuum and a vacuum without existence. If we strain the boundaries of our thought, surpassing the dual antagonism of existence and vacuum, it would mean their disappearance. But what can we call this new entity without the existence-vacuum duality? This is the second important question. Some immediately may give the customary reply of "God" but, if we apply our minds, we may arrive at a more meaningful answer. We may even arrive at the meaning of life or the answer to the mystery of life.

In the third place, and in combination with the action-reaction principle, the particle characteristic of light waves should be included in our notion of potential aliveness. This characteristic is a prerequisite for action and reaction to occur. The "black hole," which absorbs all light, makes things even more mysterious. If the energy of the radiation is absorbed, what is left? This is one of the most difficult questions to be answered. If we define black holes as pure energy islands, what can we then call the energy radiation? Matter is concentrated accumulation of energy—we all know Einstein's famous equation. Could the universe be composed just of the dual antagonism of a humongous black hole and matter? Is matter non-matter that makes itself visible? Does this mean that we can see the universe, which has made itself visible, as a big, living being? Can it be that all dual antagonisms in life are reminiscent of this universal dual antagonism? Can love and hate, good and bad, beauty and ugliness, right and wrong all be the reflections of this universe?

Questions can be multiplied, but what is crucial is that the relationship between aliveness and lifelessness can no longer be interpreted metaphysically—as was done by religious dogmatism—or be viewed in terms of capitalist modernity's distinction between spirit and body or subject and object. The richness of life neither can be explained through the dogma of an external creator nor through the spirit-matter dichotomy. To increase our chances of understanding development in the universe—including aliveness and lifelessness—we need to consider, and become adept in observing, the richness of life in the human being. Furthermore, those who are looking for justice have the duty to look for the how and the why of life.

No entity comes into being without explanation or circumstance; nature is more than just that. (If we are unable to see the explanation, we should hold civilized society responsible for losing our ability to observe.) Thus, the development of the human being too was a meaningful one and ours is the duty to uncover this meaning.

This perspective enables us to analyze the great diversity and evolutionary processes in the biological world. Understanding the transition between animate and inanimate molecules enables us to understand the transition between the plant and the animal kingdom.

Significant scientific progress already has been made in this area and, despite shortcomings and unanswered questions, we have developed a much better understanding of the evolutionary process.

The plant kingdom is a miracle in itself—from the most primitive plant to an extraordinary fruit tree; from grass to roses with thorns—showing the strength of the ability to be alive. And the relationship between the beauty of the rose and its thorny self-protection may hold a key to another mystery: The most striking aspect of evolution, as manifested in our botanical examples above, is the ability for the subsequent phase to contain in itself the previous phase, protecting the previous as part of its richness. Hence, contrary to widespread belief, evolution continues not by eliminating the other (as according to dogmatic Darwinism) but by multiplying the self through enrichment. What we have is development from a single species to a multitude of species, from a primitive fungus to the endless diversity of living beings. And all these diverse beings have a principle in common, namely to defend themselves in some way or another.

Another aspect of biological evolution we need to heed is sexual and asexual reproduction. Asexual reproduction is found in very primitive forms whereas sexual reproduction is the dominant principle. Hermaphroditism, where female and male parts are found within a single unit, is due to the transition between the different stages. In order to multiply and diversify into different species the sexes need to be represented in different units. Thus, we can attribute the female-male duality to the general development principle of the universe, namely progress based on conflict and mutation (in other words, positive dialectic!) We ought to learn this lesson from nature: insistence to remain "the same" is denial of progress. It is also clear that all the different kinds of quests for absolute truth did not result in the ability to interpret the universe.

We should also pay attention to the question of why the universe wants to flourish. Is this not proof of the universe's aliveness? Could something devoid of life flourish? The plant kingdom makes it easier to answer this question.

Another important question with regard to biological development is whether planet Earth is unique. The belief that another planet with life forms cannot exist—because such a planet has never been encountered in the observed universe—is a delusion of metaphysics that claims that the human being can know everything. It is in fact akin to believing in creation by god. We are just beginning to make sense of our world; we should not dismiss out of hand the saying "each living being has a universe"; neither should we just dismiss the concept of parallel universes. Let me clarify with an example. Any cell from any part of the human tissue is a living being in its own right. If thought develops within the brain cells, then can these cells claim that the universe is only what we think it to be? On the other hand, although these cells are unaware of the human being and of the extraordinary universe, it does not mean that the human being and the micro and macro universe do not exist. Can we then not see the human as such a cell within the macro universe? If we dare do this, we can conceive of the existence of other universes too.[5]

Although the animal kingdom is a system in its own right, the existence of the plant kingdom is a precondition for the existence of the animal kingdom. (In fact, cells common to both the animal and plant kingdoms do exist.[6]) More importantly, a rich variety of plants is also a precondition for a rich variety of animals. Potential aliveness in plant cells have led to an advanced form of aliveness in the animal kingdom, namely sensory and emotional awareness such as vision, hearing, pain, desire, anger and affection.

Animals feel pleasure and pain—emotions distinctly associated with aliveness. In the continuous search for food amongst animals, we encounter yet again the relationship between energy and aliveness. Hunger is the impulse that leads the animal to feed and thereby store the needed energy. The sexual drive has much the same function—it springs from the desire to live and from the fear of extinction. We can thus interpret eating and sexual reproduction as forms of self-defense.[7]

The development of awareness is a miracle in itself. Let us take sight as an example. This sensory awareness is an advanced aspect of aliveness.[8] Sight, like all other forms of awareness, is a form of thought. (Aliveness itself can be seen as the ability to learn: "I think, therefore I am.") Should we not understand the following saying in this light? "God created the universe to observe himself." According to Hegel, the reification of *Geist* for self-awareness is related to the act of seeing. Can it be that to see and to be seen is one of the fundamental aims of creation?

All the characteristics of aliveness encountered in the plant and animal kingdoms can be seen in the human being. In terms of the ability to learn and think, the development of the brain is at its peak. The incredible power latent in the human being's ability to think may even make a new evolutionary form unnecessary. The universe recognizes itself through our eyes: "To be known, I created the human being."[9]

3. The human being has realized the most advanced forms of social life.

For a meaningful method and regime of truth it is important to consider the human (as a species that has realized its own society) as a unique subject of study, separate from the rest of the animal kingdom. Undoubtedly, not only in the animal kingdom but also in the plant kingdom, we encounter many examples of existence in groups. By nature, all species have the need to live in close proximity to each other, or even live as a group—trees have forests and fish their schools. However, the human society has a qualitative distinction. The society itself maybe the *Übermensch*, the over-man.[10] If we put a human child back into the forest right after its birth (and, of course, securing its life), it cannot but live the life of a primate. If similar humans have to meet there, a social period akin to that of the primates will develop. This indicates the distinct value of human society, the role society plays in forming the human being and the role of the human being in constructing society.

Of course, without humans there would be no human society. But to view society as nothing but the sum of humans is a fallacy. A human without society cannot surpass being a primate. *With* society, the human becomes an incredible power. All things realized within the human individual must be socially developed. It is impossible to attain knowledge and establish the regime of truth in the absence of society. The human being is not only the inheritor of the plant and animal kingdom, the physical and chemical universe; it is a being that has been realized in society. All civilized systems, including capitalist modernity, have studied the human being detached from history and society. In fact, all thoughts and structures discussed and established by human beings have been represented as the work of individuals superior to society, detached from history and society. This has made it easy to invent the disguised and naked kings and the masked and unmasked gods. Hence, with a better understanding of society, we will not only be able to analyze the roles these kings and gods have played but we will also be able to pinpoint which tyrannous and exploitative social systems they originated from.

A serious problem regarding any method is to establish in a meaningful way the relationship between human being and society. It seems that both the Bacons and Descartes were unaware of their own societies as they discussed questions of methodology. Today we know very well that the societies they were part of and were affected by were the societies of what we today call England and the Netherlands, societies that built capitalism as a world system.[11] As a result, the methods these three scientists constructed were imbedded in those societies and brought forth ideas that left the door to capitalism wide open.

What could be our main observations if we were to consider human society as a fundamental category?

a. The society itself is a formation that qualitatively differentiates humans from animals, as has been indicated above.

b. Although the society is built by human beings, it in turn builds human individuals. The main issue that needs to be understood here is the fact that society or communities are constructed by the human mind and competency. They have profoundly affected the human memory and, although they have been projected to be everything from a totem to a god, it is clear that they are mere human constructs. If the human being ceased to exist there would be no society for the totems or gods to rule.

c. Societies are under historical and geographical restrictions (i.e., every society conforms to the dictates of the time when and the geographical circumstances under which it is constructed). History, for all living beings, but especially for humans, denotes dependency on time. The connection between history and society is tightly knit and is of a short time span.[12] We can talk about millions of years in connection with the universe, but for societies going beyond a few thousand years it is only possible in the context of the notion of long time span.[13] Geographical location of societies is determined by distribution of plant and animal life. The rich flora and fauna in some regions constitute the basis for numerous societies; societies at the poles and in arid areas are rare.

Many of the schools of thought and religious structures formed within societal and state traditions impose a system detached from history and geography on the human consciousness, as if this system is their fate. We are told that capitalist modernity bases itself on science. Why, then, does this system take great care to think of the individual as isolated from society? The time span and geographical location of a society constructs the individual and in turn, the individuals construct the future. Therefore, historical and geographical location are the two foremost prerequisites in order to deal with any problems of methodology and perception of regime of truth.

d. Social realities are constructs. People mistakenly believe social institutions and structures to be natural realities because the regimes striving to construct legitimacy for these social systems present them as unchangeable and sacred. They preach that these systems are divine establishments, so designated by the god. Capitalist modernity claims that the ultimate word has been uttered, that there are no alternatives to liberal institutions. There is much talk about unchangeable and unalterable constitutions and political regimes. However, a quick look at history shows that these "permanent, unshakable" structures have only been around for the last century. Hence, the rulers and exploiters need ideological and political rhetoric to constantly enchain the thoughts and will of human beings. To administer today's society in the absence of a strong ideological and political rhetoric is truly difficult. This is why the media is so well developed. And this is why, in general, scientific and intellectual schools have been tied down by the rulers and exploiters.

The realization that social realities are constructed realities will bring the awareness that they can be demolished and re-constructed. There is no social reality that cannot be demolished or changed, including all its ideological and material institutions. Under the appropriate time and geographical circumstances social realities in all social fields (such as language, religion, mythology, science, economy, politics, law, morality and philosophy) are continuously established, demolished and restored and new ones are formed as needed.

e. It is important not to view the relationship between society and the individual as a theoretical one. Individuals are born into established structures that have been shaped within the depths of history and within a distinct language and established traditions. They cannot participate as they wish—they participate on the basis of the society's carefully and previously prepared institutions and traditions. An extraordinary educational effort is needed for the socialization of the individual. In fact, in a way the individual becomes a member of the society only after the culture of the society has been absorbed. Socialization can only be achieved through continuous effort. Each social act is at the same time an act of socialization. Therefore, individuals cannot escape being constructed according to the dictates of its society. But because classed and hierarchic societies are prone to being oppressive and exploitative societies, the individual will always demand freedom and hence resist. The individual will not readily accept societies that construct slavery. Yet, there will be endeavors not only to transform these individuals as they pass through the oppressive and educational social institutions but also to eliminate them. However, the resisting individual will always find space for itself because of the contradictions between institutions and the equilibrium based on compromises within the society. Although the society does not have the strength to totally dissolve the individual, the individual too does not have the ability to detach itself completely from society.

In short, methodological work and regimes of truth based on a human sample that perceives society for what it is may end up with more meaningful results.

4. The human being has access to a highly elastic and free intellectual world. The flexibility of the human mind enhances the possibility of a meaningful investigation. In the absence of a sound knowledge of the human mind, any ideas about method and truth will be worthless.

We have referred to the dual structure of the human mind before: the right lobe of the brain (the seat of emotional intelligence) is more advanced and older in terms of evolution than the newer part (in the left lobe of the brain), where analytical intelligence is based.

In the animal kingdom, the developmental level of emotions and thought is nearly on an equal level—emotions are triggered by things learned through conditioned and unconditioned reflexes, they are momentary reactions. The same structures exist in the human being—for example, our bodies respond to fire immediately and there is no need to think analytically. But to climb Mount Everest there are hundreds of things that need to be considered before departure. Analytical intelligence may take years to mature. With emotional intelligence, there is no margin for error and action is based on intuition.

The primary characteristic of our mind is its flexible structure. There are very few entities in the universe that possess the ability of free choice. We may think of the areas of freedom as narrow intervals. We do not know how free choice occurs within subatomic particles and the structures in the macro universe. However, we can deduce from the observable outcomes and the diversity within the universe that flexibility in behavior and ability have to exist in the worlds of particles and in the macro universe in order to make a free choice. But in the human brain, this interval of flexibility has widened quite substantially. At least potentially we have unlimited freedom of movement—but let us not forget that this potentiality can only become active when coupled with sociality.

Another characteristic of our mind is that its structure allows not only correct but also false perceptions. The combination of this characteristic and its flexibility allows it to be led astray under physical and emotional oppression. That is why mechanisms of oppression and torture are used in conjunction with deceptive and erroneous promises. The extraordinary effect of the coercion of the human mind by the hierarchic and statist orders has been the construction of a mind favorable to themselves. However, the structure of our mind also allows us to resist, to attain the truth, to choose the right path. An independent mind has been decisive in the rise of those personalities that have contributed to humanity. Free choice can best be realized when minds work independently. There is a close tie between rich conceptualization and independent thought.

By "independence of mind" I mean the ability to act in accordance with the principles of justice. As discussed before, there is a universal order that determines the relationship between reality and justice. Thus, if the mind has the ability to be just, we can say that it has used the opportunity decreed by the universal order to make the best use of its ability to freely make a choice. Therefore, the history of freedom (that is, social history), which is the best educative power, prepares the mind for the right choices.

Psychoanalytic approaches try to measure the depth of our mind and it gains importance as a new field of information. But psychoanalysis on its own lacks the ability to arrive at the correct and necessary information. This is due mostly to its perception of the human being as an independent entity. Detaching the human being from its society may lead to an insufficient and unsound collection of knowledge. At present, the attempts of psycho-sociology to remove the insufficiencies look unpromising. If sociology has not been constructed properly, how can psycho-sociology bear the right results? Psychology may provide knowledge about the animal mind and can even provide knowledge of the human being as a super animal. But we are only at the start of knowing the human being as a social animal.

It should be clear now that without knowledge of the structure of the mind, successful results in constructing a method and a system of knowledge can be nothing but a mere coincidence. If we achieve a true and insightful definition of the mind and if we secure the human position to make free choices (that is, if we secure social freedom), our method and regime of knowledge may deliver a competent response to correct perceptions. Under such conditions, methodical study and a less flawed collection of knowledge increase our chances of being free individuals in a free society.

5. The human being is capable of metaphysical thought.

The metaphysical character of the human being is a unique phenomenon in terms of methodology and system of knowledge. The method and science of arriving at information (epistemology) can be improved by analyzing these characteristics of the human being. In metaphysics, an important area of study is the comprehension of the human being itself. The least analyzed social aspect is the definition of the metaphysical human. We still need answers to questions such as:

- How is it possible that the human being is metaphysical?
- What need does this arise from?

- What are the positive and negative aspects of the metaphysical character of the human?
- Is it possible to live without metaphysics?
- What are the main characteristics of metaphysics?
- Does metaphysics only prevail in the intellectual and religious areas of the human life?
- What is the connection between society and metaphysics?
- Is metaphysics counter-dialectic and can dialectic be limited by metaphysics?

If the human being is the fundamental subject of our knowledge, then, in the absence of knowing its metaphysical thought and institutions—which are its fundamental features—we cannot claim that we have attained sufficient information from it. We are talking about an area that has been neglected by both sociology and psychology. The question of metaphysics becomes doubly difficult to handle as especially religion, but many other schools of thought as well, are perceived as metaphysical. In approaching the question of metaphysics, we should not forget that it is a fundamental characteristic of the human being. Metaphysics is a societal construction and a reality that a social human being cannot do without. If we isolate the human from metaphysics then we shall end up with a mere animal, or a mere machine. What chances does such a humanity have of living? Let us examine what a metaphysical human is like:

- Morality is a metaphysical human feature.
- Religion is an important metaphysical feature.
- Arts, with all its branches, can only be defined as metaphysical.
- Institutionalized society, and even society as a whole, fits the definition of being metaphysical.

Why and how can the human being be metaphysical? Firstly, it is due to man's capacity to think. The human being, as a universe that becomes conscious of itself, is compelled to construct a meta-physics in order to overcome its dismays.[14] Without the meta-physical, it is not possible to deal with the intense physical pain and pleasure. To endure war, death, lust, passion, beauty, etc. metaphysical thought and institutions are indispensable. This need can only be satisfied by the creation of a god, creation of art and development of knowledge.

If we look at it from a different perspective and think of metaphysics as that "beyond the physical," the need to either condemn or praise it, disappears. Through metaphysics, the boundaries of the physical world are being pressed back by the human being. Man lives meta-physically because of its ontological character. It is meaningless to claim that there is nothing besides a physical life. Besides, such a condition would only lead to the definition of a mechanical human being.

Secondly, the fact that in the absence of morals society cannot be upheld, necessitates our being metaphysical. Society can only be engineered through morals, which is free judgment. The disintegration of the Soviet Union's Russia and the Pharaohs' Egypt, despite all its rationalism, can be linked to lack of morality. Rationality alone is not sufficient to uphold society. It may robot-ize and turn its members into fully developed animals, but it cannot retain them as human beings. Some of the qualities of morality are:

- endurance of pain and the strength to counter it;
- the ability to restrict pleasure, desire and lust; to set social—not physical—rules for reproduction;
- the ability to decide whether to abide by traditions, religion and laws.

For example, sexual intercourse needs to be bound by rules because of its reproductive feature. We need to take care when it comes to population growth so that the society can be maintained. Hence, this topic alone shows us that there is a great need for moral metaphysics.

Thirdly, humans create a universe of their own through arts. Society is sustained through creations in fundamental areas such as music, visual arts and architecture. It is impossible to think of a society without music, literature or architecture. All creations in these areas are of a metaphysical character. For the sustenance of society, these creations are indispensable. Art, as a metaphysical construction, satisfies the human need for aesthetics. Just as the human being gives meaning to its moral behavior through its choice between good and evil, it also gives meaning to artistic behavior through its judgment on beauty and ugliness.

Fourthly, the field of political rule abounds with metaphysical judgment. This field is the strongest metaphysical construction of all—we cannot define politics through physical rules. Governance solely through physical rules is at best robot-like and at worst the "flock herding" of fascism. If we add that the political field also has the connotation of choice and freedom of behavior, then we would once again arrive at the metaphysical character of the political person. Aristotle's statement that "Man is a political animal" is more reminiscent of such a meaning.[15]

Fifthly, we should emphasize that law, philosophy and even "scientism" are loaded with metaphysics.[16] All these areas are qualitatively and quantitatively full of metaphysical works of art. Keeping in mind the important status of metaphysics in the life of the individual and society, we can continue to develop a more meaningful approach:

1. Metaphysical approaches have either been hailed as the fundamental truth or have been regarded as fictitious, as words and tools to deceive man. These approaches are either completely unaware of the history of society or they are exaggerating. What both of these approaches are unaware of is the social and individual need that gives rise to metaphysics.

   Those that hail the metaphysical have denied its relationship with the physical world and perceive it as boundlessly free. In denying the relationship between thought and spirit, or in confusing the metaphysical with the physical world, they have fallen into obsessions or exaggerations of transcendental divine orders—even exalted humans as god. The hierarchic and statist order has had an important effect on these developments.

   Those who deny the importance of metaphysics (for instance the rationalists and the positivists) have attacked it intensely and have hailed the materialist world and civilization: anything reminiscent of metaphysics is a tool of deception and should be rejected completely. In retrospect, we understand that rationalism and positivism paved the way for the "fascist flock," the "robotic and mechanical human being," and the "simulative" perceptions of life, destroying the environment and the history of society. Extreme adherence to the laws of physics cannot prevent the destruction or the dissolution of society; "scientism" has thereby proven that it is the worst metaphysics of all. I do have to emphasize that "scientism" is the shallowest materialism and the most knowledgeable expert of power and exploitation. Whether knowingly or not, it is the biggest deceiver and the representative of the worst form of metaphysics.

Those who say that they do not belong to any of the sides, whom we may call nihilists, claim that there is no need to be pro- or anti-metaphysics and that one could live in total independence. Although they may seem the most harmless of the groupings, in essence they are the most dangerous—at least the other two have great ideals and are aware of what they represent; they strive to reform society and to re-construct the individual. The nihilists, who believe that total independence is possible, pay no attention to these discussions. Their number has been increased enormously by capitalist modernity, in which they constitute the *déclassé* elements of the dissolved society. While presently football hooligans are the most outstanding example of this grouping, the number of similar movements is on the rise.

2. The difference between two opposing approaches to metaphysics, the pro- and anti-schools, in actuality falls away in modernity. While the religion of the anti-school is positivism—which is disguised metaphysics—the god of both groups is the nation-state. The god that has removed its mask is being sanctified in the form of the nation-state in all modern societies.

3. I believe there is a need for and the possibility of developing a more balanced approach. I do realize that metaphysics is a societal construct, hence I feel obliged to develop a metaphysics in morals, art, politics and thinking that will be closer to the ideal of *good, beautiful, free* and *true*. The essence of a *virtuous life* is the continuance of the quest for the good, beautiful, free and true, as it was in historical societies. I believe that a meaningful life within society is only possible when lived according to this art of a virtuous life.

We are not, of course, obliged to metaphysics but we cannot just give up our quest for finding and developing the "best, most beautiful, freest and truest." Just as we are not obliged to the ugly, evil, unfree and untrue, it is not impossible either to live a good, beautiful, free and true life. Neither are we obliged to go through life as nihilists. This argument has continued since the beginning of time, since the era of early social construction. What is unique about this issue today is that we are at the dissolution phase of capitalist modernity, exactly the period where a struggle for the good, beautiful, free and true is needed for the new social re-constructions. And, we do not only need a love-like passion but also the most scientific pursuit—that is a method and regime of truth.

The arguments that I have set out above for overcoming capitalist modernity and developing and spreading democratic modernity need to be developed further. In order to achieve this, we need to criticize the method and regimes of knowledge that have led to the official institutions of modernity and to clarify post-modernity's groundbreaking method and systems of knowledge. This is my intent with this material.

I explained how and why we should focus on the human being. The correct definition and perception of both the individual and of society remain important. The efforts of sociology, psycho-sociology and anthropology are not productive because they are distorted by modernity and jammed in its knowledge and power networks. Precious individual efforts, on the other hand, are unsystematic and disorganized. Although important contributions have been made, especially by Nietzsche, the Frankfurt School, Fernand Braudel, and later Foucault and Wallerstein, the new method and regimes of knowledge (the dissolution of modernity and the new post-modernity, which we would like to name "democratic modernity"), are far from being systematized. There are numerous and precious efforts but they are fragmented. The fundamental reason for this is the poisoning by the capitalist system, as Wallerstein has already demonstrated. They all suffer under the clamps of the modernity. Let us look at a few examples:

Nietzsche talks about how society is made to adopt wife-like features and is enslaved by modernity. When he uses the phrase "blond Germanic beast," which defines fascist flocking, it is as if he could see fifty years into the future.[17] It is clear that he thinks modernization and becoming a nation-state sooner or later leads to fascist flocking. He can almost be called the prophet of the capitalist era.

Max Weber had also embarked on an important finding when he described modernity as "the trapping of the society in an iron cage." He underlined the material characteristic of the civilization when he described rationality as the reason behind the disenchantment of the world.

Fernand Braudel directed harsh criticism against the social sciences that are detached from a historical and geographical dimension. He called them a "trivial pile of events." This is an immense contribution to the question of methodology. New horizons in writing history have been opened up by his notions of *la longue durée* or geographic structures, *conjuncture* or medium term socio-economic cycles, and *événements* or short term or episodic events.[18]

The Frankfurt School's criticism of the Enlightenment and modernity is ground breaking. Adorno's analysis of modern civilization as the "end of an era in darkness" is a competent evaluation. With the phrase "the wrong life cannot be lived rightly," he acknowledged that modernity has been founded on the wrong method and knowledge.[19] His criticism of the Enlightenment and rationality also opens up new horizons.

To Nietzsche's declaration that God is dead, Foucault added that "the end of man is at hand."[20] He ascribed modern power to constant wars, inside and outside the society. His notional chain of power, knowledge, prison, hospital, mental institution, school, military institution, factory and brothel has not only made methodological contributions but also has made indirect contributions to how a system of free knowledge can be established. Due to his premature death, he was not able to complete his analysis of power, war and freedom. He seems to conclude that it is modernity that kills man. From that, we can deduce that freedom is communal life that has managed to exclude war. Therefore, we have to abolish industrialism and militarism, which produce all the destructive tools and aim for profit and regular armies. Yet, freedom cannot be realized if we cannot replace industrialism and militarism with self-defense and an ecologically sound society.

Immanuel Wallerstein is confident with his perception of the capitalist world system. He paints an excellent picture of the modern system from the 16th century until today. But he is not always clear in his evaluation of the system (as with Marx, he considers the capitalist phase as a necessity and tends to see it in a positive light), his opposition to it and finding a way out of it. Wallerstein has shown great wisdom with his theses that the socialist system—especially that of Soviet Russia—strengthens capitalist modernity instead of overcoming it and that its dissolution will not eventually strengthen capitalist liberalism but weaken it. He does not show the same competence when it comes to dissolving the system and finding new ways out of it. He states that we cannot foresee when and how the structural crisis of capitalist modernity that started in the 1970s will end, yet each small but meaningful intervention may lead to enormous results. He has distanced himself from strict determinism. In conclusion, we can say that Wallerstein is one of the most powerful evaluators of method and system of knowledge.

Undoubtedly, there are many other intellectuals that should be mentioned. The criticism and proposals produced by Murray Bookchin in relation to ecology and Paul Feyerabend in relation to method and logic are groundbreaking. However, none of these intellectuals are able to competently combine knowledge and action. (Without a doubt, capitalist modernity's tremendous power to tie everything to itself has had an effect.)

The Marxist school claims to be the most scathing and most scientific critique of capitalism but ironically this has not prevented Marxism from being the most useful tool in terms of knowledge and power *for* the system. It could not escape being liberalism's left wing—150 years of experience sufficiently proofs this. Its method and its entire collection of knowledge can be categorized under the heading "economic reductionism." Scientific socialism (which has handled the metaphysical and historical characteristics of society in a most simplistic way, reduced the notion of power to a government committee and gave a magical role to economic and political analyses) could not escape being yet another version of positivism. Although much was expected from sociology and its founders, Émile Durkheim and Max Weber, its method and theory of knowledge (epistemology) could never amount to more than being liberalism's left wing. Yet again we see that what is important and decisive is not the intention but the assimilating and integrating power of the system (its method, knowledge-power, technical power) that dominates society. Economy certainly is an important power that should be taken into account; however, in the absence of a proper historical and social analysis of political power and other fundamental metaphysical forces, any effort to transcend the system of capitalist modernity cannot but end up being a vulgar positivism. The present theory and practice sufficiently prove this.

The anarchist schools that emerged as the radical critique of capitalist modernity are competent in issues such as methodology and the theory of knowledge. Unlike the Marxists, they do not talk about the progressiveness of capitalism. They were able to perceive society from many different perspectives and did not limit themselves to economic reductionism. They play their role of the system's "rebellious children" quite competently. However, despite all their good intentions, they could not ultimately avoid becoming a sect that stubbornly protected itself from the system's sins. My critique of Marxism fits these movements as well: In the absence of a valid definition of the system, these schools failed to formulate the relevant questions that would have provided democratic modernity with the competent use of method-power and knowledge-action, thus enabling it to overcome the system.

A similar evaluation of the theory and practice of the ecological, feminist and cultural movements can be made. They resemble the nestling partridges that have just escaped modernity's iron cage. We are continuously worried about where and when they would be hunted down. But they are important movements of hope. They will have much to contribute when the main alternative movement has developed.

The social democrat and national liberation movements have integrated with the modern system above all the others and continue to be its driving forces. They have managed to become the two strongest denominations of the main movement, which is liberalism.

As we near the conclusion, it would be useful to state my anti-Orientalist approach. Taking stock of my position relative to modernity, I realize that I am at odds with it. I can immediately give two reasons for this.

Firstly, it is the effect of the classical Middle Eastern culture that has deep-rooted differences with capitalist modernity. In the first place, Middle Eastern culture radically differs from capitalist modernity in the priority it assigns to society. Individualism is not easily welcomed by society. Loyalty to the society is the fundamental criterion in the assessment of the personality and is praised above all else. Detachment from the society is scorned and ridiculed; changing societies is also regarded negatively. Occupying a place within the hierarchy and state is envied. (Religion, tradition, and the traditional state culture of the Middle East have strongly influenced these values.) As a result, it is not easy to submit to foreign and modern cultures. Stated differently, it is really difficult to assimilate. Thus, it is not surprising that the strong tradition of the *Ummah* culture (the Community of Believers) is still preferred to the nation-state. This is because the nation-state is the product of capitalist modernity: it is foreign. When political Islam and the nation-state are compared, (both being nationalistic at heart) Islamic nationalism is still preferred.[21] This comparison alone proves the historical and social permanence of this cultural structure.

Secondly, although I never stayed committed to any of its movements for long, I was always very interested in Western schools of thought. In my quest for truth, I became aware of the method and accumulation of knowledge and science that led to modernity. I see its clear-cut mastery. As a result, I feel the same affinity with modern culture as I have with the Middle Eastern culture. Albeit late, I realized that they were of the same material and I saw the real source of both cultures to be the five thousand year-old hierarchic and statist structures. After this realization, I had no hesitation in daring to criticize the common aspects of both of these cultures.

It is not difficult to see that individualism is eroding the society. Neither is it too difficult to understand that capitalist liberalism is not the freedom of the individual it proposes to be, but that it is the art of human society's erosion. It has its origins in the traditional merchant culture. It can be shown that the merchant culture is linked to many of the ancient traditions, including the three major monotheistic religions of the Middle East. Commodification and exchange of commodities, which are the roots of commerce, have played the leading role in the erosion and disintegration of the communities and societies. The merchant mentality is a deep-rooted tradition of the Middle East. It has played a decisive role in enforcing negative elements of symbols, identities, languages and structures on society. (The creation and sanctification of god, the turning of the art of state administration into one that is conspiratorial, and the permanent insertion of deceit and hypocrisy into morality, are only a few examples.) The contribution of Western Europe lays in its ability to take this system from the Middle East, combine it with the outcomes of the Renaissance, Reformation and Enlightenment and then to make it the dominant social system. The Middle Eastern societies do not esteem the merchant and its institutions highly. On the contrary, they have always aroused suspicion. The success of European capitalist modernity, however, is to make the commodity system society's most precious element and to put all the sciences, religions, and arts at the service of this new society. As a result, people that were undistinguished and of little importance in the Middle East became the chosen and the all-important ones for Europe.

It has become quite fashionable in today's Middle East to criticize European modernity and to violently oppose it through radical Islam. However, these critics (from approaches like Edward Said's to organizations like Hezbollah) that seem to be anti-Orientalist and an enemy of Western modernity are nothing but establishments within the boundaries of this modernity—just like Marxism. As a result, they cannot escape serving capitalist modernity dishonorably. Since they owe their existence to modernity, it is in their nature to beg modernity and to defend it—whether successful or not. These organizations have only put on the clothes and the beard of tradition. Their soul and body are loaded with the most backward remnants of modernity.

While presenting the framework of my method of criticism and my evaluation of knowledge, I have tried to shed some light on the method and science that has led to the formation of capitalist modernity. It may not be absolutely correct in all aspects, but this framework does provide us with a chance to develop our own method and science for the preferred option of freedom and democratic life at a time when capitalist modernity is going through a period of structural "chaos."

The cornerstones of this narrative (as discussed either in this section or in my earlier books) are summarized here for clarity.

1. There is a relation between the methods of Roger Bacon, Francis Bacon and Descartes—the scientific paradigm—and capitalism of which we should be critically aware.

2. The intensification of the distinction between subjectivity and objectivity and its reflection in various dichotomies allows the individual (the subject) to utilize society (the object) as a source open to all sorts of exploitation.

3. This results in the distinction between the bourgeoisie and the proletariat being perceived as natural and thus paving the way for the proletariat to be used as an object.

4. The realization that "knowledge is power" lays the foundation of the union of science and power. Hence, the union of knowledge and power was turned by the system very early on into its fundamental weapon.

5. Science has been turned into a new religion in the form of positivism, capitalizing on the exposed absurdities and obsessions of religion and metaphysics. In the name of a struggle against religion and metaphysics, the new religion has been formed to ensure domination.

6. The most powerful ideological hegemony has been realized by declaring liberalism to be the official ideology of capitalist modernity. This is then used on the one hand as a tool of immense compromise and on the other hand as a weapon to assimilate and integrate all opposing ideologies.

7. Liberalism and positivism are officially sanctioned to discredit many other schools of thought and ideological movements. This will continue until all the opponents of the system are integrated.

8. Philosophy and morality are discredited to reduce the chances of opponents developing their own perspectives and taking a stand against the system.

9. The internal unity of science and its power of meaning is fragmented through its division into a multitude of disciplines. This excessive fragmentation makes science dependent on the power structure and thus it can easily be turned into profitable technology. The aim of knowledge is no longer the discovery of the meaning of life but making money. This enables the transition from the unity of science and wisdom to the unity of science, power and money. The unity of science, power and capital is the new sacred alliance of modernity.

10. In capitalist modernity, in addition to the completion of the housewifization (the most advanced form of slavery) of woman, the housewifization of man—after his castration through citizenship—has also been achieved.[22] As a result, the society's control has been attained through housewifization.[23]

11. In modernity, political power has meant continuous war both within and between societies—a "war of all against all," in Hobbes' words.[24] Genocide is the extremum of these wars.

12. In the system of capitalist modernity, the period of center and periphery expansion has been completed; damage to ecology has reached unsustainable levels, unemployment and poverty are at its worst levels, wages are low, there is an excessive bureaucracy, religious society is collapsing, going through the age of the global finance hegemony, which is the most parasitic form of capitalism. However, the fact that networks of resistance are established in all areas and amongst the majority of society generates a structural crisis.

13. In periods of structural crisis, revolutionary and counter-revolutionary movements, democratic-libertarian movements and totalitarian-fascist groups all vie to shape the future. Those who develop their methodology and scientific systems the most competently and make it the basis of their actions have the best chance of determining the new social system.

14. Thus, during such periods of structural crisis and chaos, the democratic, ecological, libertarian and egalitarian movements may be able to form the establishments needed to determine the far future through small but effective moves.

To this end:

1. Sociology should be used as the blueprint for action—but a sociology imbedded in the historical and geographical dimensions of society.

2. Capitalist modernity should be seen as the malignant structure that it is and (keeping in mind point 14), a solution should be sought outside the boundaries of this system.

3. We have to ideologically overcome all the vulgar dichotomies based on the subject-object distinction, such as idealism-materialism, dialectics-metaphysics, liberalism-socialism and deism-atheism. Instead, we

should apply the art of interpretation that takes all scientific gains into consideration.

4. We should constantly and critically develop a human metaphysics based on goodness, beauty, freedom and truth.

5. Democratic politics should be the norm.

6. Based on democratic politics, thousands of non-governmental organizations should be established in areas where there is a crisis of power.

7. A new social nation should be constructed as the democratic nation. It can be separate from the nation-state but one should not disregard the possibility that these two can also exist next to each other or within each other.

8. The political administrative model for the democratic nation should be developed on the basis of local, national, regional and world democratic confederalism. Different nations can be organized in a single democratic nation. The same nation can be organized as both a nation-state and a democratic nation. Regional democratic confederalisms and World Democratic Nations' Confederalism are quite essential and can be more effective (much more than today's UN) in the resolution of local-national problems.

9. Democratic society should be anti-industrialist and economy and technology should be ecologically sound.

10. The defense of the society should be ensured by people's militia.

11. A new family system, based on deep-rooted freedom and the equality of woman, should replace the system based on the deep-rooted slavery of women. Such a system will help to abolish the male-based hierarchic and statist order.

The era of capitalist modernity is also the period in which the ideal of a utopia of freedom and equality has revived. Much blood has been spilt for this ideal: there are numerous cases of torture and inflictions of pain. It is unthinkable that this suffering has been in vain. On the contrary, we have to attain a proper historical interpretation of our problems and let that illuminate our future. Then we should be able to make the transition into a life where love reigns. However, the transition to such a utopia requires a serious effort.

I am not so insolent as to re-initiate the quest for method and regime of truth with myself. But what I tried to demonstrate in all the topics I examined was that there is something terribly wrong that is fundamental to our world perception. I emphasize that my analysis should be seen neither as an effort to construct a new system nor as the total rejection of that which I criticized. After all, it is important to criticize the system of capitalist modernity that has led to millions of cases similar to my own, to countless massacres, genocides and wars. This is especially true of the people and region of which I am part—the Kurds and the Middle East—who are going through the most brutally tragic period. The least contribution I can make, as an intellectual, is to examine all of the factors that are responsible for this terrible situation. I am being tried as the head of a comprehensive and effective organization and my primary duty is to look for solutions to the questions with which we are faced. If, at a given place and time, that oppression, exploitation, dissolution and deadlock is so profound that to live is worse than being dead, then there is no alternative but to replace the existing world-view with a profoundly new approach. Hereafter, I shall advance such an approach.

The Main Sources of Civilization

As argued in the previous section, the best way to obtain insight into a specific society is through an examination of its historical and geographical conditions. We will turn to this now, as I try to analyze the main factors that have led to today's civilization.

From our earliest primate beginnings, it seems to have taken us at least seven million years to arrive at the agricultural revolution about 8,000 years ago. Paleontological evidence indicates that hominid species evolved in Africa from approximately 2.5 million years ago and spread from there to Asia and Europe. Homo Sapiens seems to have evolved in East Africa, around 150,000 to 200,000 years ago, and soon afterwards started spreading around the globe from the East African Rift Valley during the so-called "first exit" out of Africa.

In Africa, and later in other parts of the world, all hominid species are believed to have lived in clans of twenty to thirty people, sustaining themselves by gathering and hunting. Ownership and family had not yet developed but the clan system functioned as the extended family. It is believed that early Homo species mastered a communication system consisting of body and sound signs, but were not yet able to transform sounds into symbols. Nevertheless, this communication system brought many advantages such as the ability to act in unison when hunting or fighting.

Research indicates that approximately 150,000 to 200,000 years ago, Homo Sapiens developed something akin to language. These studies also indicate that around 50,000 years ago a second wave of migration from East Africa, via the Rift Valley took place. Prior to the second exodus from Africa, humans had already obtained a communication system consisting of sounds with symbolic meaning—the origin of modern languages.[1]

We can assume that the early humans, both inside and outside of Africa, lived in larger communities and hunted intentionally, that they used caves as dwellings and that women specialized in gathering and men in hunting. Some archaeological findings point to the fact that the species advanced rapidly during this time due to their obtaining symbolic thought. For instance, the incredible cave drawings from this period in the region of the French-Spanish border and in Hakkari, Kurdistan, attest to the fact that these humans possessed symbolic thought.[2] There may even be a connection between the complex communication system of modern humans and the elimination of the other hominid species (amongst others the Neanderthals, who disappeared between 30,000 and 40,000 years ago).

The Contribution of the Taurus-Zagros Arc to Humanity

It is my contention that the Taurus-Zagros Arc—the so called Fertile Crescent—was the main gathering and dispersion point for humans as they exited Africa through the East African Rift. In the first place, the Arc forms the end of the natural path of the Rift. The Great Sahara and the Arabian Desert block off the eastern and western entrances into Asia and Europe, leaving the Suez and the eastern Mediterranean shores as the natural paths for human expansion. This ideal path is the arc formed by the Taurus-Zagros Mountain range, off the eastern Mediterranean shores. Secondly, the suitable weather conditions, the huge numbers of shelters provided by the caves in this area, the abundance of streams and rivers, and the fertility that led to the creation of the image of "Paradise" in the memory of humanity—all made the Fertile Crescent the ideal gathering point, a "place of incubation" for civilizational development.

With their newly acquired ability of symbolic language, the extensive area of the Fertile Crescent provided its inhabitants a unique opportunity for societal development with its safe shelter and a ready food source.[3] For the first time, humans made the transition from a nomadic life style to a culture of a settled life. The four seasons could be now be experienced together in all of their beauty. The new circumstances brought about a new life style—that is, a new cultural era, the Mesolithic. New terms were coined to name the new society, along with other concepts, new objects, new plants and animals, and all of them became part of the newly developing languages of the widespread communities of the Arc. Hence, new communities with new identities were formed in the Fertile Crescent.

In comparison to the Palaeolithic era that lasted a few million years, the Mesolithic period in the Arc was short-lived. Despite its short span, the Mesolithic period had a profound effect on this region, as attested to by the Hakkari caves and hewn stones. But the real progress was made in the Neolithic—an era we can call *the Era of the Farming, Field and Village Revolution*. It is a cultural era of which the importance has not yet been fully understood and which has not yet received the attention it deserves.[4] The Neolithic inhabitants of the Fertile Crescent brought numerous inventions and revolutionary developments in areas such as agriculture, arts and crafts, transport, housing, administration and religion; inventions and developments that truly shaped the modern era.

It is here in the Arc that the shepherd culture was likely introduced by the Semites during a period of favorable weather conditions at the end of the fourth ice age around 10,000 years ago. The impact of this new life style is clear from the cultural importance that the accumulation of sheep, camels and goats still have in the Semitic culture today—in its essence the Semitic culture still is a shepherd culture. Furthermore, from the Sumerian and Egyptian tablets of the time, it is clear that they too valued the importance of the shepherd culture. It seems that the Semitic culture has left a permanent mark on a vast area from the Sahara and Eastern Arabia to the lands suitable for agriculture in the North.

However, the Arians of the Arc were the pioneers of crop farming. (The

Kurdish word *ari* means "related to earth, place, field.") Archaeological evidence (charred seeds and chaff from barley, wheat and pulses) indicates that the earliest transition to agriculture took place in the Fertile Crescent during the Neolithic, more or less 1,000 years before pastoralism was introduced. The favorable weather conditions of the time, the soil structure, the streams coming from the glaciated mountain peaks, all contributed to the Arc being extremely suitable for growing olives, nuts, grapes, cereals, dates, pulses, and so forth. Wild sheep, goats, cattle, pigs, etc. roamed around in flocks. The forests on the mountain slopes provided the building material needed for the settled life style of crop farming and the copious streams and rivers offered suitable areas for settlement. In fact, under conditions like these, the development that took place here was almost inevitable.

By about 6,000 years ago, agriculture had spread from the Fertile Crescent into Europe, northern Africa and central and southern Asia. As agriculture spread, so did village settlement and farming techniques such as irrigation and terracing. And, as the culture spread, so did the Aryan language and cultural group.

Thus, contrary to the common belief, the birth place of the Aryan language group is not Europe, India or the regions in-between (the areas of the northern Black Sea, the Russian steps or the Iranian plateaus) but the Fertile Crescent. It is of utmost importance that we understand this, because the history of the expansion of this big language and cultural group is vital for understanding the societal development of the urban civilizational phase and of modernity.

Another contribution that is vital for modernity and has its origins in this period in the Fertile Crescent is monotheistic religion.

Problems with the Expansion of Aryan Culture and Language

To fully understand modernity, we need to trace and understand the origin of the Indo-European civilization on which modernity is built. Historiography usually defines core cultures with reference to the time and location within which they exist. Historical conceptualization without reference to origin is, however, delusive and irresponsible. Instead of producing meaningful interpretation of historical knowledge, it produces misconceptions.

I received some criticism on my analysis of the source of modern civilization as set out in *Prison Writings: The Roots of Civilization* (the published form of the argument for my submission before the Court of Human Rights of the Council of Europe). I have been criticized for being excessively reductionist in postulating the Euphrates and Tigris basin, and hence the Sumerian civilization, as the foundation of modernity. After thorough consideration of this criticism, I still maintain that this postulation is valid. Just as today's dominant civilization—capitalist modernity—rests upon Indo-European cultural roots, the Indo-European culture rests upon Aryan cultural roots and its Sumerian and Egyptian branches.

Of course the issues we are trying to analyze are not solely a matter of culture and civilization. But, if we do not determine the relative contribution culture and civilization made to social development, historiography will indeed be no more than "the trivia of the past" from which nothing meaningful can be learnt. Such numerical records of the succession of religions, dynasties, kings, wars and peoples are no more than ideological efforts to disguise social development and to prepare the social memory and mind for exploitation by the rulers. Without correctly identifying the main source of our civilization and its branches, we will not be able to understand today's society nor solve its problems. Even if we wish to understand and end the atrocities in today's Iraq, we need to acknowledge that our knowledge of sociology and historiography has failed. Only then may we be able to propose a new framework for historical and sociological analysis that will render meaningful results. All I am trying to do here is to make a small contribution to end this human tragedy.

A further point of criticism against my analysis was my claim that Kurds are descendants of the Aryan language and cultural group—it was felt that, because Hitler laid claim to the notion of Aryanism, it may have a "racist" connotation. Let me just ask this in return: Because Hitler's political party was the National Socialist Party, does this mean we should abandon the word *socialism*? Fascism quite successfully utilized various scientific and ideological notions for its own benefit, but this doesn't mean that we should abandon science and ideology. I have no intentions of fostering a nationalism based on Aryan language and culture. On the contrary, I have argued strongly against nationalism.

I am compelled to summarize the arguments I set out in *Prison Writings: The Roots of Civilization*:

a. Both the formation of a language and its being the foundation of a deep rooted culture depends on the historical and geographical preconditions. The period 10,000 to 4,000 BCE defines the "long term" (*la longue durée*) in which this language and cultural group institutionalized itself. During this period various inventions such as pottery, the plough, animals for farming, the wheel, weaving, manual grinders, arts and religion were institutionalized. A rich list of plant and animal products enabled the great increase in the population. Metals were not only used for tools, it was used to make rich works of art during the Chalcolithic period (Copper Age). We are still discovering examples of these today—houses and religious architecture made of hewn stone and many tools made of metals have been recovered from the archaeological sites of Bradostiyan at the skirts of Zagros, Çayönü (Diyarbakir) and finally Göbeklitepe (near Urfa) which is said to date back 11,000 years.

    The cultural tools and words used even today by the local people to name these tools shed light on the identity of the core region. Words such as *geo* (location), *ard* (location, soil, field), *jin* (woman, life), *roj* (the sun), *bra* (brother), *mur* (death), *sol* (shoes), *neo* (new), *ga* (ox), *gran* (large, heavy), *mesh* (to walk), *guda* (god) are still used in European languages. These words are also used by Middle Eastern and Central Asian peoples such as the Kurds, Persians, Balochi and others—clues that the Aryan language and cultural group is not of European or Indian origin. Sumerian tablets and other archaeological findings prove that this culture has existed at least around six thousand years ago, when Europe and India were still in the "Old Stone Age."

b. While I do not wish to deny the rich contribution of the Semitic language and cultural group, I cannot envisage that around 4,000 BCE the shepherd culture could have led to urban civilization culture.

    Although the civilization of the Egyptian Pharaohs is in the Semitic region, one cannot find evidence of contributions from the Semitic culture. The Egyptian documents also show that the Semitic culture is foreign to them. There are no similarities in the language structures. The

Semitic culture takes its initial place in the written history around 2,500 BCE with the Akkadian, Babylonian, Assyrian, Canaan and Hebrew identities. The Arabic identity can be seen much later in history—around 500 BCE. Conceptualizations such as Arameans, Amorites and Habirus have first been used by the Sumerians and the Egyptians. It is thought that Phoenicians, Palestinians and even Hebrews have been integrated into the Semitic language and culture group at a later stage (as with the Egyptian Pharaoh culture). There is evidence that they initially had been immersed in the Aryan culture, but that they lost this identity under waves of Semitic migration.

The Sumerian sources and various archaeological records indicate that Semitic language and culture groups have attacked or migrated to the Aryan language and cultural region, possibly as far back as 5,000 BCE. Akkadians, Babylonians, Assyrians, Arameans and Arab colonies especially left their traces in Upper Mesopotamia. However, Assyrian and Arabic influences are much greater than the others. (When combined with Islam, it meant a greater force of assimilation, as Islam and Arabization are intertwined.) The Aryan language and culture group was able to resist these efforts of colonization, assimilation and incursion by counter attack, incursion, colonization and assimilation. The initial founders of the Sumerian civilization, leaders of the Egyptian civilization as well as the Hyksos and the Hebrews are examples of this.[5]

I think that the most acceptable interpretation is that the initial leaders of the Sumerians migrated to Lower Mesopotamia, carrying the Aryan core culture with them and transforming it to a more advanced level. This Aryan culture reached its peak in the Upper Mesopotamian region—Tell Halaf—around 6,000–4,000 BCE. Thus, the Sumerians should be viewed as responsible for the cultural expansion of the Tell Halaf era instead of some migrating groups. It does not make sense to look for Central Asian or Caucasian influences, as at the beginning of the Sumerian civilization (around 5,000 BCE): these areas were still in the Stone Age and had just begun encountering the Aryan culture. At the time, they simply had no means to sustain a culture such as that of the Sumerians. Physically, they would not have been able to overcome the Aryans.

Just as European culture is propagated all around the world today, the Aryan language and culture too was propagated around the world, especially after it completed its institutionalization and experienced a population boom (especially in the Tell Halaf period between 6,000–4,000 BCE). Just as today a variety of poor cultural groups and laborers are lured to the safety that Europe offers, at the time such groups arrived in the Fertile Crescent and the Sumerian zone.

c. Thus, the Arian culture established and institutionalized itself at the Fertile Crescent. From there it moved further to the east—to the regions that are today called Iran, Afghanistan, Pakistan and India. I must emphasize that it was not the groups of people that migrated but the culture itself. Initial signs of this culture are encountered around 7,000 BCE in the Iranian plateaus and the culture was effective in India around 4,000 BCE. Its influence reached the Turkmenistan plateaus around 5,000 BCE. There is a school of thought that claims the previous cultural layer there had been of African Stone Age descent.[6] Cultural remnants seem to substantiate this thesis. Just as in Egypt and Sumer, there is no theoretical or empirical evidence of a culture in this region that is solely the product of local development.

Although some of my critics find this line of argumentation too reductionist, we should keep in mind that a limited number of cultural revolutions took place in history and that those were achieved only with the greatest difficulty. Furthermore, though European culture is quite unique in the world, the above-mentioned culture did have similarities with European culture and with the culture of the Fertile Crescent. In the third place, there is no theoretical evidence or archaeological remains indicating that groups that have lived according to the same habits for hundreds of thousands of years or groups that are at the threshold of being annihilated suddenly could come up with a fundamental cultural revolution. Hence we can assume that there was a cultural expansion to the east around 3,000 BCE leading to the urban civilization centered on Susa to the west of Iran in the Elam region. This expansion we can assume originated from Sumer. Further east, the establishment of the cities of Harappa and Moenjo-daro (at the shores of the Punjab River in today's Pakistan) in around 2,500 BCE, also embodied Sumerian influences. It is impossible to reason that they were the original institutions of some other cultural structures. If this were the case, then one would need to question why thousands of other groups at much more fertile geographical locations were unable to develop a civilization or a grand cultural revolution.

Undoubtedly, each and every region would have made its own contributions. Expansion and local acceptance of the culture is intertwined and mostly voluntary. Expansion is not that of the exploitative groups but rather of the more advanced material and moral values of production. The expansionist cultures that have demonstrated their abilities in this regard have always been seen as "sacred miracles of the gods." It is important that we do not confuse cultural expansion that elevates the value of life both morally and materially with that of colonialism, occupation and forced assimilation. In fact, only a small number of cultural expansions have been achieved through brutal attacks, colonialism, and forced assimilation. The majority were accepted because they brought an advanced quality of life. However, because of the narrow nationalistic conceptualizations of history, the concept of cultural expansion is still not well understood. It is important not to fall into the traps of nationalism, which lead to denial, exaggeration, disguise and distortion—especially here, where we are attempting to establish a meaningful method of obtaining and interpreting knowledge.

d. The relationship between the Aryan language and culture groups and that of the Indo-European language and culture groups may be one of the main problems of historiography and therefore it is important to determine this relationship. There has been much speculation on this topic but a common interpretation has not been attained. In the 19th century, when it became clear that the Indo-European languages had much in common, much research was done. Various interpretations were made in relation to the main source of these groups. Some said the source was Greek or Indian while others claimed it to be North European or Germanic.

Establishing that all modern humans originated from the East African Rift and that the Neolithic-agricultural revolution took place in the Fertile Crescent excludes many possible hypotheses. The next step is to establish which language and culture group was the original group in the Fertile Crescent during the Neolithic. As argued above, the proto-Kurdish, Persian, Afghan and Balochi groups gained prominence as the Aryan groups of the time. Furthermore, a better understanding of the language structure of the Hurrians—the proto-Kurds—broadened our insight of the Aryan language and cultural identity. Thus, I postulate that this is the language and culture that formed the core of the Neolithic revolution, and that this language and culture formed the center of the Aryan language and culture group.

It can be assumed that, similar to the expansion to the south and east, there would have been an expansion to the north and west—toward Europe. This wave of expansion is estimated to have begun around 5,000 BCE and to have been completed in 4,000 BCE in Eastern Europe and around 2,000 BCE in Western Europe. This is now the main opinion and many important historians, including V. Gordon Childe, date the beginning of European history to this timeframe. Prior to this period is the period of "Old Stone Age." It is estimated that around thirty thousand years ago Homo Sapiens became the dominant species in the region between the South of France and Spain with roots in Northern Africa. Thus, its expansion around the world was most probably during the Mesolithic period or the middle part of the stone age.

I am not about to embark on an examination of the European Neolithic and the agricultural revolution. But because of the importance of what the main source is, we need to shed some light on it. Again, I propose that the expansion to the west was not physical or colonial but cultural. However, Europe is unique in that it had absorbed the Neolithic period with all its creative aspects. It digested an accumulation of around ten thousand years in a short period of time. Just as Western Europe has turned the modern world into a cultural expansion region over the past four hundred years, it was once the region of expansion of, initially, the Neolithic culture from the Fertile Crescent, then the Roman civilization and finally the Christian revolution. The expansive bases for all these three big revolutions in Europe were cultural more than anything else. Expansion was not based on colonization, imperialism and forced assimilation alone. It has mostly been achieved through the acceptance of the more advanced cultures as "god's gift." As a result, the foundation for the later "Big Revolutions" of Europe has already been laid (such as the Renaissance, Reformation, Enlightenment, Political, Industrial, and Scientific Revolutions). Europe did not have special talents with which it created these big revolutions. They resulted from the core and peripheral cultures. On the other hand, the retreat of the Ice Age brought weather conditions quite suitable for all kinds of development. The synthesis of all these conditions has paved the way for a civilization that has determined our future.

The Evolution of Social Structures in the Fertile Crescent

In this section, I will look at the effects that the time and location of a specific social development have on a specific way of life.

As explained in Section I of this book, social realities are constructed by human beings. If we do not fully understand this, all attempts to acquire the knowledge and understanding needed to construct a meaningful life will only result in ignorance and meaninglessness. I repeat that our ignorance in the time of capitalist modernity is worse than it was at the onset of the major religions and that the fundamental reason for this is positivism.[7]

Adorno's statement "Wrong life cannot be lived rightly" (*Es gibt kein richtiges Leben im falschen*), although used to express his dismay with the Jewish Holocaust, applies to life in modernity in general. What then, is the fundamental mistake that caused this *wrong life*? Adorno has linked the root of the problem to the period of Enlightenment and to Rationalism. However, he did not attempt to clarify the problem itself—the form of life that is wrong. Who is responsible for it? How has it been constructed? What is its relationship with the dominant social system? Similarly, Michel Foucault states that "Modernity is the death of man" but leaves it there, without investigating this critical subject further.[8]

It is not enough to just blame modernity. In the first place, can only life constructed by capitalist modernity be described as *wrong*? Was the life enforced by previous civilizations *right*? Were not the Sumerian priests and god-kings, the Egyptian god-kings, the Iranian Khosrows, Alexander the Great, the Roman Empire, the Islamic sultans and European monarchs all responsible for constructing life on the wrong foundations? Were they not links in the chain around the neck of social development whereby the foundations of *wrong life* were strengthened? It is not sufficient to put the responsibility for the *wrong life* on modernity, its wars and genocidal order, without further investigating what it was caused by and how it can be rectified. Just as the root of the problem, its solution is profound.

Although we cannot understand a society solely through its culture—many elements need to be included in its definition—culture is at the basis of any society. But what do I mean by culture?

A culture, in a narrow sense, is the mentality, forms of thought and language of a particular society. In a broader sense, the material gains (the tools and devices used to satisfy the needs for production, storage and processing of food, for transportation, worshipping and beautifying, etc.) form part of its culture. The similarities and the differences between the mentalities and devices of different cultures determine to what degree their life styles correspond.

Generally speaking, the social realities constructed in the Fertile Crescent during the Neolithic are still in existence today. Both the mental and the material cultural elements—despite some quantitative and qualitative changes—are essentially still the same. In essence, the languages spoken today are the same in terms of their main structure. The mental effort is still divided between the fields of science, religion and art. Defensive and offensive wars existed then and are still waged today. The family structure continues to be the fundamental social institution. The differences are due to the growth of the state institution. The state has continuously expanded its field of operation against society. As it began to take possession of the mental and material cultural accumulation it has changed these constructs qualitatively and quantitatively. Contrary to belief, social developments have been achieved *despite* the state. I will continue to point out the consequences that the state formations (from the very beginning of the Sumerian priest-state to the nation-state of the capitalist modernity) had on society and what the real function was of the civilization that grew from these formations.

I believe that the role of Fernand Braudel's concept of plural temporalities (different modes of periodization, different time scales) in social development has not been analyzed sufficiently. Especially Braudel's notions of *longue durée* (a historical relation that allows an open and experimental approach to the theoretical reconstruction of long-term, large-scale world historical change) and structural time (that is, historical temporalities beyond direct human or social intervention) in relation to culture, civilization and society can make a strong contribution to our understanding of history. In the discussion that follows, I will attempt to apply these notions to the social development in the Fertile Crescent.

a. La longue durée

For the society of the Fertile Crescent, *la longue durée* implies the period starting with the end of the fourth ice age and ending when it can no longer continue its physical existence due to some natural or nuclear disaster.[9] Cultures with Chinese and Semitic roots have taken their place within this *longue durée* society as two branches. Other smaller cultural branches also take their place within this main river as streams. It is important that the logic of the thesis is well understood: The constructed society is so strong, together with its mental and material cultural elements, that no internal social event can destroy it within this duration. I will thus refer to the society of the *longue durée* as the "fundamental cultural society."

In my opinion, this interpretation of *duration* and *society* can contribute much to social science. Liberal sociologists, through the construction of a false metaphysics, wish to enforce their societal conception formulated as the end of history to be eternally valid.[10] Marxist and other messianic approaches promise all an era of eternal prosperity, detached of time and location. The notion of long duration is much more scientific than all these social theories. It presents understandable arguments not only for concrete conditions but also for both the beginning and end of the social system. It neither congests history by treating it as a pile of events nor does it fragment history by emphasizing the periodic existence of isolated social forms. The meaning of life cannot be profoundly interpreted by examining either instantaneous events or social forms in isolation.

Within the scope of *la longue durée*, there is room for various fundamental institutions such as religion, state, art, law, economy and politics in the fundamental cultural society. These institutions continuously change both qualitatively and quantitatively. Some shrink dramatically and in return its counterparts grow. While some diminish, their function is continued either in other institutions or in the new ones. In more general terms, there is a dialectical creative relationship between all its constructs and institutions. The fact that there is a single main cultural society does not deprive it of strong partners and new internal formations.

In the light of these concepts, we can better understand the quarrel between the evolutionists and the creationists. The creationists are aware of the *longue durée*; in fact, they gain their real strength from this knowledge. We can explain the religious verses on the duration of god's creation of the universe and its end in cultural terms. If we, however, interpret it sociologically, we see that the creationist perspective is aware of the sacred, supreme and glorious characteristics of constructed society. In fact, all three Holy Books of monotheistic religion, the Torah, Bible, and Koran, are attempts to explain the captivating and "sacred" life at the Fertile Crescent. Maybe the reason why the majority of humans belong to these religions lies in the quality of these interpretations. These books succeeded in turning into the fundamental belief of humanity the claim that the new cultural life—which has "miraculously" occurred—will continue eternally; an indication of just how influential this culture is.

Sociologists such as Émile Durkheim did not move beyond defining society as groups of human beings who are the sum of events and institutions. Class, state, economic, juridical, political, philosophical and religious narratives cannot surpass the mentality of events and institutions. However, these scientists never really question why these are not held to be as precious as the Holy Books. Their main weakness is that they have not understood the importance of the *longue durée* society. Humanity possesses a profound memory of its own story and will not abandon it so easily. The belief in the sacred religious books are not due to an abstract god and some rituals, but because humans can feel the meaning and traces of their own life story in these books. In fact, these books are the memory of living society. Thus, whether the events and notions in them are true or not is of secondary importance. Fernand Braudel draws our attention to a fundamental methodological and scientific mistake with his apt comment that "sociology and history make up *one single intellectual adventure*, not two different sides of the same cloth but the very stuff of the cloth itself."[11] Unless we meaningfully determine the relationship between duration and society, separate historical and sociological narratives will harm the societal realities and their meanings.

Hence, even though the evolutionists have a much better understanding of the events and processes involved, they will never free themselves of criticism because they do not understand the notion of *duration*. Societal memory is more important than the evolution of events and processes. The reason why the god is not abandoned lies with the power of social memory—society equates the concept of *god* to its past memory. In fact, positivism is a disease of modernity and as long as it stands in the way of society's memory—and hence its metaphysics—it will not be free from criticism. And rightly so, because societies that have lost their memories are easily exploited, conquered and assimilated.

Although the positivists claim that they define society scientifically, this school of thought least understands how society evolves. By interpreting society as a history-less and vulgar materialistic pile, they pave the way for many dangerous social operations. The idea of social engineering is also related to positivism, as the positivists think they can shape society through external intervention. This is also the understanding of modernity's officialdom, and thus it gives legitimacy to exploitative power and warfare.

b. Structural time

The concept of *structural time* can be applied to analyze the fundamental institutional transformations in social development. If we define the construction and collapse periods of fundamental structures in these terms, we may obtain a better understanding of social realities. Humanity has a history of oppression and exploitation, and differentiating between slave-owning, feudal, capitalist and socialist societies may be the subject of a meaningful discourse. In fact, relating structural time to these social forms has led to a considerable literature. However, because no meaningful connection between the long and short terms has been made, such discourse cannot be very productive and turns into repetitive clichés.

A meaningful analysis of Neolithic society can be made by investigating the interrelationship between the structural term and the fundamental cultural society term. Neolithic society has its own unique institutional structures, mentality and accumulation of material life that can be explained in terms of structural time, but it can also be explained through the concept long term because of its cultural influences that will exist until there is a physical destruction or collapse. Science, religion, arts, language, family, ethnicity and peoples as well as the different forms of mentality and diverse human groups—who go through various changes but will most probably always exist—constitute the fundamental cultural society, that is to say the *long term*. In addition, ecology must definitely be a subject of concern. It must be interrelated to the conclusions drawn from all the other branches of science. It can be examined as science of economic institutionalization. Democratic politics needs also to be continuously kept alive as a science and as an institution.

The fundamental institution of a structural term is the establishment and life of a state as well as those things that originated during its existence, such as hierarchy, classes and state borders as well as property, territory and homeland. Different forms of state, such as the priest-state, dynastic state, republic and nation-state, mark some of the important topics. Different types of religion also constitute an important subject. Propositions that distinguish societies based on their mode of production (Neolithic, slave-owning, feudal, capitalist, socialist), as well as the collapse of institutions, can also be regarded within the structural term.

c. Medium and short term

The medium- and short-term matters consist of qualitative and quantitative multiple events and notions.[12] The subject matter of the short and medium term is all the cultural and structural changes and transformations of events. The medium term is involved with changes that take place within the same structural institution. Economic depressions, political regime changes, the establishment of various types of organizations (economical, social, political, and operational) are examples of such changes. The main topics of the short term are all the various social (and socialization) activities of the individual. The media is usually concerned with the short term events and notions. The daily events in each structural institution are also within the compass of the short term.

There really should be a branch of sociology that examines the influence of events. Since it will base itself upon events within the short term, it could be called the August Comte sociology. It may be suitable to call it "positive sociology" (without ignoring the fundamental criticism directed against positivism). Especially during chaotic periods, events gain significance and become a determining factor. I believe that only when the fundamental cultural sociology, structural sociology and positive sociology are united shall we achieve the integrality of sociology.

In addition, all universal events and formations, including social events, require a quantum or chaotic environment because they are the moments of creation. Although they have not been profoundly examined, they definitely do exist. Science is each day more concerned with the fundamental issue of how the "occurrences" of both "each instant" and "short intervals" sustain all long, medium and short-term formations. We should not neglect the "quantum moment" and the "chaos interval" as these can be seen as "moments of creation." The possibility of freedom in the universe occurs at this "moment" and is thus itself related to the "moment of creation." All structures in nature and society, whether in the case of their construction, sustenance or period of life—despite their different qualities—require "moments of creation." There is thus a need to find a name for the sociology that is concerned with the issues of creation at the shortest possible term. I propose the name *sociology of freedom* for the sociology that deals with the moment of creation in social events. Moreover, I think it is a necessity to have sociology of freedom as a branch of sociology. It could also be viewed as the sociology of mentality because of the incredible flexibility of the human mind—due to socialization—and the creativity that has resulted from it. At the top of the list of subjects to examine should be thought and the desire for freedom. We should add that the development at the moment of creation is a development with a component of freedom—hence such a discipline could also be called sociology of creation. Since this shortest *quantum moment* and *chaos interval* encompass the entire social field, the sociology of freedom should be at the top of the list of all the sociology subjects that are in need of urgent development.

Let us then investigate the developments at the Fertile Crescent through this perspective. I will try to implement the method of sociological examination as I go along. However, it should be kept in mind that this examination is experimental and thus can have only experimental value.

In terms of social history, the sociology of freedom observes the most fecund chaos interval in the Fertile Crescent during the Neolithic revolution. The groups that used to sustain themselves through hunting and gathering now embarked on a quest to sustain themselves in settled life through farming. The old clan communities, hundreds of thousands of years old, are replaced with broader structures. This marks an enormous mental transition. Instead of the old clan mentality and the language structure, we see the transition to a broader mentality of people sharing a village and of ethnicity. The introduction of numerous nutriments, means of transport, weaving, grinding, architecture, religious and artistic matters necessitate new mental forms and a new order of nomenclature.

The new society is now based mostly on village life and the clan ties transform into ethnic ties. The new material structures could not have been sustained without a more meaningful mental framework. Although the *totem* (the identity of the old clan society) continues its existence, the symbol of the Neolithic society is the mother-goddess. In time, the size of the totems decrease and the size of the mother-goddess' figures increase. This symbolizes the increasing role of woman. This is a higher level of religious realization and it results in the formation of a very rich conceptualization. Grammatically, the female suffix becomes dominant—a characteristic that can still be observed in many languages. An intensely sacred meaning is bestowed on the mother-goddess as well as on socialization.

The new society also means new notions and nomenclature. Since mental revolution requires creativity, we need to examine this in the sociology of freedom. Historians like V. Gordon Childe suggest that such a period has indeed been experienced.[13] The occurrence of thousands of events means thousands of mental revolutions and names. History shows us that the majority of the terminologies and inventions that we utilize today were created in this period. Religion, arts, science, transportation, architecture, grain, fruits, animal husbandry, weaving, pottery, grinding, kitchens, feasts, family, hierarchy, administration, defense and assault, gifts, farming tools and many other concepts, tools and their related terms continue to exist as the fundamentals of society despite obvious changes. Examining the structure of the village and family of the Neolithic period shows that the most treasured moral values, the values that strengthened society, were societal morals such as respect, affection, neighborly relations and solidarity. These are much more precious than the capitalist modernity's moral values. Society's fundamental forms of mentality are the remnants of this period and they will never lose their value.

From the perspective of positive sociology, the events of that period are also quite rich. When compared with the clan society's monotonous life of hunting, gathering and defense, the events and new notions that developed in the Fertile Crescent are manifold and very exciting. It can be deduced from the narratives of the Holy Books that the fundamental meaning carried over from those times in the minds of the people had later developed into the concept of *paradise*. This is the most prosperous moment of positive sociology and humanity is faced with an incredible development.

In terms of structural sociology, one could see at the Fertile Crescent the traces of all the institutional orders that resulted in societal development. The period from 6,000 to 4,000 BCE in particular was a period of institutionalization. Areas for villages and cities had been determined and settled, hierarchy was born, religion was institutionalized, sanctuaries appeared, ethnicity came into being, customs for interpersonal relations were established and administration on the basis of morality was at its peak. It appeared as if Neolithic society and its agricultural and village revolution came to stay. The social structures that form the backbone of structural sociology exhibited theses strong formation for the first time at the Fertile Crescent during the Neolithic. Much can be learned by examining these original institutions. In fact, studying these structures of the region—the initial institutionalized values of humanity—will enable us to draw sound conclusions about the establishment of structural sociology. Today's structural sociology has a serious lack of meaning. If it is revised as a component of general sociology, it can become an effective, meaningful branch of sociology.

The language and culture whose foundation was laid at the Fertile Crescent is an original source and is a subject for fundamental cultural sociology. The society established in the region is a very long term society. As mentioned earlier, unless through some natural disaster human life deteriorates to a major degree, the social culture and civilization based in the Fertile Crescent has the capacity to continue to play a leading role. Although in terms of capacity it is not impossible for a civilization based on Chinese or Semitic culture to become a hegemonic power, practically it will be very difficult. There were very big Islamic and Mongolian originated assaults, yet the Indo-European culture (hence the Aryan language and culture which is the source culture) has never lost its hegemonic character.

Fundamental cultural sociology may be equated with general sociology. We may thus consider topics such as mental formats, family institution and the change and transition of the ethnic-national entities under general sociology. More importantly, the chaos and decay environments that are encountered and that are the base as well as the result of both the sociology of freedom and structural sociology, can also be examined under general sociology.

The second phase of society that arose at the Fertile Crescent began with the Sumerian Priest State, which is also the onset of "civilized society." Civilized society is in fact based on the culture present at the Fertile Crescent, bu t with hierarchic and dynastic roots from elsewhere.[14] The state was seen as the Leviathan in the Holy Books.

In the next section, I will examine the bloody, exploitative and at times genocidal march of this monster. I will also look at different forms of exploitation—whether they are under the rule of masked, unmasked, disguised or naked kings—as well as at the ways these kings have managed to legitimize themselves.

At the Skirts of the Mountains

The fundamental postulate of this section is that communality as a constructed reality is a human creation. Despite our criticism, there are things that we have and can learn from this fragmented state of the sciences. The reason behind my frequent emphasis on the distinct perception level of social reality is to clarify its difference with other sciences. Without understanding this difference, we will not escape but fall into the scientism of the positivists that have resulted in the genocides of capitalist modernity. Genocide was the great crime that Adorno based his term "wrong life" on. Positivism holds that despite these genocides communal life can be sustained. What I am attempting here is to expose the sources that made this "imprudence" possible and to look for possible methods of transcending these sources, so that we can gain an understanding and identify the appropriate steps to take. We cannot ignore the fact that the continuing existence of modernity leads to institutionalized centers of genocide. The example right before us, the reality of Iraq, shows all of us—not only those who burn in it but also those who observe it from outside—that all the regimes in the Middle East are partners in this crime, whether it be overt or covert. On the other hand, there is also the quest for free life. Free life or genocide—this cannot be an acceptable alternative. We cannot be partners in this crime by living the way we do. How did it happen that this region and history that led to such a meaningful life ended up as it did? With, on the one hand, the wars between the ethnicities that have led to the initial meaning of life, and on the other hand, the wars for leadership of the last great god of modernity? It seems clear that we cannot move on if this issue is not thoroughly addressed.

I feel obliged to express the taste of life in the Fertile Crescent in a more literary way. Let me begin with a quotation by Robert J. Braidwood, who initiated the excavations at Çayönü (Diyarbakir). He said, "Life could not have been more meaningful than at the skirts of the arching range of the Zagros-Taurus Mountains." I really wonder what it was that made this person, grown up in the distant cultures of today, say such a thing. As an archaeologist and a historian who knows this civilization best, why has he seen the most meaningful life of all to be that of this cultural region? Despite this observation, today's inhabitants wish to flee from this land to Europe as if to run away from plague, even though it means working for the lowest wages. They look at migration as if it is their destiny, as if there is no sacred or aesthetic value left in this region, as if there is nothing that can once again be attained.

I admit, at some stage I too fell for the disease of modernity and wanted to flee from everything, including from my mother and father. I often admit to myself that this was my biggest delusion in life. However, I had not totally detached myself from what Braidwood observed. As a child of those skirts, I always thought the peaks of the mountains to be the sacred throne of the gods and goddesses, and its skirts to be the cornerstones of heaven that they created in plenitude and I always wanted to wander around. As a young boy, because of this, I was described as "mad for mountains." When I learnt much later that such a life was reserved for the god Dionysus and the free and artistic groups of girls (the Bacchantes) who travelled before and behind him, I really envied him. It is said that the philosopher Nietzsche preferred this god to Zeus and that he would even sign many of his works as the "disciple of Dionysus." When I was still at my village, I always wanted to play games with the girls of my village. Although this did not conform to the religious rules, I have always thought that this was the most natural thing. I never approved of the dominant culture's way of shutting women behind doors. I still want to engage with them in unlimited free discussions, in games, in all the sacredness of life. I still say an unconditional "no" to the slavery and bonds that smell of possession and that is based on power relations.

I remember how I have always saluted the free women of these mountains with the morning breeze of goddesses and how we tried to understand one another. I also remember the unique anger I have always felt against men—family, clan and state—for the deaths of truckloads of south-eastern women who died in car crashes on their way to other regions for seasonal work. How is it possible that they fell this low from being the descendants of the goddess? My mind and soul have never accepted their fall. I have always thought that a woman should either have the sacredness of a goddess or not be at all. I agree with the statement that "the degree of emancipation of woman is the natural measure of general emancipation."[15]

To me, my mother always was reminiscent of the mother goddess. But then modernity's construction of a superficial mother veiled the sacredness within her to my eyes. Although I experienced extraordinary pain in my life, I have never seriously cried about anything. But now, in the aftermath of shattering the constructs of modernity, I remember my mother and all the mothers of the region with tears and sadness. Now, I again value the meaning of the water I used to drink from the copper buckets that my mother carried home with such difficulty. They are my most vivid and my saddest memories.

I plead that everyone will reconsider their relationship with their mother and father after having shattered modernity in their own minds. And then for everyone to reflect upon all of their relationships in the village from the same perspective. The biggest success of modernity is its achievement in shattering the fifteen thousand year old constructed culture and reducing it to nothing. Of course one cannot expect a noble and free perspective, resistance and passion for life from individuals and communities that have been shattered and reduced to nothing.

The flora and fauna on the skirts of the Arch's mountains have always been objects of passion for me. I used to consider them sacred. The one thing I can still not forgive myself for is snapping off the heads of the birds I hunted without any pity. There is no better example of the profound danger embedded within the object-subject dichotomy modernity enforced on us. My concern for the ecology is strongly related to this passion and the crime of my childhood. My only remedy was to pull down the masks of the "strong exploiter and ruling man" who is a mere hunter and whose only talent is power relations and warring. Unless we understand the language of the fauna and flora, we will neither understand ourselves nor become ecological socialists.

I have the most intense feelings when I remember how the valleys that began at the skirts of the mountains were prepared for production from the onset of spring to the onset of autumn by my farmer father. I cannot forgive myself for the inability to mourn his death—an inability brought on by the relationships imposed by modernity. I have big regrets: Why could not I fully understand these travelers of god and befriend them?

At one time, I thought that the moment for village relationships had come and gone. Today, I have no doubt that the ideal life for humanity can only be sustained in the villages that are in harmony with the ecology—not in the city structures of modernity. The only way that cities can become fit for human dwelling is to transform them into ecological villages.

To my mind, the people living in the range of the Nur and Zagros mountains are the sacred passengers of the gods and goddesses who reside at the thrones located at the peaks of the mountains.[16] I reject the insult, from the perspective of modernity, of being "backward" because *progressiveness* and *backwardness* are just ideological judgments. I not only think that *modernity* is backward, but I also believe that a profound analysis of capitalist modernity's mentality (which I view as an enemy of humanity) will lead us back to the fundamentals of humanity. When we rid ourselves of modernity's hellish shackles, namely profiteering, industrialism and the nation-state, we will be able to live a meaningful life again. The city—that has opened its doors to the life of profit, the capture of the human being in an iron cage and the industrial monsters that are the murderers of life—is an even more meaningless copy of the old "Babylon with seventy two languages." I have no doubt that the liberation of humanity lies in the collapse of the cancerous structure of this kind of urbanism. And I do believe that I was able to make the grand return to freedom.

I have told this short story to evoke memories of the life-culture that is our roots. We need to fully and effectively understand the lifestyle that is the product of this constructed social reality before we can escape playing the role of modernity's fool. If we do not rid ourselves of this cancerous life of modernity that has taken all of us hostage—including the shepherd in the mountains—we cannot live a free life. We shall, sooner or later, understand that "the wrong life cannot be lived rightly."

Urban Civilized Society
The Age of Masked Gods and Disguised Kings

The most critical damage resulting from positivism (capitalist modernity's official ideology) lies in the area of the social sciences. In the name of being scientific, the reductionist objectification of social phenomena has created problems that will not be easily overcome. Scientific socialism's employment of this method in the study of the social and economic areas has complicated the problems associated with establishing a meaningful scientific method to such a degree that it will be very difficult to resolve. The mental attitude resulting from this physical approach has given capitalism the strength that no weaponry could. Opening up the proletariat and the poor to the study of society through its objectification and inducing within them a mindset that accepts such an approach has disarmed them from the outset. But the scientific socialists are not even aware of this. We will try to show that to conceptualize society as a phenomenon like the biological or even physical nature is to already surrender to capitalist modernity.

It is with pain and anger that I have to admit that the noble struggle that has raged for the past one hundred and fifty years was carried out on the basis of a vulgar, materialist positivism doomed to failure. The class struggle underlies this approach. However, the class—contrary to what they believe—is not the workers and laborers resisting enslavement, but the petit bourgeoisie who long ago surrendered and became part of modernity. Positivism is the ideology that has formed this class's perception and underlies its meaningless reaction against capitalism. This class of urban tradesmen is totally ignorant of the way society is really formed and has always been the basis of forming unproductive factions. Ideologically, they constitute a social stratum easily defended by the dominant official order.

The social approach of positivism can be seen as contemporary idolatry. In fact, idolatry is worshipping a divinity which has lost its meaning. In the past, the concept of *divinity* served enchanting and sacred functions for society and the loss of these functions constitutes idolatry. It is understandable that those lacking insight in this matter worship idols. They do not realize that the need for idols lies in the functionality of the idols. On the contrary, they believe that idolatry will produce meaning and hence equal the sacredness and supremacy of believe in divinity. It might be quite enlightening to analyze the anti-idol religions. I have no doubt that those positivists who restrict themselves to positive facts and phenomena are nothing but contemporary idolaters.

Marx and his school attempted to evaluate society, history, the arts, law and even religion by means of economic analysis. But let us not forget that social institutions are also constructs of the human mind. The human mind continuously produces meaning and willpower in a social environment. The mind administers society. Hence, societal economy is also a product of the mind.

I must reiterate that, to make a meaningful contribution, it is of the utmost importance that we look at sociology from a historical perspective and history from a sociological perspective. One of the advantages of this method is that it comes close to a realistic interpretation of history—history as it happened. I do not deny the importance of speculative thought but for speculative thought to be beneficial, we have to understand how history has truly evolved. This cannot be done by proclaiming "history is determined by infrastructure" or "history consists of the state's actions." Such an approach cannot explain what happened in history and thus in society. This amounts to social physiology and not understanding history. Explaining how social institutions (the "tissues" in physiology) have effected or determined one another cannot be considered a narrative of history. It is indeed a very vulgar positivism.

The key to obtaining a meaningful interpretation of history is to determine how the power of its flow is achieved at the instant of that flow. What is important is to understand the nature of the mental attitude and willpower effective at that specific instant in history—whether it is economically or religiously driven. Metaphorically speaking, what is important is not the kind of weapon that was used but the moment the weapon was triggered by the hand. This is the true interpretation of history. As those who have had strategic responsibilities in history well know, history is a weapon always at the ready.

This introduction, before I embark on the history of civilization, is an attempt to ensure that the question of method is not disregarded—it is an attempt at making some contribution to epistemology, the science of knowledge. The value of an interpretation does not only lie in its power to explain history. For those who can influence history, the value lies in how it can be utilized. For the victims of history—the oppressed and exploited—the real value would be realizing that they can attain the power to obtain their freedom, the recapturing of their willpower. If an interpretation of history eternally condemns the victims to the victors or if it forestalls liberation with the dictum "in no time liberation will be achieved" then, despite the fact that they claim to represent the victims, the analysts are, at the least, gravely mistaken.

An Analysis of Sumerian Society

I am searching for the answer to the following question: *How can the Sumerian example be utilized when interpreting history? In other words: How can it contribute both to clarity of method and to our understanding of history?* Let us analyze the Sumerian example from multiple aspects to see what we can learn.

a. Intertwining functions of the Ziggurat

The Sumerian civilization developed in the alluvium rich region where the Tigris and Euphrates rivers met in Lower Mesopotamia. Further to the north, during the Tell Halaf period (6,000-4,000 BCE), the institutionalization phase of the Neolithic period had taken place. During this period, for the first time, abundant and diverse food resources were procured. This revolution resulted not only from newly developed production techniques but also from village society itself, as it was this new societal form that had given rise to the mentality that led to the discovery of these techniques. Sedentary life brought not only agriculture but also the development of social institutions that nurtured one another. (In a sense, institutionalization is the organization of social mentality—it is being collective.) Archaeological findings in Upper Mesopotamia point to many village settlements that were on the brink of developing into cities. However, limited irrigation and dependence on rainwater constrained further expansion and population growth. On the other hand, the Lower Tigris and Euphrates presented favorable areas for irrigation and fertile and plentiful soil. So, around 5,000 BCE, the initial village settlers of Lower Mesopotamia arrived from the North, from the Tell Halaf culture. Due to population growth villages spread out in all directions. As they moved further to the South, the rainfall decreased and irrigation became mandatory. This, in turn, required being extensively organized. The ideal organization was achieved within the temples called the Ziggurats.

The three intertwining functions of the Ziggurat are of key importance for the understanding of Sumerian society. Its first function was to house the field workers, who were owned by the Ziggurats, on the lowest floor. This floor also housed the makers of the tools and various other devices. Its second function was to host the priests, who did the administrative duties, on the second floor. The priests had to be in a position not only to calculate the ever growing production but also to provide the legitimacy (the persuasive power) to ensure cooperation from the workers. Thus, they simultaneously had to administer the religious and the secular work. The third function was to house the divinities, whose role was to influence all spiritually, on the third floor (the original example of the pantheon?). As argued in *The Roots of Civilization*, the Ziggurat functioned—to a greater or lesser degree—as a model for later civilizations. This initial model led to an urban society that now exceeds millions of people. It is in fact the womb of all state-like organizations. Ziggurats, at the time, were not only the center of the city but the city itself. Today's cities too are divided into three main parts: the temple (the house of the god) where legitimacy is derived, a larger section for urban administration and the largest section—dwellings for the workers.

The priest was the early entrepreneur: he was the capitalist, the patron and the Agha of his time. He played a historical role as founder of the city and ultimately the engineer of the new society. His task was daunting. The period of forced enslavement had not begun and the gathering of a workforce from people belonging to close knit clans and ethnic groups was not as easy as today, when unemployment has become institutionalized. His only possible advantage was the use of the god-weapon. And this was the most extraordinary function of the priest: the task to construct god. This task was of critical importance. Failure in this regard would mean failure to construct the new city and society, and therefore failure to produce an abundance of food. This is the reason why the initial state administrators were priests.

The Ziggurats did not only have the task to re-invent and re-construct the city, abundance of production and the new society, but a whole world of concepts—including the concepts of *god, calculation, magic, science, arts, family*, and even the initial exchange of product had to be constructed. The priest was the initial social engineer, architect, prophet, economist, businessman, foreman and king.

We need to look at the main tasks of the priest in more detail.

b. Constructing god

The most important task of the priest was constructing the new religion and god. In my opinion, the missing link between totem worship and the Abrahamic religions, that progressed beyond idolatry, is the Sumerian priests' invention of religion. This religion was a mixture of the god, that is the power regulating the skies, and the totemic religion, that is the power determining the identity of the society—the identity of both the clan and the tribe.[1]

During the Neolithic, the driving force had been the mother-woman to whom attributes of sacredness were ascribed—sacredness reminiscent of the male priest of the Ziggurat. In the Ziggurat, totemic and celestial representatives of god and the symbols of fertility and blessedness both gained importance in the form of mother-goddesses. Later, the mother-goddesses would become entangled in an extraordinary struggle with the Sumerian priest-gods as witnessed in the main theme of the Sumerian legends, namely the rivalry between the crafty male god Enki and the leading female goddess Inanna.[2] Underlying this theme is the transition from the Neolithic village society, which had *not* allowed exploitation, to that of the urban society, newly constructed by the priests, which *was* open to exploitation. This transition constituted a clash of interest. For the first time serious social problems emerged (though, of course, the terminology and notions involved were determined by the mindset of the time). Society itself was represented as semi-divine—the human mind was not yet able to conceive of an abstract identity.

At the time of the Ziggurat, nature was seen as animate, abounding with gods and spirits.[3] Tampering with the deities could result in disaster. They had to be approached with the utmost care and respect; sacrificial offers were needed to pacify them. Pleasing the gods and other sacred entities became so important that a tradition of sacrificing children and youths developed in an effort to uphold society. The various types of relationships between the human groupings of the time were reflected in the relationships and conflicts between the sacred beings and gods. Lacking the modern-day language of positive science, these notions were reflected in myths. We should not forget that the language of positive science—or rather the religion of positivism—has come into existence only in the past two hundred years. Any attempt to interpret history should not omit this fact.

The struggle between Inanna and Enki thus reflected a crucial social struggle. (Doubtlessly, this struggle had a material basis as well.) The fact that the celestial god Enlil and the earthly god Enki were both masculine reflected the coming into prominence of male power in the Sumerian urban society. Masculinity was being transformed into sacredness, turned into god. Maleness was viewed as so sacred that the new, holy male leader was in fact society itself. As the Inanna belief had reflected the social strength of the creative and leading power of the Neolithic—namely woman—the priest class was being exalted in the new religion. This struggle remained in equilibrium (although the balance in the Sumerian society turned to the disadvantage of women) until around 2,000 BCE.

The priest reserved the top level of the Ziggurat for the gods, ever decreasing in number, and kept this level extremely secret. Apart from himself—the high priest—no one else was allowed on this floor. This tactic was important for the new religious development as it stimulated respect, curiosity and dependence. Society was told that it was on the third floor that the high priest continuously met and talked with the gods. Thus, anyone wanting to hear the word of god had to listen to the high priest. He was the only authorized spokesperson of god. This tradition was passed on to the Abrahamic religions. The prophet Moses spoke to god at Mount Sinai where he received the Ten Commandments. Another name of the prophet Jesus is "God's Representative." His attempts to speak to god were thwarted by the devil but in the end he succeed. The Prophet Mohammed's ascension shows that the same tradition continues in Islam. Whereas the top level would be adapted in the Abrahamic religions as the synagogue, the church and the mosque, in Greco-Roman religion it was re-arranged as the magnificent pantheon.

The high priest was not only the inventor, but also the presenter of new ideas. His dialogues with the gods dictated the rearrangement of the new society. For the first time, statues representing the gods are placed on the third floor, further increasing people's curiosity.[4] This practice resulted from the need to symbolize the new conceptual god as idols and figures. With humanity still under the influence of sign language, which is more or less a figurative and body language, the contemporary human mind was better able to understand figurative mental schemes than abstract ones. Thus, it was easier to relate to figurative conceptualizations of god.

Thus, the Ziggurats' top floor was the initial residence of god—the pantheon, temple, church, mosque and university. These formations, which are historically linked to one another, denote society's sacred memory and identity. Theology teaches this memory by philosophizing about it, thereby dissociating and isolating it from the initial example. The biggest distortions of history are made in the field of theology. No-one can deny the importance of theology in the development of science and philosophy but the social roots are never revealed. Because of the sociality they constructed, the priest-class is the group bearing the biggest responsibility for the formation of both the civilization of modernity and of civilization in general.

Doubtlessly, theological interpretations that take their true origins into consideration contribute much to our understanding. However, since theologians are influential in all the official state and bureaucratic orders, it is important that we are aware of the distortions—whether they are made deliberately or unintentionally. In order to understand the Middle East of today, I shall attempt to analyze the new forms of these distortions.

c. Constructing society

The second most important task of the priest was that of social engineer. He not only planned and constructed the new society but also administered it. This task was carried out on the Ziggurats' second floor, the priests' floor. At a later stage, a vastly increased number of priests developed into a sacred class under the leadership of the high priest as the god's deputies. They, the elite administration of the city, formed the initial bureaucratic caste. They housed the people on the first floor to facilitate the production of the material goods—a first step into subsequent enslavement. But on the second floor, they dealt with god and science. The foundations of writing, mathematics, astronomy, medicine, literature and, of course, theology were laid in the rooms of the priests on the second floor—the initial school and university. The priests' main task was to administer the requirements of the growing urban society.

It should be understood that producers of material goods have never done so of their own accord or indeed, as Marx puts it, production is never done by "free laborers." In no classed society, including that of the capitalist period, do private or collective property owners have access to free laborers. Nobody, unless enslaved through oppression and legislation, works of his own accord for someone else's benefit.

For the most part, the priests accomplished their tasks through legitimation, which they obtained by selling themselves as the deputies of god and by their monopoly on science. These positions gave them extraordinary administrative powers. Let us not forget that even in the capitalist era *knowledge is power*. The foundations of science were laid during the Neolithic period, especially during the Tell Halaf period when the contributions of the mother-woman-goddess were marked. Woman's position as the first teacher, especially with reference to the uses of various plants, domestication of animals, pottery, weaving, grinding, housing and creating sanctuaries, cannot be underestimated. The mother-goddess Inanna in her struggle against Enki always claimed that she was the legitimate owner of the hundred and four *Mes* and that they were stolen from her by Enki.[5] Many of the early discoveries were in fact made by women; the male administrators *did* later steal this knowledge. As we will see, the Sumer civilizational phase was indeed built on this stolen knowledge.

The contributions made by the priests cannot be underestimated. Inscription, astronomy, mathematics, medicine and theology undeniably played an enormous role in the scientific foundations of civilization. The Sumerian priests played a leading part in the commencement of science. The initial Sumerian kings, the priest-kings, were the first kings of urban society. Every city had a priest-king. They received their legitimacy from their scientific and theological inventions. However, these inventions later constituted their main weakness. During the era of dynasties, "the strong man" would lead the dynasties with his military force. Military force would beat the priests at their game.

d. Establishing the workforce

At the lowest level of the Ziggurat were the workers. The first level workers must be understood well because they laid the foundation for slavery, serfdom and workforces. Where and how were they obtained? What was the role of force and of persuasion? From which community and in return for what were they obtained? Were there women amongst them? What was the role of woman and family? Answers to these questions will greatly enlighten us.

In the formation of the initial working groups, the priests' power of persuasion was probably the dominant factor. Furthermore, as food production increased with the use of irrigation, we may assume that the workers were fed better in the Ziggurat than they were in their places of origin. As the population and migration increased, it is possible that some fell into dispute with their tribe, eventually finding refuge in the temple. The sacredness attributed to working in the temple could have played an even more significant role. In Middle Eastern tradition, families and tribes often gave their children to service at the temples—forced labor at the temple brought honor to those who worked there; society exalts them, as with Christian monasticism. Even today, to work for the sheikh is not only honorable but a good deed.

Ziggurats are remarkable in that they are the first examples of pure collective work. The workforce, including the craftsmen, is the first example of the implementation of communist ideals. Sociologists such as Max Weber have called it "Pharaoh Socialism."[6] It is redolent of factory production. The excess production is stored, thereby providing for times of famine. This would enormously increase the priests' power. None of the families or tribes could obtain the same strength. The Ziggurat clearly was the embryo of the new society and state.

e. Reconstructing the role of women and family

It is important to see what happened to the woman and family in the Ziggurat system. The opposition of the mother-goddess religion to that of the religion of the Ziggurat priest can be seen in the Sumerian texts. Each city had a designated woman as guardian-goddess. In fact, the adventures of Inanna, the Goddess of Uruk, provide an example worth studying as Uruk was the first Sumerian city-state. (Could the name *Iraq* have *Uruk* as its roots?) It is also a famous city since it was the city of the first male king, Gilgamesh. It is highly probable that Uruk was the first city-state in history and the period 3,800-3000 BCE is designated as the Uruk period. The fact that the founder goddess of Uruk is Inanna shows that she is far more ancient than Gilgamesh and that the role of the mother-woman was still the leading one at the time. However, Uruk's struggle against Eridu (the city of the god Enki and perhaps the first priest-state) is legendary (an excellent example of gender struggle). Over time, less and less figurines of the woman-goddess were made and apparently, with the onset of the Babylon period, the woman-goddess had been destroyed: Woman now was an official public and private prostitute as well as a slave.[7]

In a designated section of the Ziggurat, woman played her role as love object. At the time, this role seemingly was an honorary role preserved for the daughters of the best families. Only the distinguished and privileged girls were picked for this task. They received many lessons on beauty and mastered some forms of art before, if they agreed to marry, they were offered to the distinguished males of the surrounding regions. The result was a dramatic increase in the income and influence of the temple. Only the males from the noble families could obtain a woman from the temple. The temple education would thus be represented in the new tribes; new allegiances to the new society and new state were formed. In fact, women were the most productive agents of the priests' new society and state. The collectivization of woman in this way is indeed the prototype of the brothel. As woman's position declined from being the noble goddess and the temple's woman of love, she turned into a desperate brothel worker, putting herself on the market.

Sumerian society has the honor (or is it the *dishonor*?) of being the first of its kind. However, had this method of schooling women not been abused to the extent that it became a brothel system, it would have been the ideal system due to the difficulty for girls to obtain a sound education in systems where either the mother-woman or the father-man is dominant. But the male dominant society, through the usage of oppression and exploitation, toppled the original institution. The Sumerian training institution was the envy of society—everyone wanted to give their daughters to the temple. Initially the girls had the opportunity to develop themselves immensely; their first goal was not to find a husband for themselves but to become the leaders of the new society and state.

f. Organizing trade

Thus, the priests' approach to women served the development of the new society and state. The way the priests organized the new society and state was close to ideal. Trade was still in the developing stage. Although there is no evidence of this in the texts, we can assume that the Ziggurat also functioned as a trading house. The surplus product and the production of tools by the craftsman attached to the Ziggurats were probably the objects of trade. History considers the period from 4,000 to 3,000 BCE as the era that trade began. The era of the Sumerian society coincides with the transition from the gift economy (parting of gifts amongst the members of the society and families) to commodity (or exchange) economy. Commodification during this era developed extensively, resulting in production for exchange value. The Sumerian society can thus be seen as the initial trade society.

The Uruk colonial system probably began between 3,500 and 3,000 BCE. Within the Taurus-Zagros system, the Uruk colonies were probably the first colonization offensive of the new state structures. Although the dynastic colonies were more ancient, these divergent tribal colonies cannot be considered real colonies. A prerequisite to having colonies is to be a metropolitan city. Uruk, as a very famous metropolis, must have had many colonies. Later Ur (3,000-2,000 BCE) and Assyrian (2,000-1,750 BCE) colonies became very famous. The ancient cities of Harappa and Moenjo-daro in the Punjab area, together with the Egyptian civilization, were all, in a wider sense, colonial orders with roots in Sumerian civilization since their roots also rested in the Tigris and Euphrates rivers.

One reason that trade played such an effective role in the priests' system was that in the lower valleys of Mesopotamia many of the cities' material needs were absent. Therefore, trade, expropriation, or both, were a necessity. The colonial order developed exactly for the purpose of obtaining material needs. Many of the colonies on the banks of the Tigris and Euphrates were established due to this need. Especially widespread were colonies needed for the timber, metal and weaving trades.

Thus, it is clear that a prototype of the new society and state was formed within the Ziggurats. The concrete development of the state-society that has influenced our system of civilization has the Sumerian Ziggurat system as its origins. Indeed, the other examples, from Egypt to China, follow the same path. To date, no counter-examples have come to light to prove this thesis wrong.

So, from our analysis of the Ziggurats, we can conclude that the beginning of the Sumerian society was also the beginning of the era of masked gods and disguised kings. The initial masked gods were the Sumerian priests but just behind them, with much fanfare and pomposity, were the disguised (politically clothed) kings.

g. The emergence of dynasties

The priest-state society was a precursor to the dynastic system. For a societal development such as state-based society to be successful, it needed to be guaranteed first. Initially, intelligent people are needed to make and legitimize the new arrangements. This cannot be accomplished by political or military power—before coercion can be applied, there needs to be a society and an administrative system that is conducive to trade and surplus products. Only when this aspect of the new society is well established can the seizure of power by political and military forces be meaningful; if not, the attempt would bring nothing but chaos. In the case of Sumer, this required the priests.

The dynastic system had a long and powerful history in Mesopotamia. As ethnic identities developed and strengthened, dynasties emerged within the clan and tribal order as those who had gained experience in protecting the tribe, locating it in fertile regions and resolving its internal problems gained prominence. Inevitably, one or more of these families or clans would grow stronger than the others—either by taking part in the administration of the tribe or by seizing it. Undoubtedly, the approval by the members of the tribe would have been the decisive factor—strong kinship bonds amongst them did not leave much room for strangers (unless an appropriate form of participation and assimilation could be found). A strong clan identity emerged during its formation stage. Such a development occurred around 5,000 BCE in Mesopotamia, but the Sumerian society was not the first to undergo this development. A similar development had been experienced in the Semitic tribes between 9,000 and 6,000 BCE. Dynasties continued to gain strength until around 5,000 BCE. During the Ubaid period, which likely preceded the Uruk period, there were strong dynasties, but there was no transition to a state structure. However, there is evidence suggesting a trend toward colonization when distinguished Semitic families settled in the Aryan cultural stratum between 5,000-4,000 BCE. The initial Semitic colonization took place at the Upper Tigris and Euphrates river basin, today called South East Anatolia.

It is important to understand this particular aspect of dynasties, as it still concerns us today: Familism and the desire to have as many male children as possible constitute the cornerstone of the dynastic ideology.

Whereas the priest attains his leadership on the basis of his intellectual power, the strong man of the dynasty attains leadership through political power. Political power is associated with coercion. Whereas the power of the priest is a cautionary, moral power—akin to the "curse of god"—the real source of political power is the military associates of the strong man.

In the period of the hunter-gatherers, when women were the dominant influence, men had no power. To understand this, we have to understand the matrilineal system and the notion of familism. In the matrilineal system, the father is either unknown or insignificant. Women don't choose the men fathering their children for love. They are not bound to any man through housewifization. The male, on the other hand, is not in a position to dominate a woman or to call her "his wife." If not performed well, hunting is a job lacking esteem. The woman doesn't seek sexual intercourse for pleasure—sexuality is solely for the purpose of reproduction. The children belong to her. By giving birth and nourishing them, she attains this right. The notion of fatherhood rights at a period when fatherhood has no social significance is non-existent. The woman's brothers have some significance because they grew up together. (The custom of uncle-hood and aunt-hood—on the mother's side—attains its strength from this ancient woman's law.) The matrilineal family consists of the uncle, the aunt—and their children if they have any—and the mother's own children. This can be seen as the social expression of the mother-goddess cult. Apart from the uncles, the males are insignificant; the practice of fatherhood and husband-hood non-existent.

A dynastic system can only develop ideologically and in practice once the matrilineal system has been inverted. A dynastic system—or patriarchal system—roots itself in a society through an alliance of "the old man's" experience, "the strong man's" military associates and the legitimization given by "the spiritual leader"—in the pre-priest period, the shaman.

The experiences of the old man signify lifelong lessons. He is the sage that everyone consults and asks for advice. The community needs him. And he in turn tries to overcome the difficulties of old age by making use of his experiences. This is the pact he negotiates with society.

The strong man is the one desiring to escape the shackles of the mother-woman through productive hunting. Physical strength and superlative hunting techniques enhances his chances as a hunter. The pact he establishes with the youngsters wishing to benefit from his skills affords him even more success. The alliance established with the elderly of the tribe strengthens patriarchy in the face of the matrilineal system.

The final link to the alliance is the shaman, who fulfills the functions of the priest as well as the wizard. He is an educator and perhaps the initial expert in the society. Although at times mixed with charlatanry, the expertise of the shaman establishes itself in the society. Shamans are mostly male. In the construction of the dynasties, their alliance with the strong men strikes a huge blow to the matrilineal system. The Sumerian texts indicate an intense struggle between the male alliance and their female antagonists.

In this new order, the male is both the owner of the children and the acknowledged father. He wants to have many children, especially male children, for work purposes and to acquire the accumulated possessions that are held by the women. Thus, we witness the onset of ownership. The private ownership of the dynastic system develops in parallel with the collective ownership of the priest-state. For the inheritance to pass on to the children (mostly the male children) fatherhood needs to be constructed—another reason why there is a need to be acknowledged as the father of the children.

Dynasties, patriarchy, and fatherhood are indicators that a classed society is emerging, and indeed the Sumerian tablets speak of the kind of struggle and political turmoil that indicate the emergence of such a society. The Ur city-state system, which was constructed after the Uruk city-state, had a dynastic character. In comparison to the theological administration of the priests, the dynastic administration had a more secular and political character. New gods were constructed and the priests were reduced to deputies of the political leaders. They still played an important role, but increasingly they lost their power and became mere propagandists of the system. The masked gods, who gave birth to the state, became progressively subordinate to the disguised king. The dynastic kings had no hesitation in calling themselves god-kings, thereby making use of the shield of legitimacy provided by the priests. Day by day the class divisions intensified, the numbers of cities increased and, as a result, the Sumerian civilization-type society proved its permanence and institutionalized itself.

This ancient tradition of dynasties still prevails in the Middle East. The reason why republics and democratic systems have not developed in the Middle East is because the initial states were based on theocracies and dynasties.

The model of the Sumerian civilized society has determined the development of civilization in the Old World at least as much as the Neolithic model. *Civilization* as a notion differs from that of *culture* because of its connection with class division. Civilization *is*, in fact, all about a class-culture and class-state. The dominant indicators of the new civilized society are urbanism, trade, institutionalization of theology and science, development of political and military structures, law taking prominence over morality, and male gender discrimination. To a degree, the sum of all these characteristics can be called "the culture of civilized society." Hence, the two notions are often equated and given the same content.

The big expansion of the Neolithic society-culture of the Fertile Crescent was followed by a second big expansion—that of civilized society. It was the daughters of the mother-goddess that institutionalized the Neolithic as they expanded into each region. Civilized society, which is in reality male dominant culture, institutionalizes its sons wherever they expand. The generation of the civilized male, who binds the female child through housewifization, will always breed males; hence, the masculinity of our civilization will continue to strengthen and multiply.

An Analysis of Civilized Society

Increasing our efforts to analyze the Sumerian society will enhance our understanding of our own society. All that needs to be done is to analyze civilization—to pull off the masks that cover its mentalities and institutions so that the true faces and the actual status of the different role-players within the society can be seen.

Our society tries to pass itself off as the youngest society, calling itself "contemporary" or "new age." It claims that ancient civilization is old. This is peculiar—after all, adolescence is closer to birth than maturity. If, as argued in the previous section, the Sumerian society represents the birth of our own civilization, then the term "adolescence" should be bestowed accordingly. If this is the case, then attributes such as "new" and "young" are misnomers when they refer to our society. Rather, we are the oldest society of this civilization. This misnaming indeed is a continuation of the masking used by civilized (that is, the classed, city-state) society.

The fundamental question that must be asked is: Why did civilized society, which can also be called the "urban civilization," require such intense masking? The Sumerian priests' art of masking was maintained endlessly. While initially the concept of *divinity* had a meaningful and noble content, why did it later become the foremost agent of degradation and meaninglessness? Many opinions have been expressed in favor of or against civilized society, but what has not been attained is the formulation of a radical criticism of civilization and the development of a set of guidelines to progress beyond it. This is indicative of the degree to which all interpretations thus far have failed.

Still, it is widely accepted that there is an extraordinary suppression of humanity's desire for freedom—suppression so intense that the desire for freedom has long ago reached a state of unsustainability. In fact, there is not a single year in the history of civilization without wars. Living a life of suppression has become "natural." Exploitation is seen as "the way of life," accepting it as honesty, and innocence and morals are deemed to be idiocy.

What is needed is an analysis of civilized society conducive to the kind of criticism that will enable us to progress beyond this civilization. A critique that focuses only on capitalist modernity will not lead to such progress, as is quite clear from the failed efforts of many schools, including the Marxists. The fundamental reason behind this failure is the fact that civilized society, which capitalist modernity is bound to, has not been included in the analyses. A Eurocentric philosophy of life seems to have silenced even the fiercest opponents. Just as in our analysis of the relationship between Neolithic culture and European civilization, there is a dire need for a comprehensible analysis of the relationship between European civilization and previous civilizations in terms of history and society. The fact that I am convicted under the harshest possible suppression of this civilization justifies my attempt at such an interpretation despite its amateurishness.

a. In defense of a free life

The analysis of civilization is a matter for structural sociology. If the main provision for being scientific is not to flounder in the swamp of positivism but to obtain the knowledge and understanding that will exceed the subject-object dichotomy, then there is a dire need for it in structural sociology. The primary duty of general sociology is to diagnose and treat society. *There can only be one reason for knowing: to make some sense of this life that we love.* This in turn will give us the opportunity to understand the structural issues and, if there are any unsound elements, to restructure them.

The society of civilization is a structural heap, a conglomerate that epistemology difficultly tries to make sense. The existence of this heap is closely related to the distortion of our understanding. It is not enough to just make an effective diagnosis; urgent treatment is necessary. If our structural sociology and our sociology of freedom wish to evade becoming a heap of rubbish like its predecessors, then it must prove its strength in diagnosis and treatment.

Civilization is worse than just the "great slaughterhouse" Hegel called it.[8] It is a continuous genocide of freedom—which is the sole reason for human life. All else is just the residue of life. Civilization is what is left of life when the meaning of free life has been pumped out of it! Is the history that we are taught not the chronicle of the construction and collapse of states and their subsidiaries? Is acquiring power not the sole aim of this? Which of the heroic tales are innocent of violence and exploitation? Have those who claim to rebel for their tribe, nation, or religion done anything but claim the crown of power? Does civilized society, that has not had a year without war, deserve to be called anything other than "the slaughterhouse"? Would the development of the sciences, arts and technology that we hear so much about have been possible if it were not for the real inventors, either giving their lives for their inventions or having it seized from them? Can this reality that is told as the story of order, stability and peace have any other meaning than that of theatrical performances of how human beings are subjugated? We can multiply the number of questions concerning civilization, but what is really dreadful is the boldness and arrogance with which this story is told as the undeniable fate of humanity, as a story of friendship, genteelness and alliance, a glorious history, sacred religion, legend of love and beauty, magnificent inventions, the dream of reaching for heaven.

My purpose in raising so many questions lies in my interest in, respect for, and devotion to the last unspoken words of all those who took up resistance in the name of freedom. It may just be that a meaningful method will empower us to fight in defense of a life of freedom.

b. The role of class struggle in civilized society

It is important to have a clear understanding of the notion of *class* as used by the opponents of capitalist modernity. If not, opposition will never go beyond demagogy; a vague and hazy understanding will serve only as a tool to keep the essence of capitalist modernity disguised. What we need to determine, is whether class has any role to play on its own, whether it has the ability to act as subject—as an agent determining action.

Class constitutes the hands and feet of power. As with hands and feet, on its own class has no power. But the power within modern society—and the Leviathan within civilized society—is the most organized power there is. We can describe the state as the unity of the power relations through which the general coercion and exploitation of classed society is enabled. Does this not entail that those coerced and exploited are an inseparable part of this network of relations? Is it not true that civilization—that is, organizational and structuring power—lies not only in the organization of the state, that it can also be found in fields such as religion and the economy? Is it not the main function of this power to create the slave, serf, worker and the numerous other horizontal and vertical strata of society?

In the organization of power, the hands and feet will never be given the opportunity of being "subject"—the agent determining the action. If power relations have been successfully installed, an absolute domination over the laborers has been achieved. This means that, even if the laborers previously did have acting power, under these circumstances they would lose it. This is exactly why the slave-laborer rebels of the Spartacus era and Paris Commune never had a chance to succeed. Only on one condition would success have been possible: if the powers of the time had seen them as "fresh blood" that could have rejoined civilized society. The one hundred and fifty years of attempts at socialism bear witness to this reality.

Whether it is the class's upper stratum of master, seignior, patron, or the middle stratum of bourgeoisie or the lower stratum of slave, serf, worker—these strata all have the same ideological and political approach concerning power relations. Internal disputes do not have any value at all. The relationship between the different strata forms a network with many knots. If you reject one of these, the others will come into motion. The system is such that severance of any of the knots will be repaired, the upstart more devoted than before or—if needed—his life taken.

Let us examine the worker and the laborer of the tribe working in the "first draft" of the state—the system of power relations devised by the Sumerian priests and the dynastic chiefs. The worker who was being turned into a servant by the priest was under the spell of the enormous legitimization attempt of the newly manufactured gods—if he was not under their spell, he would not have been accepted. Secondly, in the Ziggurat he was fed better than before and thus bound to the system. Thirdly, his dreams were continuously decorated with the beauty radiated by the houri in the temple.[9] (The offerings of women must have contributed much more to obedience and submission to the system than the present-day offerings of media and armies!) Thus, this new subject was anything but a rebel fighting for freedom—he was totally drained from any desire for free life.

The dynastic chief used a similar approach as he built its own state-power relations. The first step was to secure a strong organization based on more visible and sound interests among the main allied forces. The dynastic family had a feared and respected legitimacy within the larger family. The tribal traditions continuously extolled the hierarchy. All disputes were resolved either peacefully within the tribal assembly or through conflict.

If the class characteristics of a dynasty on its way to becoming a state were so pronounced, we have to conclude that *class division is a fundamental characteristic of civilization*. Of course, while theoretically it is not impossible that this characteristic forms the strategic basis for a class revolution, in practice such a revolution can't succeed—history teaches us that all civilizations and power systems that have been overthrown were overthrown *together with* their subjects and proletariat. In the few cases where they were overthrown *by* their subjects and proletariat, the new administration has usually been far worse than the previous oppressive and exploitative regime.

While asserting that class is fundamental to civilization, at the same time we have to acknowledge that to view history as nothing but a series of class struggles is a highly reductionist approach. The maintaining of civilization, and hence the history of civilization, is indeed based on oppression and exploitation, but the ideology, policy and even the economy of this system works on a different basis. In other words, the course of history has not been determined purely by a struggle of class versus class. With this statement, I am not negating the dreadfulness of enslavement, the degrading characteristics of the system or its denial of freedom. My contention is that the struggle between classes could not have been the sole cause of the establishment and collapse of systems of political power and the various systems of civilization. My interpretation is that opposition to the system always ends in becoming part of it—either by knowingly joining the existing political power or system of civilization as a new political force or, despite rejecting it, by not being able to escape being the "new blood" for the system, as happened in the Soviet and Chinese experiences.

This approach may be criticized as being lenient toward power reductionism and of not pointing a way out. I will discuss this issue in detail in my forthcoming book, *The Sociology of Freedom*. For the time being, let me just say that freedom has its own social area, mentality and strategy, just as political power has its own ideology, policies and organization.

c. The role of conflict in civilized society

Although the question under discussion is that of conflict or alliance between civilizations, its historical meaning is much more comprehensive. Civilized society is a structure that generates conflict both within and between civilizations. To achieve the aim for which this society was generated and to institute the class division that it bases itself upon, requires oppression and exploitation combined with continuous diversion and disguise. This explains the need to continuously generate conflict. Political power and class division by their very nature mean conflict, whether internally or externally. It does not matter how we categorize a civilization in an attempt to hide its essence. Whether warlike or pacifist, monotheist or polytheist, fertile or infertile, cultured or ignorant, from the same tribe or from different tribes—these attributes do not change the essence of civilized society. Its guiding force is its perceived duty to conquer the whole world. The desire to become a world power is a structural disease. Its source is political power. The moment it stops expanding, it starts to regress—it does not end up as a "normal" power but ends up in collapse. Like cancer, it must either eradicate or be eradicated. There have been many simple tribal chiefs who deified themselves with the powers of civilization.

Behind the assertion of divinity lies the power to destroy humanity. Mass destruction creates the belief that mass creation is possible; an uncontrolled ego develops into limitless megalomania. The civilization system offers a society in which this disease can flourish. It has been said that there is not a single social value and personality that political power cannot corrupt—truly an insight into the essence of political power. Civilizations are societies of political power and hence systems in constant conflict with life. There is not a single value that one would not sacrifice in order to attain political power, nor one's own brother, partner or friend. An in-depth examination of the administration of civilizations will make evident the many murders and conspiracies. Indeed, the systematized lies are called "politics."

d. Subservience of society as a whole

Attention should be drawn to a characteristic that has become institutionalized in civilized society, namely the susceptibility of society to political power. It happened in a way quite similar to the remaking of women according to the institution of housewifization. Political power cannot be sure of its continued existence before it has recreated society, just as it did with women. Housewifization, as the most ancient form of enslavement, has been institutionalized as result of woman's defeat by the strong man and his attendants. It required a long and comprehensive war and resulted in the domination of the sexist society. This action of domination has positioned itself within the society before the civilization was fully developed. This was such an intense and fierce struggle that it has been erased from our memories, together with the consequences thereof. Woman cannot remember what was lost, where it was lost and how it was lost. She considers a submissive womanhood as her natural state. This is why no other enslavement has been legitimized through internalization as much as woman's enslavement.

This had a twofold, devastating effect on society. Firstly, it paved the way for society to be enslaved; secondly, thereafter, all enslavement was based on housewifization. Housewifization is not just about becoming a mere object of sexism. It is not a biological characteristic either. In its essence, housewifization is a social characteristic. Enslavement, submission, acceptance of insults, crying, the habit of lying, being unassertive, self-sacrifice and the like are all considered a part of housewifization. These characteristics also indicate a rejection of the ethics of freedom.

This aspect constitutes the social grounds for degradation. In fact, it is the true reason for enslavement. It is the institutionalized grounds that have given breathing space to all forms of enslavement, from the most ancient forms to the most modern. In order for the system of civilized society to function, society as a whole must be made to adopt wife-like characteristics. If political power is identical to masculinity, then the housewifization of the society is inevitable. Political power doesn't recognize the principles of freedom and equality because—should it do so—it could not exist. There are essential similarities between political power and sexist society.

In ancient Greece, which is considered to be a milestone of our civilization, male teenagers were offered to the experienced men as "boys." The philosopher Socrates maintained that the contact between *erastes* (the adult male) and *eromenos* (the youth) could be aimed not only at sexual love, but also at obtaining moral wisdom and strength—in other words, to prepare the boy for a code of behavior "befitting" to women. Greek society quite openly wished to create a housewifized society. As long as there still were noble and dignified youths, such a society wouldn't be possible, hence housewifized behavior had to be internalized. *Eromenoi* were widespread in this society: it reached a point where it was customary for every master to have a "boy." Thus, we can't view this custom as sexual perversion or a disease; in fact, it was a social phenomenon caused by the classed society. In all different shapes of civilized societies similar trends exist. In other words, the grounds for power relations within civilized societies have been carefully prepared and on the basis of housewifization. The tradition of civilization sees women as "men's field." A similar view exists with regard to society. Men must offer themselves to political power as women offer themselves to men. Those that rebel or refuse to offer themselves will be readied through warfare.

The creation of power systems is not sudden, nor are they created by any individual, class, or nation. Governments may be formed suddenly, but political power and political systems have been prepared as a culture of domination by hundreds of brutal emperors and various other dominating forces. Societies—just as the wife waits for her husband as if it was her destiny—wait to be used by their political powers. Political power exists as a dominant culture within society. Therein lies the true importance of the quote attributed to Mikhail Bakunin, "If you took the most ardent revolutionary, vested him in absolute power, within a year he would be worse than the Tsar himself."

This degeneration is elicited by the power system. The seat of power, composed of the blood and exploitation of thousands of years, will of necessity corrupt the one sitting on it. There is only one way of not getting corrupted: by being devoted to protecting oneself! One of the most striking examples of the corruptive force of power can be found in the experience of real socialism. One cannot doubt their intentions or their devotion to their aims; why then did, did those who set up the system voluntarily gave themselves up to capitalism—the very system that they fought so hard against? In my opinion, the fundamental reason for this historical tragedy is the way in which power was obtained and exercised. The founders of socialism came to power through the culture of civilized society. Although they claimed to oppose this bloody and exploitative heritage and claimed that they refused to become a power resting upon it, they fully embraced it. Kropotkin's criticism against Lenin for the quick transition from soviets to the adaptation of state power was even seen as opportunism.[10] Immanuel Wallerstein comes close to the truth when stating that the Soviets did not have the inherent strength to surpass the capitalist world-system and thus were destroyed by the impact of that world-system. But this is still not the essence of the problem. Michel Foucault, with the insight that the soviets reintegrated with the system because they used the system's method of handling knowledge and power, is much closer to the truth.

The same happened with the Paris Commune, numerous national liberation movements, and initiatives by both communists and social democrats. Just as each field is sown with only one crop, freedom and socialism cannot be generated in the millennia old fields of knowledge and power. To succeed, activists and theorists of freedom and socialism must prepare their own fields, continuously diagnosing and treating contagious diseases that are generated by power relations and, even more importantly, keeping a distance from power relations and all its institutions and characteristics. If rich democratic forms are not implanted and nurtured at the same time, they will not escape the power net and only repeat the thousands of failed attempts which, in the end, were not at all different from the systems of power they sought to escape. Keeping in mind the limited understanding of the human being, claiming that we understand the whole universe would be arrogant. Therefore, to attribute to divinity the things that cannot be explained with the humans' limited knowledge and information must be seen as "good" metaphysics.

e. Religion, science, philosophy, the arts, morality and law in civilized society

It is important to understand the role that such institutional practices as religion, science, philosophy, the arts and morality play in civilized society.

The bedrock of religion lies in the extraordinary value attached to food. During the Neolithic, the attainment of abundant and diverse types of food was gratefully received as a blessing from a divine entity that humans equated with their own social identity. Even today we do not understand the reason behind life; during the Neolithic an effort was made to attach a meaning to it through the concept of divinity, a concept which is in fact closer to a creative principle than to magic and enchantment. It is important that we don't confuse this idea of *divinity* with Allah. The concept of *Allah* was constructed in the atmosphere of the Semitic culture; as illustrated below, it had a different and particular course of development.

Attaching moral aspects to the gods they manufactured eased the Sumerian priests' task of selling themselves to the society that they had constructed. The priests were probably the first to attribute punishment and sin to the notion of *god* in order to develop the sense of obedience. *God* was slowly turned into *the state*. This is the reform brought about by the Sumerian priests. From many of the wall reliefs it is clear that much was done to increase the status of the state's administrators, and thus to increase the administration's authority over society. The king managed to mask his own interests very well as he went to war in the name of his god. In all the drawings and narratives from Sumer the administrator is always the beloved son of the god; its enemies are the devil that must be conquered. Slowly a group of gods took shape—a clear reflection of the new administration.

The indistinguishability of god and administrator has never been displayed so openly in any other society. The question of who was masking whom no longer held much importance. The more god was turned into the state, the more he attained attributes such as "supreme creator," and as the priests developed into the administrative class attributes such as "administrator" were assigned to god as well. In time god and administrator became equated; distinguishing between them impossible. This is the point where the constructed divinity turned into bad metaphysics. In all the later stages all civilized societies would discover and use the magical power of religion and god in the legitimization of administration. Although the god of old—the sacred and creative divine force—would occupy a place in the thoughts and emotions of the oppressed, the god and religion that would become the state played their roles through their administrative agents.

There is a notable relationship between the number of gods and the form of a society. Polytheism occurs during an era of tribal equality. The decrease in number and the ranking of the gods according to supremacy is closely related to the administrative protocol. The gradual rise to a primary god is a development in line with the distinction between the administrators. We need to investigate the relationship between the invisible god of monotheist religions, who may not be represented in images, and the state that no longer depends on individuals and no longer has a need to institutionalize itself.

The gradual decrease in the number of gods amidst the administrative forces means on the one hand their unmasking; on the other hand, it clarifies what the state really entails and whose interests it represents. This decrease signifies that religion was no longer needed for legitimization. Nevertheless, civilized society has always used the legitimization effect of religion as much as it has used tyranny. Turning religion into state and its privatizations is part and parcel of civilized society, specifically of the development in its administration. This explains the formation of different religious orders and of religious conflicts. Contending civilizations are contending religions and sects. The battles are taken up in the name of religions and sects so that the whole society can be drawn in. The big and long civilization battles have always been disguised as religious battles. The wars waged in the name of Islam, Christianity and Judaism were in essence struggles for dominance over the Middle Eastern civilization, as became apparent when they were later declared official state ideologies. But, as with any phenomenon that reaches its peak, their importance has decreased. As well as reflecting class conflict, dissident sectarianism has always signified the rebellious attitude of the marginal societies excluded from civilized society. During the construction of capitalist nation-states, sectarianism was transformed into a type of nationalism—a pretext masking the real reason behind the bloody wars.

Although the significance of philosophy is small compared to that of religion, it is still highly important. The inadequacy of religious explanations for the phenomenon of life makes apparent the need for philosophy. Sagacity, which has a history as old as religion, can be seen as the beginning of philosophy. The sage, who represents the thinking human, is a different source of understanding than the theologian. The opinions of the sage were valued as highly as those of god's spokesman. They were never at peace with the state or civilization, having been more devoted to the part of society that falls outside the boundaries of official society. They have played a distinct role in the development of morals and science. Strong traces of the wisdom associated with the mother-goddess survived in the Sumerian society. The rise of the prophets certainly had a lot do with such wisdom. The tradition of wisdom and philosophy in the Middle East certainly warrants more research.

Just as the Sumerian priests were able to conduct the construction of religion and god in parallel with state and society, the Greek philosophers helped to construct and perpetuate a new, more developed civilized society partly by means of both religion and philosophy. The method the two groups used is the same, namely the artful use of concepts. Whereas in Sumer, state and society resulted from concepts used for the construction of religion, in Greece state and society were given shape through philosophic concepts. The masked gods had begun to give way to unmasked gods and naked kings. Development in the thinking of humanity is related to development in philosophy.

Philosophical thought, which played a relatively limited role in Greco-Roman society, underwent a dramatic revolution in capitalist European society. Here, the turmoil in religion was reflected in philosophy. The biggest contributor to this turmoil was the emphasis on national and class interests to meet the requirements of the system. When conflicts were not resolved through religious wars the duty fell on the shoulders of philosophy. The last religious wars were fought between 1618 and 1649. The 17th century was the very same century of philosophical revolution. Philosophy became the leading ideology in the new civilized society, as can be witnessed from the rise of the many philosophic schools at the time. While on the one hand the "death of god" is declared, on the other hand, disguised kings are dethroned. This marked the beginning of the period of nation-states—which themselves have become divine—and capitalist states—which are nothing but naked kings.

The Neolithic agricultural revolution also led to a revolution in arts. Cave drawings were followed by mother-goddess figures, the forerunners of sculpture. With the onset of civilized society, the figures of god and administrators were drawn alongside each other. Increased class division and administrative authority gave rise to the nationalization of the arts as much as religion did. Especially in the art of Egypt, China and India, gods, kings and priests competed in a show of strength as symbolized through enormous statues and reliefs. Architecture followed the same path in the houses of religion and administration. Temples and palaces of vast dimensions were constructed. Huge tombs were built—horrible indications of the level that human exploitations and repression can reach in civilized society. For the construction of a pyramid or a temple alone thousands of people were sacrificed. As trade increased, the merchant became a frequent figure in art. Often other powerful figures besides kings were honored with monuments.

The rise of Greco-Roman civilization brought a revolution in urban architecture. Cities, previously consisting only of the inner and outer periphery of the castles, went through structural transformations which evoke admiration even today. The underlying labor cost, to a large extent, was the enslavement of society. Most of the slave labor was used for the urban building projects. The indicators of enslavement are the enormous tombs, temples, castles and cities. These structures are also indicative of the lives and labor that civilized society required. With their sculptures, attempting to immortalize beauty and superiority, Greco-Roman society reached new heights in the world of the arts.

Greco-Roman art and culture, revived during the Renaissance, was the inspirational power of European civilization. Feudal Europe, ruled by religion, could only free itself intellectually through Renaissance culture, which was partially open to free thinking. Only with the development of the bourgeoisie, the new civilized class, would the arts effectively influence large numbers. Yet popular art has never reached the magnificence of the past. Art forms, such as urban architecture, music, painting and sculpture, have degenerated in the hands of capitalism, losing their sacredness and distinct identity by turning into an arts industry and thereby declaring their own death.

Oral legends tell with great eloquence of the sacredness of the initial tribal identity and the yearning for it. These legends are the main resources of the written legends. The *Epic of Gilgamesh*, the first written text of substantial length in history, may be the main source for not only literature but also for the sacred texts. The Sumerian literature and religious texts were inspirational not only for the Greek literature and theology—Greek legends (especially all the mythological constructions) were the transformed versions of the Sumerian legends that travelled throughout Anatolia.

Although the distinction between good and evil in the myths and legends is also linked to the fundamental social division within civilized society, in essence it defines the distinction between good and evil within society. Its essence is socialist: good morality is equated with devotion to society, whereas remoteness from and conflict with society denotes evil. Social constructions always have had a moral character. The initial "constitution" of society was its moral rules. Morality lies at the heart of society—a society that loses its moral basis cannot but disintegrate. Adherence to the rules of the government is considered a sacred duty; social rules can be seen as devotion to the social identity, divine existence, language and other aspects of society. This devotion may include having to risk one's life. Being excluded from society is equal to a death sentence.

Law is an important invention of civilized society. It only came into existence with the development of social and class divisions and nationalization. Its origin is in the morals of society. In the same way that nationalization of religious sacredness led to state religion, the nationalization of morality led to law. The law denoted the governing rules of the new sate-society and the interests, property and security of the ruling class and in effect was the constitution of the new society.

The earliest sets of laws we know of come from the Sumerian society. Pre-dating the well-known Code of Hammurabi by three centuries, there is the Code of Ur-Nammu (written about 2100 BCE). Though the birthplace of law is, therefore, not Rome or Athens but the Sumerian city-state, much emphasis has been placed on the link between law, the republic and democracy during the Athenian and Roman eras. The birth of the republic and democracy necessitated a code of official, written laws—a constitution—to ensure a collective administration by an aristocracy, preventing the establishment of monarchies and despots. Although precursors existed in the Sumerian society, the first republican system emerged in Rome and the first democracy arose in Athens. In the civilization of the European bourgeoisie, constitutionalism, republicanism and democracy have been some of the most important

123

issues concerning law. The latest development concerns human rights. With this development, individualism and representation are carried to the social level. Thus, the pendulum has now swung to the opposite of where it was during the Neolithic, when morality demanded the individual's devotion to society.

History recognizes three major revolutions pertaining to scientific development. First, there was the institutionalization period of the Neolithic (6,000-4,000 BCE, i.e. the Tell Halaf period) and the contribution of Sumerian society. Next was the period of the West Anatolian-Athens society (600 to 300 BCE). We are currently in the third period, that of the Western European society (commencing in the sixteenth century). The connection between these revolutions and the stages of civilization is obvious—each stage of civilization was built upon its own scientific revolution.

Scientific development cannot be separated from the other categories of the interpretation of knowledge discussed above (that is, religion, philosophy, literature, arts, morality and law). Science's only "privilege" is that it deals with the part of knowledge that is empirically verifiable.[11] Science does not contain *all* knowledge—only the knowledge that pertains to empirically verifiable phenomena. In a broader sense, there is no knowledge that cannot be empirically verified. The division of knowledge into categories (such as verifiable or unverifiable, positivist or metaphysical, theoretical or empirical) has been created by civilized society, and has much to do with the relationship between knowledge and power.

As a whole, the relationship between civilized society and these categories of knowledge can be expressed as the conflict between meaning or interpretation of knowledge and power. These disciplines resulted from the experience of human society. But, since that section of civilized society that represents the state came into being, the practical manifestations of this experience and the development of the human mentality that led to it in the first place have been distorted and expropriated. One of the first things that the administrators have always done with the onset of a new stage in civilization is to reorganize the categories according to their own social paradigm and the source of their practical power. Each stage of the civilization is arranged on the basis of a new, fundamental paradigm. All this rearranging is a means of disguising, of obscuring and of *enchaining* those who are ruled. The legitimation that the new paradigms allow for has always been preferred to undisguised tyrannical administration. The administrators' main endeavor with this rearranging has always been to present their interest as the interest (and even the destiny) of society as a whole. The more successfully they do this, the more they can prolong the lifespan of the so-called civilized societies. No civilization—even a world civilization—that loses its legitimacy can escape collapse. The collapse of the Roman civilization is an example of this. It lost respect and appeal because of the growing Christian community internally, and the migration of other ethnic communities externally. When these communities united as new religious and ethnic communities, the extraordinary Roman power lost its legitimacy and fell apart. All major civilizations have been religious civilizations. But when religion loses its ability to provide legitimacy (whether through philosophy, science or a new religion) this usually means the end of that civilization.

All of these facts show the critical importance of the major categories of interpretation (religion, philosophy, arts, law, science and morality) for the civilized (that is the classed, city-state) society. While the task of structural sociology is to explain these categories within the civilized society, the task of the sociology of freedom is to interpret how these categories should be criticized and then combined with a free and democratic social life.

If studied in isolation, investigating the social institutions—which can also be seen as metaphysical categories—leads to the distortion of meaning. But metaphysical disciplines, which are so harshly and fiercely criticized, cannot be evaluated as "good" or "bad" per se. Since the human mind and human society cannot make do without metaphysics, it is more meaningful to make methodological evaluations of good and bad metaphysics in relation to one another and the society in question.

f. The role of economics in civilized society

Historically, studies of economics are both complicated and open to distortion. Capitalist civilization has made economy a field of theoretical and empirical research. Economics is indeed research of the "material" of the social reality. Capitalist civilization, which has recorded itself in history as the material civilization, can also be called the "economic system."[12] In the same way that we can call all of the previous systems of civilization "metaphysical systems," calling capitalism "materialist" may have explanatory value.

All societies, from the Neolithic society (or even the initial hominid societies) to the pre-capitalist civilized societies, have appraised sacredness, meaningfulness and, on the whole, metaphysics itself and have not able to interpret life in any other way. Capitalist civilization, on the other hand, has presented itself as "unmasked gods and naked kings" (a development so profound that it warrants exhaustive studies into its importance and extent). Ironically, this is the society with the highest power to obstruct, mislead and dissolve within itself (that is, to assimilate).

My personal opinion is that seizure and theft, organized in the name of "economy," constitute the essence of its social form. The Greek word *oikonomia* means "household management." It denotes the material rules of subsistence, its periphery, supplies and other materials. If we extrapolate this to civilized society, it denotes the subsistence rules of smaller communities. This constitutes the least nationalized and privatized social reality. It is the fundamental tissue of social collectivism, its privatization and nationalization are inconceivable because privatization and nationalization of the *oikonomia* would devastate this fundamental social tissue. It is to deny society its most critical rule of life. Therefore, no other society but capitalism perceived the idea and had the courage to make privatization and nationalization the leading characteristics of society. There is no doubt that all social areas in civilized society have been nationalized and the economy—its most fundamental tissue—has been the subject of both private and state ownership. No other society but capitalism has ever officially and openly declared private and state ownership as its system.

It is important to note that the privatization and nationalization of the economy has been seen as seizure and theft from very early on. Karl Marx expresses this in a more *scientific* way when he says that the surplus value is stolen as profit. This is an issue that needs to be analyzed exhaustively. We can interpret economy—which has become the subject of private and state ownership—to be a seizure and theft beyond that of the surplus value (or surplus product before that). Hence, all the different types of ownership of the economy, including private and state ownership, are immoral and can be seen as seizure and theft. I will deal with this issue in more detail in the section on capitalism.

Commodification has developed as a very important notion within civilized society. There is a close-knit connection between commodification and the civilized society—be it the society of private ownership, classed society or the city-state. Seeing that commodity and commodification are the prime indicators of attaining the state of being civilized, we have to clarify the term "commodity." An object becomes a commodity when it gains an exchange value that is not determined by the satisfaction of a human need. The idea of exchange value was foreign to society for a long time—it was not even entertained as a thought because it was considered a shame: precious objects were made gifts to society or to a valued individual. Replacing the gift system with the exchange system is the invention—or rather deception—of civilization. For pre-civilized society and the societies that have remained outside civilization, exchange has been shameful and should be refrained from unless absolutely necessary. Such societies have known from experience that when the economy overproduces and its production becomes an object of exchange, grave trouble might be in the offing.

As commodities acquired exchange value, merchants and trade have become important categories of civilization. Here I have to note that I do not share Karl Marx's concept of *commodity*. The opinion that the exchange value of a commodity can be measured by the workers' labor has initiated a conceptualization period fraught with disadvantages. This may be better understood if we look at the disintegration of a society which has no value that has not yet been commodified. The mental acceptance of the society's commodification is to abandon being human. And this is beyond barbarity. Beneath the societal harm sits the interest rate, of which trade is the basis and of which, in turn, the commodity is the basis. There is a strong causal link between trade and ecological disaster. When the economy stopped being social tissue it marked the beginning of a fundamental break with nature. This happened because of the profound distinction that was made between material and moral values, which form a natural unity. In a way, this severance cultivated the seeds of bad metaphysics. By leaving the material without spirit and the spiritual without matter, the path was being paved for the most confusing dichotomy encountered in the history of thought. Throughout the history of civilization, the bogus distinctions and discussions that have divided every aspect of life into either materialism or morality have destroyed ecology and free life. The concept of inanimate matter and an inanimate universe, combined with an incomprehensible spiritualism, are occupying, invading, and colonizing the human mind.

I have some doubts about another aspect of Marx's concept. I am quite doubtful that social values (including commodities) are measurable. Commodities cannot be regarded as a mere product of abstract labor but, rather, as a combination of many non-quantifiable, non-natural properties. To claim the opposite paves the way for fallacy, extortion and theft. The reason is clear: How are we to measure the total amount of non-countable labor? Moreover, how are we to measure the labor of a mother at birth and that of the family that raises the worker? Then, how are we to measure the share of the whole society in which this object called "value" is realized? Hence, exchange value, surplus value, labor-value, interest rate, profit, unearned income and so forth are all forms of theft through official and state power. It may be meaningful to develop other measures or new forms of a gift economy to replace the exchange system. I will delve deeper into this topic later when I discuss modernity and free life.

Even in Greek culture trade was a despised occupation—the Greeks were aware of the connection between trade and theft. Nor was the position of the merchant in Roman society considered honorable. Commodification pertained only to a limited number of objects; serious precautions were implemented to restrict it. In other words, the morality of Neolithic society still existed as far as commerce was concerned. Although, due to favorable circumstances, there were occurrences of capitalism before it became the dominant system, even the civilized societies did not allow it to flourish. It was always kept at a marginal level. The fact that it flourished in the 16th century in what is today the Netherlands and England resulted from very special circumstances. It is entirely possible that the capitalist system was a necessity for the existence of the Netherlands and England. Within 400 years it had spread around the world.

My aim with this very short introduction to civilization was to provide the historical and sociological background needed to develop a meaningful method of interpreting knowledge. Our respect for free life demands that all of us who believe that we have a social duty should work from a historical and sociological perspective, so that we can arrive at a meaningful interpretation. In order for us not to be deceived and not to deceive anyone else, a profound analysis of civilization in general—but especially of capitalist civilization—must be combined with the sociology of freedom so that free life can be constructed.

Problems Associated with the Expansion of Civilized Society

There is general agreement in the scientific discussion of our key question: *when and where did the world's current dominant civilization develop?* The location of this development was in the Upper and Lower basins of the Tigris and Euphrates rivers. And, indeed, my analysis in the previous two sections indicates that the mountain basin skirting the Upper Tigris and Euphrates is the root of civilization—the ovule. The fertilization of the ovule by the Sumerian priests led to the foundation of civilized society. The process that I have described in one sentence, however, took place over thousands of years of trial and error.

As there is not a single event, notion, institution, action, personality or society that does not bear the effects of time and location, a method of investigation that takes these two factors into account will necessarily add to a meaningful result. Thus, in agreement with Fernand Braudel, I hold that it is essential for the establishment of a meaningful sociology that the concept of *term*—or *duration*—forms a fundamental part of the methodology. But I want to go further than Braudel and propose that location should also be included. (It remains a puzzle to me why Western scientists generally ignore the factors of location and time. Could it be a result of a Eurocentric approach or a tendency to universalize Europe?) A methodology of sociological investigation that includes history and location will reveal not only what we have been and what we are now, it will also reveal how life *could* proceed. If past and present are within reach of one another, and if locations complement one another like the steps of a staircase, then it follows that humanity is a whole and it can live up to this unity without the need for ethnicity, religions, nations, states, alliances, and international bodies like the UN and Socialist Internationals.

These introductory notes indicate the approach I will follow in my analysis of civilization's expansion over location and time.

a. Problems with the expansion of the Sumerian and Egyptian civilizations

As previously stated, the Neolithic institutionalization was the ovule out of which civilization grew. Without this ovule, the Sumerian fertilization would have been meaningless; there was no other ovule from which it could have sprouted. Just as we can't think of the United States without the existence of Europe, one can't think of the Lower Tigris and Euphrates becoming what it is without the existence of the Upper Tigris and Euphrates civilization.

An important question regarding expansion is why were advanced settlements in the Middle Tigris and Euphrates region, and even in Anatolia, unable to make the transition to urbanization. Looking back 5,000 years, we see that there were many regions that nearly reached the civilization stage and many big villages that entered into the stage of urbanization. However, for reasons still unclear, they collapsed before making the transition to a more advanced level. Examples of this are Çatalhöyük in southern Anatolia and the excavated villages in the border region between Iran and Turkmenistan.[13]

Urbanization will occur only in the presence of a sizeable and permanent population. Populations expand drastically only when there is a surplus in food production. Oversupplies of food occur only where there is artificial irrigation of the alluvial earth at river mouths, as in the alluvial region around the Nile and the Tigris-Euphrates rivers. Besides the preconditions of population size and permanence, certain cultural factors must be present in the surrounding regions. No single alluvial region could have formed the Neolithic culture because the pre-conditions were not all met. On the other hand, not all the pre-conditions needed for urbanization existed in the Neolithic culture.

At around 3,500 BCE, the Uruk urban civilization developed at the lower end of the basin. It established a colonial order and developed a system that multiplied the number of cities under its domain. It has the honor of being the first civilization in history. It collapsed around 3,000 BCE—likely due to the rivalry of systems with more fertile and numerous cities—but the survival of the cult of the goddess Inanna and the Gilgamesh legend attest to the immortality of the culture.

The dynastic period of Ur began at about 3,000 BCE. It continued to exist in the form of three dynasties until it collapsed at around 2,000 BCE. The first written law codes, literary epics, academies, conflicts between cities just as ruthless as those of today (striking examples of this are found in epics such as the *Nippur Lament* and the *Curse of Akkad*), are just a few things that come to mind about this period. It seems that Ur had an extensive colonial system. In fact, many of the early colonies in the Zagros-Taurus arch were theirs, but they ceased to exist just as quickly as they developed. One may conclude that this was due to the cultural strength of the society within which they formed their colonies.

The age of Babylon began at around 2,000 BCE. Although it adopted the written Akkadian language for official use, Sumerian was retained as sacred language. In essence, Babylon formed part of the Sumerian civilization and Babylon, especially with regards to science and institutionalization, can be seen as the apogee of the Sumerian civilization. The city of Babylon can be likened to the European city of Paris. It was a city of science, culture and commerce; cultures from all over converged there, and there, for the first time, cosmopolitanism occurred. The age of the Nimrods (the initial strong kings) started in Babylon. Keeping in mind that many of the Greek philosophers (including Solon) took their first schooling in Babylon, will help us appreciate that its influence spread like a chain reaction. The Enuma Elish myth, depicting the sorrowful story of women's plight, is renowned for its description of the struggle between the god Marduk and the goddess Tiamat. Its astronomy, its sages' prophecies, its captivity of the Israelites, its huge written literature and its resistance to the Assyrians are some aspects of this culture that cannot be forgotten. Despite it being conquered and ruled by, amongst others, the Kassites, the Assyrians and the Persians, Babylonian culture never lost its influence in this region. The Babylonian era, in total a period of 1,500 years, has left a strong imprint on human memory, albeit nowadays not always consciously noticed.

The Assyrian era can be divided into three periods. The first period (about 2,000-1,600 BCE) was the period of the merchant kings. They constructed trade colonies in Cappadocia, for instance Kanesh (close to today's Kültepe in central Anatolia). The trade colonies stretched from the eastern Mediterranean to the shores of the Punjab and from the Black Sea to the Red Sea, with Nineveh—located near today's Mosul—as the center of their activities. This was a blossoming period not only for trade but for architecture too, as can be seen from the remains of temple-palaces in ancient cities like Nineveh. In the next period (approximately 1,500-1,300 BCE) Assyria lost its influence when it became a vassal of Mitanni, a Hurrian-speaking state. In the Neo-Assyrian Period (approximately 1,300-612 BCE) Assyria became the most powerful and largest empire the world had ever seen. Neo-Assyria is infamous for its brutality in war, for ethnic cleansing and for the total evacuation of a region. In the Assyrian era, strong resistance grew amongst the various peoples; the strongest resistance coming from the proto-Kurds (the Hurrians) under the leadership of the Urartu kings.[14] The fact that the Kurdish people still exist in this area is due to that resistance. As a matter of fact, the alliance of the Medes (who also had Hurrian roots) with the Babylonians led to the collapse of this huge empire around 612 BCE. Assyria was the last empire of Sumerian origin and made a huge contribution to the development and expansion of this civilization, especially with regard to trade and architecture.

Central Mesopotamia was the likely conduit through which the Sumerian civilization expanded when the first centers of civilization (aside from those of Lower Mesopotamia) developed, even though differences of form and essence occurred in the new centers of civilization. This area was the homeland of the Hurrians. The Hurrians are the first group to be identified in written sources as being related to the Aryan language and culture group. It may be meaningful to postulate them as the proto-Kurds. The structural similarities of the languages, as made obvious by etymological and linguistic analyses, show their connection to the Kurds. What information we have about them came from archaeological, linguistic, and ethnological research. The records indicate that they were an ethnically identifiable group since 6,000 BCE. They probably settled in the Zagros-Taurus system during the last ice age, where they were part of the Neolithic village and agricultural revolution and the development of animal husbandry. It seems that some Hurrians lived a sedentary life in the open plains while others lived a nomadic life in the mountains and plateaus.[15] During the Neolithic, the inhabitants of this zone had the most contact with the Sumerians, followed by the Arameans—a Semitic group.

Indications of the first civilization with Hurrian origins (if the period of Neolithic institutionalization from 6,000 to 4,000 BCE is ignored) can be seen from 3,000 BCE. Those Hurrians that settled in the Sumerian region made an early transition to urban civilization; those that stayed behind turned their settlements into city-states as well, but this happened very slowly due to irrigation and weather conditions. Findings at archaeological sites in the Tigris and Euphrates river basins such as Kazane, Titriş, Gre Virike, Zeytinlibahçe and lately Göbekli Tepe (close to Urfa), including castle walls, internal and external settlements, structures resembling temples, statuettes and samples of trading goods, prove the formation of cities.[16] With some of these cities going back as far as 3,000 and 2,750 BCE, it is realistic to say that they were the first non-Sumerian city groups.[17] New archaeological work may well show that the Middle Tigris and Euphrates river basin was the next big center of the civilization. The findings and the consequent analyses at Göbekli Tepe may even rewrite history.[18]

The next civilization of Hurrian origin expanded to such a degree that its political administration resembled that of an empire. The state of Mitanni, with its origins in Central Mesopotamia, lasted from 1,600 BCE until the rise of the Assyrian empire around 1,250 BCE. The Mitanni capital city, Washukanni, was probably located on a tributary of the Euphrates, the Kabhur River, in Syria.[19] At its height, the Mitannian Empire controlled northern Mesopotamia and Syria—from the Tigris and the region of Assyria to the Mediterranean. The fact that Thutmosis I described Mitanni as an important military force, indicates just how influential the empire was.—as does the fact that it was able to hold off the Assyrians and Babylonians for four hundred years and prevented Thutmosis III from expanding over the Euphrates. The Mitannians used hieroglyphics and cuneiform script. Their cultural legacy includes a unique architecture and a manual on chariotry by a Mitannian named Kikkuli. Recovered tablets indicate that the language structure of the

Mitanni differed from Hurrian, but the two languages had the same origins. The Mitanni and the Hittites both spoke Aryan languages.[20]

It is often claimed that the Hittites came through the Straits or that they were Caucasian and came from the east through Iran. Neither of these assumptions seem plausible. From the significant traces of Hurrian language and culture in the Hittite artifacts, we can deduce that the Hittites were a ruling group of Hurrian noblemen. Their gods, literature, diplomatic relations, and remnants of Egyptian palaces display their similarity to the Mitanni of Central Anatolia. In the same period that the Mitanni took control of the center of the Assyrian empire, the Hittites overwhelmed the Assyrian colonies and established the Hittite empire. It lasted from about 1,600 to 1,250 BCE. It is quite possible that the Mitanni and Hittite states were actually two large regions of one huge Hurrian state that we know nothing about, with a "missing link" between the Mitanni and Hittite regions. I believe that further investigation may yet uncover evidence to this effect. Excavations of the important Hittite centers, such as the capital of the empire, Hattusa, indicate the significant contribution the Hittites made to the progress of civilization. For instance, Hattusa far surpassed the sacred settlements of the Ziggurat: temples for religious activities, palaces for the administration, residence for the workers and storage rooms for produce were separated and a larger area was protected by castle walls. Many similar cities can be encountered. As far as governance is concerned, significant political reforms were proclaimed in the constitutional edict of Telipinus—for instance, he prescribed that nobles should have legal means to seek redress should they be dissatisfied with the conduct of the king or royal family and to not take the law into their own hands. He also decreed that the *pankus* ("whole body of citizens") should constitute the supreme court for punishment of lawbreakers. Furthermore, in the military field, the Hittite state was the most advanced of its time.

The cities of Troy and Ahhiyawa to the west of the Hittite empire, Aşkava and Kaska to the north, and Cilicia were all neighbors of the Hittites and had relations with their infamous rival in the south, the Egyptian pharaoh-state.[21] In the central region lived the unique people, the Hattians. They called themselves the people from the "country with thousand gods"—an indication that their relationship with their gods was one of friendship, not of rivalry.[22] One of the most famous documents in history is the treaty between the Egyptian pharaoh Ramses II and the king of the Hittites, Hattusili III.[23]

Much has already been said about the Egyptian civilization on the banks of the Nile. Although this civilization seems to have developed independently, we have to acknowledge that it carried traces of Aryan cultural values, as shown below. Neither the inner dynamics of the society on the Nile nor that of its close neighbors had the ability to produce such a civilization. There is a third possibility, namely that the Egyptian culture is a reflection of the Aryan culture, absorbed through the widespread reciprocal migration of the time. The greatness of the Egyptian civilization cannot be disputed, but neither can the fact that it did not permanently expand beyond the Nile, nor the fact that there was no native culture in the Nile area capable of developing into the Egyptian civilization. The development of the Nile culture, then, must either be a miracle from above or the result of the Neolithic revolution in the Taurus-Zagros system. On the other hand, I believe that the influence the Egyptian civilization had on the Sumerian civilization was far smaller than its influence on the Greco-Roman civilization.

The center of the Old Kingdom (more or less 2,700-2,200 BCE and encompassing many dynasties) was the alluvial area in Lower Egypt around the capital Ineb-Hedg (called Memphis by the Greeks) close to modern-day Cairo. The numerous monumental gravesites that were built by the pharaohs during the Old Kingdom, also known as the Age of Pyramids, display the god-like power of the kings. The abundance of temples built during the Middle Kingdom (about 2,030-1,640 BCE) reflects the strong influence of the priests during this period. During part of the Middle Kingdom, the capital was in Upper Egypt at Waset (Thebes) at today's Luxor; Amenemhat I built his capital at Itj-Tawi in Lower Egypt (probably at today's town of El-Lisht, close to Cairo). The Middle Kingdom ended when the Hyksos, a group of mixed Semitic-Asiatic origin, overthrew the pharaoh regime in about 1,630 BCE. This accomplishment, something that no one before them could achieve, shows their cultural and organizational strength. They ruled Egypt for about one hundred and fifty years. The period of the New Kingdom started in about 1,550 BCE. This period coincided with a period of development in trade, just as it did in Assyria. Initially, the New Kingdom had its center in Upper Egypt (the formidable temple complex of Karnak is an indication of the power of the Theban priests); later, the capital was moved back to Lower Egypt—to Avaris (close to the Nile Delta) and Memphis. Although the priests were still strong during this period, they were secondary to the kings—except in isolated cases as during the reign of Ramses II, when the high priest of Amun at Thebes in effect ruled Upper Egypt. The Semitic Hebrew tribe arrived in Egypt in about 1,600 BCE (that is, after the arrival of the Hyksos) and returned to the Middle East after three hundred years, in about 1,300 BCE. Their stay in Egypt thus coincided with the rule of King Akhenaton (1,350 to 1,334 BCE), famous for declaring the first monotheistic state religion in history. Many princesses from both the Hittite and Mitanni kingdoms were sent to the Egyptian palaces as brides.[24] Since about 1,000 BCE, tribal attacks from the south by groups of Sudanese-Abyssinian origin, and attacks by the Assyrians since 670 BCE, weakened the Egyptian state. In 664 BCE, the Assyrians conquered Memphis and Thebes. Egypt, then, was no match for the Achaemenid Persians, and in 525 BCE it became part of the Persian Empire. Alexander conquered Egypt in 333 BCE. When in 30 BC, toward the beginning of the Christian era, the Ptolemaic queen Cleopatra was defeated by Rome, it meant the end of the third phase of the four thousand year old civilization.

The question will always be: Sumer or Egypt, who influenced whom? The Egyptian civilization shows authenticity in terms of shipbuilding, the erecting of stone columns, wall paintings, the art of calendar making, medicine, astrology and mummification. But the hieroglyphic writing system is more primitive than the cuneiform system of the Sumerians—its functionality is limited. The Egyptian religious structure is more like a complex copy of the Sumerian system: while the Isis-Osiris tradition could be derived from the Inanna-Enki tradition, the Amon Ra tradition is very close to the Ziggurat system of the Sumerian priests.

Excavated tombs attest to the advanced architecture of the Egyptians. Though these are architectural wonders, they also are the manifestation of a frenzy that consumed a frightening amount of slave labor. This civilization, which has left as big a footprint in history as Sumer, practiced the classical slave system in its purest form. In no other civilization has the unity of slave and master reached the level it had in Egypt. As in Sumer, the promise of an after-world offered by Egyptian religion was a strong legitimization device needed to convince the slaves, who certainly did not have an easy life. It is this strong civilizational region that invented the paradigm of heaven, hell and the life to come. There is a strong possibility that Egyptian religion influenced the Abrahamic religions as much as the Sumerian and Babylonian religious beliefs did. The fact that Moses was brought up in the Egyptian culture, and that his ancestor Abraham fled from the Babylonian Nimrods, reminds us of the strong influence of these two cultures upon, and their synthesis in, the Abrahamic religions. In its original form, the Egyptian pharaoh regime shows many characteristics of what today we would describe as state communism.

Urartu was also a first generation civilization. It is believed that after a long era of being a confederation, the Urartu civilization took its first step toward becoming a centralized kingdom around 870 BCE due to a continuous struggle between the Assyrians and the Nairians.[25] The Assyrian inscription stating that King Sarduri defeated all those that crossed him with the support and protection of the god Haldi may have heralded his magnificent march to a centralized kingdom.[26] It is presumed that Urartu was the first state consisting of provinces with a centralized government. This strong, centralized state stretched from the eastern skirts of the Zagros to the western shores of the Euphrates, from the Aras valleys in the north to the Assyrian region in the south, as far as the northern border of today's Syria. The area around today's Van was their headquarters. It was named Tushpa, most probably after the ancient god of the sun, Teshup. Many castles were built in the area of their headquarters. Their system of belief was strongly influenced by the Sumerians and the Assyrians. They exchanged their hieroglyphic script for Assyrian cuneiform script. Besides Urartu (which seems to be related to Hurrian and the languages of the tribes migrating from north-eastern Caucasia) Assyrian was used as court language. After the fall of the Urartian state in the sixth century BCE, the use of Urartu was limited to the elite while the common people spoke a language related to proto-Armenian.

It may not be unwarranted to call Urartu the strongest civilization of the Iron Age. Many weapons, cauldrons, plates and clothes made of an iron-copper mixture have survived. It seems that they were the earliest civilization to have used processed iron ona huge scale. Besides advancing to a civilization stage of urbanization and having an official capital, they developed the new concept of a centralized state. Their road network was excellent—one can still make out the routes. The royal tombs carved into rocks are magnificent. Enslaved neighboring peoples were used in the construction of castles and cities. They were quite advanced in their water channel systems and the making of ponds. They resisted the Assyrians for three hundred years—a conflict that led to both states being defeated by the Medes and their allies. History has not witnessed a similar political formation in this geographical since.

The Medo-Persian Empire constituted the final, magnificent rise of this first generation of civilizations. The word *Mede* came from the ancient Greeks. The historian Herodotus said, "The Medes were called 'ancient' by all people Aryan" and, indeed, we can call the culture of the Median descendants authentically Aryan because no other group has succeeded in occupying their land. The Median culture was shaped at the Zagros mountain range and can be traced back to the Gutians and Kassites. (A common approach is to classify all these tribes as Hurrian.) These tribal clans were probably the groups that suffered most from constant clashes with the Assyrians and we can surmise that this resistance was the reason behind their statehood, although they also had clashes with the Scythians that came from the Caucasus.

The Medes had a reasonably successful confederation after the tribal clans loosely united in 715 BCE. The continuous oppression by Assur and Urartu led the Medes into an alliance with the Scythians (forming alliances seem to be a historical tradition). Despite the fact that the leadership often changed hands, they destroyed the Urartu palaces (around 615 BCE) and shortly afterwards burnt down the city of Assur—one of the capitals of Assyria—to end these last two strong civilizations of Mesopotamia. According to Herodotus, their famed capital Ecbatana (present-day Hamadan in Iran) was surrounded by seven circular walls of different colors. Their short-lived period of rule was closely linked to their relation with the Persian tribes, who were close relatives. The political formation that they had built up over three hundred years was snatched by the Persian Achaemenid Empire. The Persian Cyrus the Great, grandson of the Median king Astyages, allied with the military commander of the palace, Harpagus, in order to overthrow his overlord, King Astyages, in a terrible coup. The historical records of Herodotus claim that, faced with this coup, Astyages said to Harpagus, "What a wretched soul! Now that you have overthrown me, why have you given the power to a Persian bastard? Why did you transfer the power to the Persian and not be ruler yourself? At least it could have stayed with the Medes!"

I believe Herodotus called all those of Hurrian cultural origin "Medes." He respected them highly, seeing the Persians as secondary to them. He was correct in conceiving the cultural stamp of the region to be that of the Medes. The Persians, at the time, were at the beginning of their fame in history. The magnificence of the Hurrian culture was even then famous from the shores of the Aegean to Elam and from the Caucasus to the Egyptian palaces, as disclosed by Herodotus.

A similar role as the one played by the initial priests, namely to construct the new mentality and gods within the Sumerian civilization, was played by priest in the establishment of the Urartu and Medo-Persian civilizations. The priests called the Magi were probably symbolic figures or else *magi* was the title for the Zoroastrian priests, who had their central, sacred town at Musasir.[27] We can thus assume that the initial pantheon of their gods was established there and later taken to Tushpa, Ecbatana and Persepolis.

Without an old tradition of priesthood it is difficult to build important civilizations. The philosophers and their philosophy in the Greek culture, and the intellectuals of the Age of Enlightenment in the European civilization, played a similar role. (It may be instructive to see the sheikh of the Semitics and the Hebrew prophets in the same role.) The role played by the Magi and Zoroaster should also be recognized—especially in the rise of the Medes. It is my conviction that the Magi and the foundation of the Zoroastrian belief and morals reflect the values of the Neolithic society by seeing fire, agriculture and livestock as sacred. A belief and moral system like that could not have been contaminated with the impurities of civilization. It is different from the inventions of the Sumerian priests, such as their masked god-kings. In fact, it is the opposite. It rests on the idea that the universe is full of contention between good and evil, light and darkness. The fundamental norm within the Zoroastrian priesthood is the existence of free morality—it does not speak of how to manufacture gods, but of the sacredness of agriculture, livestock and the characteristics of free human beings.[28] These morals played a determining role in the defeat of Assur and the rise of the Medo-Persian Empire.

After the death of Cyrus, a group of Mede origin gained power during a coup in 528 BCE. However, they were easily eliminated and the infamous rule of Darius began.[29] In a very short time, after the collapse of the Ionian cities in Babylonia, Egypt and the Aegean shores, the most extensive empire was established that history had seen till then—stretching from the Aegean to the shores of the Pençav ("Five waters," the Punjab River). It was the strongest civilization of its time, excluding China. Undoubtedly, it had been influenced by the cultures of the Sumerian, Assyrian, Babylonian and Urartu civilizations. On the other hand, it had been nurtured by the free spirit of the Aryan culture. It also had relations with the Scythians coming from the north via the Greek culture and the proto-Turks from the East, and certainly had been influenced by these cultures as well. It thus presented history with a unique example of a synthesis of numerous cultures.

The Medo-Persian Empire is the final and most extensive representative of the first generation civilization.[30] It reached the highest level attainable in a first generation civilization. Their innovative architecture and the magnificence of their headquarters can still be seen in the remnants of Persepolis. The power of the state centers was almost on par with that of the Roman Empire and it prepared the ground for the Greco-Roman world. The Medo-Persian Empire is famous for its political system of multi-states, each with a degree of autonomy and governed by a satrap—a vassal king. It is also famous for its tremendous postal and transportation systems, its special security forces, the Immortals Regiment, and an army consisting of hundreds of thousands of people.[31] The Zoroastrian belief system and religious rituals were totally new. A distinction developed between the religion of the nobles, who were Zoroastrians, and the ordinary people, who continued the ancient worship of the sun god Mithra. The development they brought to the different fields of civilization was greater than the sum of those who preceded them. They were the first to unify numerous numbers of tribes, clans, religions, sects, languages and cultures. It is the last glorious and dazzling Middle-Eastern civilization of antiquity and superior in all aspects to the newly developing Greek civilization. Alexander, the student of Aristotle, was one of the new breed of barbarian invaders craving to possess this magnificence, but with a profound feeling of inferiority toward the Eastern culture. What the Roman Empire meant for the Goths, the Persian Empire meant for the Macedonian and Greek tribal chiefs and petty kings. If we look at Alexander's invasion from this perspective, a more meaningful and accurate interpretation may be achieved.

Let us conclude this section with a few additional points, the first of which concerns the Hebrew clan. Let me reiterate that from 1,700 BCE onward, the Aryan language and culture, the Semitic language and culture, the civilizations of Sumerian origin and the civilizations of Egyptian origin shared some characteristics. In the sacred book of the Hebrews the names of Suruç, Urfa and Harran are explicitly mentioned as the ancestral location of Abraham, from where the tribe seemed to have travelled to Egypt.[32] They made a living mainly through animal husbandry, although they seemed to have practiced some trade as well. Their religious belief apparently hovered between Yahweh and El (which was later to become Allah). They resisted assimilation into civilization—their monotheistic belief may have much to do to with this resistance. They have the privilege of developing tribal theism. It began with Abraham's opposition to the Babylonian King Nimrod and continued with Moses's opposition to the pharaoh, and would later continue in Palestine as conflicts with many of the tribes and their gods. They continued to preserve their uniqueness for a long time under the leadership of priests of which Aaron, Moses' younger brother, was the first.

The initial period of leadership by priests, initiated by Moses, ended with the renowned priest Samuel. In 1,020 BCE started the period of the kingdoms with kings like Saul, David, Solomon and others. They constructed a small kingdom with a strong military and political character. There seemed to have been continuous conflict between the kings and the priests. Both those who resisted and those who collaborated with the Assyrians were defeated around 720 BCE and around 540 BCE their exodus to Babylon began. They were freed when the Persians ended the rule of the Babylonians. Two collaborationist parties, the Sadducees and the Pharisees, came to the fore during the conflicts between the Persians and the Greeks. Later, resistance against the Romans resulted in the first and second waves of exiles, first to Egypt and Anatolia and later to all parts of the known world.[33] Then the resistance of Jesus followed. His death by crucifixion started the second religion of Abrahamic origin—and the troublesome relationship between the Greco-Roman and European civilizations on the one hand and the small Hebrew tribe on the other. Most leaders of the Hebrew tribe were rabbis or nabis; the long list of prophets ending with Jesus and Mohammed (though the last two are not recognized as prophets in Judaism).[34] Religious conflict accompanied by political conflict continued. The period of scribes started with the end of the Roman rule and this tradition continues to date with a generation of writers and intellectuals as strong as that of the prophets. In time, the pre-historic small step in the direction of trade played a leading role in the birth of capitalism and the dominance of today's finance capital. The Hebrew tribe has always been small in numbers but they have a strong influence on the history of civilization. The Hebrew tribe should be studied as intensively as civilization itself as, even today, they appear to be the emperors of science, law and money. My personal story reflects the history of this tribe in the miniature: I too started my resistance by making my exit from Suruç in Urfa, similar to Abraham. However, my resistance led to a crucifixion different to that of Jesus.[35]

Another point that needs to be noted is the Scythian influx from the north around 800 BCE. The Scythians had Caucasian roots. These tribes, who expanded to inner Europe and Asia and from the Russian steps to Mesopotamia, did not really leave strong traces behind, as their expansion was physical rather than cultural. However, they did play a role in the establishment and collapse of many empires, including that of the Hebrew tribe. They served as soldiers and chamber women in the palaces. This continued in the time of the Ottoman Empire and even today in the Republic of Turkey. It is evident that they could not protect their own identity as well as the Hebrews did. Scythian and similar peoples of the first generation civilized society should also be studied thoroughly.

The center-periphery model is useful when studying the formation of historical systems.[36] When talking about centers of civilization, the question of what happened in the periphery is obviously important. When Sumer and Egypt, the first centers of civilization were constructed, the Amorite and the Apiru were the peripheral powers in their areas of influence; for the Chinese it was the proto-Turk Huns and for the Romans the Goths. When the chiefs of these tribes acquired and learnt how to use the weapons of civilization, they were either in a continuous state of offense or defense with the civilized states. Their fate was either to dissolve in one of the dominant centers of civilization or to establish a similar center of civilization in the periphery. For example, the Amorite Akkadians constructed their own dynasty after being on the offensive for a long time. The Hebrews established their own kingdom based on what they learnt from Egypt. Although the Huns were one of the strongest peripheral groups, they finally dissolved within the civilization centers of China, Europe and Iran. Usually, the chief of a peripheral tribe remained in the center of the civilization as an administrative chief and became totally integrated; the clansman, on the other hand, remained marginal for a long time or made new attempts at establishing their own center of civilization under a new chief. The Gothic attacks on Rome laid the basis for the German princedoms—at times Gothic leaders even wore the Roman crown. An interesting example is the Mongolian and Oghuz tribes that developed as a peripheral force to the Byzantine Empire's central force. However, the conflict that continued for hundreds of years ended with these tribes transforming themselves into central powers. The Scythians were a peripheral force for the first generation centers of civilization, playing their role mostly in the north, especially in the Caucasus. When they became acquainted with the various civilizations and took up their arms, they became a force of extraordinary offensive strength. It is thought that they were quite active between 800 and 500 BCE. Although they played their role well as mercenaries and palace servants, they were not able to establish significant centers of civilization on their own behalf.

b. Developments in the Chinese, Indian and Native American cultures

It will be instructive to look at the developments in other systems of civilization with their own specific characteristics, namely the Chinese, Indian and Native American cultures.

China was one of the most important regions to which migrating groups from south-east Siberia had moved at the end of the last ice age (around 10,000 BCE). The fertile land at the shores of the seas and streams, and its resulting rich fauna and flora, was conducive to both the Neolithic culture and city-civilizations. Around 4,000 BCE, history notes the development of the Chinese Neolithic revolution. For us, the important question is to what degree this was an authentic Neolithic agricultural revolution or whether it was strongly influenced by the expansion of the Aryan culture. Indications are that the Aryan Neolithic culture had been established at least six thousand years before the Chinese Neolithic and thus could have influenced the latter. However, the question remains whether this was a determinant influence. History tells us that big cultural revolutions do not form very easily and that their formation needs unique conditions and the *longue durée*. I think that the Chinese Neolithic and civilization were as original and native as Chinese socialism and capitalism. (There should not be a misunderstanding here: I have no doubt that even the most nationalist capitalism is imported. This also holds true for China.) It may then follow that the Chinese Neolithic could not have expanded into Vietnam, the Indo-Chinese Peninsula, Japan, Indonesia and the Korean Peninsula before 4000 BCE.

The birth of the Chinese slave-owning civilization took place around 1,500 BCE. The initial central empire was established around this date and was considered sacred. It was the Uruk of China. Just as with the Sumerian and Egyptian civilizations, around 1,000 BCE a period of disintegration and expansion followed the establishment of the Chinese civilization. During this second period, many city-states were established and, similar to what happened during the Ur period in the Sumerian civilization, intense city rivalry caused numerous wars. During the third period (from 250 BCE to the year 250), the feudal, centralized dynasties (of native or foreign origins) grew strong once again and outweighed the rest. This continued until the beginning of the twentieth century. The Chinese civilization is thought to have expanded to Indochina, the Japanese islands and Central Asia—including the areas of the Mongolians and proto-Turkish peoples.

What is interesting is not the inventions of gods similar to that of the Sumerian priests, but the wise men's interpretation of the universe. The way they comprehended and interpreted the universe and nature was more scientific than that of Sumer, and it is instructive to see how they defined energy. They envisioned that the universe was alive. In general, Chinese philosophy can be described as Taoism—it can also be called sagacious. Confucius (500 BCE) tried to establish the principles and morals of a civilized city and state order. The cornerstone of his doctrine is that the governance of the state society must be based on sound moral principles instead of official laws. Confucius lived in the same period as Zoroaster and Socrates and influenced civilized society as much as they did. These great sages all emphasized the importance of morals and core virtues.

The Chinese made important advances with regard to material civilization. In terms of industrial development they were ahead of the West. They were the inventors of paper, gunpowder and printing. The Chinese were positioned at the east end of trade, where the ancient Silk Road began. China had opened itself to capitalism around the middle of the 19th century. Today, it has grown gigantically and, as a new Leviathan, it is watched with close interest as to what it will do and how it will expand.

The other civilizations of Chinese origin—such as Japan, Indonesia, Vietnam and Korea—advanced in a similar way, spreading the main civilization. It is not important for our topic to explore this in more detail.

A local Neolithic development cannot be observed in India. The Aryans probably entered India for the first time circa 2,000-1,500 BCE. The Neolithic revolution there was indeed related to this influx. Priests, just as with the Sumerians, led not only this revolution but also the revolution of the civilization that began circa 1,000 BCE. The Veda, the primary sacred book of the priest class, the Brahmin priests, was probably created around 1,500 BCE.[37] It is the story of the construction of the priest class on the basis of their supreme divinity. This became the foundation for the caste regime. Around 1,000 BCE, the Rajahs—the political and military strong men—appeared. They waged fierce battles against the Brahmins and established themselves as the new rulers of the state, just as it had happened in all other civilizations. They then formed the second caste. As in China, the fertile river and seashores were suitable for farming. Around 1,000 BCE, the cities started to expand, but they were still characterized by their large palaces and temples. Agriculture developed quickly and farmers and craftsmen constituted the third caste. At the bottom were the Untouchables. Even coming into contact with them was considered a sin.

The priests created a very colorful theology. They constructed, besides the main gods, numerous divine entities. A profound Sumerian influence can be detected in Hindu religion. The mind-boggling abundance of deities may be attributed to the fact that this pantheon has its origins elsewhere and a thorough synthesis has not yet been achieved.

As in all the other important civilizations of the time, in India a great religious reformist was born around 500 BCE named Buddha.[38] Buddha based his reform on morals and not on gods. Seeing the great pain in nature and society, he tried to develop a compensatory metaphysical doctrine. Buddhism is a doctrine with a strong environmentalist character and is critical of civilization. It is a doctrine that needs to be considered seriously, especially in terms of its moral metaphysics. It is a regime of vigorous implementation, self-control and self-improvement. It expanded swiftly in China, Indochina and Japan. Another religious tradition, reminiscent of the Dionysian cult, took root in India, namely that of the god Krishna. It was strongly influenced by the Neolithic and mountain cultures, nomadic life, free women and love stories— it was based on a morality that highly valued the desire to live freely. The contrast between the religion of the Brahmins and these last two religions with their radically different metaphysics and their disregard for materialistic values, reflects the complexities of the Indian society and the profound differences in life styles in this country.

The Indian civilization became a centralized political structure after the invasions of the Persians and Alexander the Great. Around 300 BCE, the Emperor Ashoka adopted the Buddhist reforms. He was the first to achieve a thorough centralization of the maverick and widespread Rajahs (reminiscent of the relationship between the Zoroastrian religious reform and the establishment of the centralized Medo-Persian Empire). Ashoka was unable to completely eradicate the maverick and chaotic life of the Rajahs. Around the year 1,000 CE, they faced incursions from the Muslim states and in the early 1,500s, they once again became part of a centralized state under the leadership of the Moghuls—Muslim emperors of Mongolian origin. A certain civilizational progress was attained and therefore expansion continued. The infiltration that began around 1,500 and that rested upon capitalism entered a new phase in the mid 19th century with the colonialism of English capitalism. After World War II India gained independence, though it lost its north-eastern and north-western parts to the new Muslim states of Pakistan and Bangladesh. Nevertheless, in order to continue its existence, the Subcontinent as a whole—from the skirts of the Himalayas to the wide shores of its seas and rivers—needs to infuse its complex cultural richness with that of capitalist civilization. It will be very interesting to see how the Subcontinent will progress as it becomes acquainted with democracy, seeing that it has such a complex religious, artistic and moral structure and such diverse language and political structures.

The expansion of civilization to the American continent occurred in two stages. The first stage may have occurred around 10,000 BCE, when some groups migrated to North America via the Bering Strait, and from there they spread to South America.[39] They became acquainted with the Neolithic revolution around 3,000 BCE and by the year 500 BCE the initial stages of civilization occurred. In the east of the Americas, from Mexico to Chile, the Native Americans established initial civilizations, known as the Aztec, Mayan and the Inca civilizations. These civilizations, which resembled the Uruk civilization of the initial Sumer period, petered out, unable to establish big cities and multiply their numbers—possibly because of weather and geographical conditions. When the Europeans arrived these civilizations were still in existence, albeit weakly. The strong structure of their cities and the remnants of their temples are impressive. If they had the opportunity to expand into the continent, they might have succeeded in establishing multiple centers and attain centralization. In these civilizations too one can see the weight of the priests, indeed, they may also be called "priest-civilizations." They practiced the frightening ritual of sacrificing youngsters.[40] They developed the use of a sign system that resembled writing. They had an advanced calendar and they introduced a variety of plant and animal species to the world. At the time, North America had not yet come into contact with civilization. The boom of the civilization in the American continent really began with the European invasion and colonization of the 16th century. In the 19th century, as part of the new capitalist development of civilization, seemingly independent nations were born in the Americas. In reality, they were nation-states of capitalism; they joined and became integrated with the world system. After World War II, America—specifically the United States—has continued its ascent as the system's hegemonic power. The exciting quest by South America (for instance Cuba, Venezuela and Bolivia) to seek a new model of civilization as an alternative to the capitalist civilization of European and USA origin continues.

The role that Europe, the huge Leviathan of our age, played during the time that the initial civilization came into being was that of institutionalizing the Neolithic culture. Around 100 BCE, at the time of the expansion of the Roman Empire, there were no signs of civilization in the rest of Europe. Many battles were waged between the tribes—the Scythians, Huns, Goths, Celtics, Nordics and so forth. Migration was common at the time. Apart from village and agricultural development, there was also a small trade in metals. I keep the Greek and Roman cultures separate from the rest of Europe because I discuss these two regions at the western end of the Middle Eastern civilization under a separate heading.

Mother Africa—where man learnt to walk, search for food with tools in hand, and attained speech—continued to be devoted to this deep-rooted culture of hers. Further than the Sudan, the Egyptian civilization was unknown and the Christian civilization only advanced as far as Ethiopia. The entire northern part of the continent became Muslim as it was occupied by the Semitic Arabs, who flourished with the Islamic civilization. Finally, in the 19th century, Africa was overrun by the European capitalist civilization. Africa, with its difficulty to digest the different civilizations due to its internal structure, is a bewildering conglomerate of different cultures and stages of civilization. As with South America and the Middle East, we are anxiously waiting to see whether it will integrate with civilization and modernity or whether it will choose free life.

c. Greco-Roman civilization and problems associated with its expansions

We examined the expansion of the Sumerian and Egyptian based civilizations together, because they developed more or less at the same time, mutually influencing each other during their development stages and continuing to do so during their periods of expansion. Furthermore, their shared Middle Eastern roots are another reason for their unison. It is a characteristic feature of this region that at birth they are already intertwined.[41] These two cultures were the inventors of many of the "firsts" of history. It cannot be denied that all the other expansions that succeeded them were formed on the basis of the essence and on the pattern of these two civilizations. Although the successor civilizations were not exactly similar, there is no doubt that they were bound by their shared roots. The initial slave-owning civilization was the Sumerian one, followed by the Egyptian civilization; this model then spread itself around the world with little change. I doubt that any civilization can be analyzed effectively if the Egyptian and Sumerian civilizations are not taken into account.

However, there are problems associated with this model. Firstly, we need to clarify what the level of influence between the Sumerian and the Egyptian civilizations was, and secondly, we need to determine whether the Medo-Persian civilization, the first to be constructed outside of the Mesopotamian centers, originated from the same or a different source. It is clear that the Medo-Persian civilization adopted many of its essential characteristics from Sumer, and later from Babylonia, Assyria and Urartu. However, they achieved areas of major and unique reform, of which the Zoroastrian moral revolution (quite similar to the moral of freedom), a centralized state system, and an immensely effective military order were the most important. For this reason, I treat the Medo-Persian Empire as a civilization distinct from the Sumerian-Egyptian civilization, but as the connecting link between the Sumerian-Egyptian and the Greco-Roman civilizations. If seen in the correct historical perspective, such similarities and differences can play an important role in determining the phases of civilization. If we discard these factors, the Greco-Roman civilization will not be analyzed properly or the analysis will be overly complex due to unscientific interpretations and because some characteristics will have to be attributed to miraculous origins.

Thirdly, there is the question of the origins of the Chinese and Indian civilizations. I believe that we should not treat them as independent. This approach will allow us to analyze the similarities and the differences between civilizations. Even if we accept the South American, Harappa and Mohenjo-daro civilizations as distinct, it is clear that they were not able to move beyond the initial city-states phase (the Uruk-type state) and faded away. As a result, Africa, Europe (apart from the Greco-Romans) and even Australia became civilized during a much later expansion; all these areas, including the Americas, became civilized only with the expansion of capitalism.

I hope that these short remarks will aid me in defining the Greco-Roman civilization and analyzing its expansion.

Undeniably, the Greco-Roman civilization was superior to that of the Medes and Persians. However, it would be a historical distortion and short-sightedness to claim that this superiority resulted solely from conditions in continental Greece and the Greek peninsula; we also have to consider the widespread expansion and the characteristics of the civilization from the Middle East—started by the Egyptians and Sumerians and then developed further by their successors, the Babylonians, Assyrians, Mitannians, Hittites, Urartus, Medes and Persians. All the inventions and the developments in the area of religion, morals, philosophy, arts, politics and science came into being during the birth, progress, strife and conflict of these civilizations. Furthermore, they came about as a result of the significant inheritance from Neolithic society. The Europeans were ignorant of these fields of knowledge until much later—such knowledge only became firmly established amongst Europeans with the Renaissance of the Greek and Roman cultures. They then proclaimed that all were the inventions and innovation of the Greeks and Romans themselves. Hence, they now carry the sole responsibility for this faulty understanding of the Greco-Roman civilization.

If Herodotus's history were read more carefully, discovering the sources of Greek culture wouldn't have been that difficult. All available historical documents suggest that continental Greece and the Greek peninsula were penetrated by the Indo-European language and culture from about 5,000 BCE, and that it underwent a Neolithic revolution.

To obtain a proper historical understanding of this period, we need to establish the source of these influences. It is possible that a later wave of migration, around 1,800 BCE, brought the inventions of the civilization to this area. These immigrants later progressed to the stage of the city-state (similar to that of Uruk) around 400 BCE. This attainment was influenced significantly by the Hittites, who referred to this region in their documents as Ahhiyawa.

Reciprocal trade within the region began around 3,000 BCE via Troy—a city vital for Continental Greece and the Greek peninsula at the time.[42] The Hittites brought to this region both the ideological inventions (gods, literature, science, etc.) and material inventions (especially things that could be traded such as metal, pottery and weaved goods) of the Middle East. They played a significant role in channeling these inventions into civilization. The Phoenicians, on the other hand, taught the early Greeks the art of navigation and their alphabet. Egypt also had a significant influence on them—both directly and through the Minoans on Crete. Thus, all the inventions of the Middle Eastern civilizations nurtured the Greek culture continuously via these four channels. Later, Solon (638–558 BCE), Pythagoras (570-495 BCE) and Thales (624–546 BCE) visited the Egyptian, Babylonian and the Medo-Persian palaces and schools in order to learn and bring back the lessons and its system of rule.

After the fall of Troy around 1,200 BCE, the area was invaded by the Ionian, Dorian and Aeolian tribes. The Egyptians called the people who made these early attacks the "Sea Peoples," and, according to the Egyptians, they were involved with the fall of Troy as well.[43] These groups, which crowded in to western Anatolia and the Aegean Islands, were seen as barbarians by the Troy and Hittite civilizations. Indeed, the Hittite country and the small kingdom of Troy were the centers of civilization in the area. Barbarians can only become civilized after a long period of settlement in an established, civilized culture and this is indeed what happened: after a long period of settlement in continental Greece, the peninsula and the Aegean regions, the establishment of cities began after 700 BCE.[44] Besides influence from the Middle East, the urbanization around the Aegean shores also had an element of authenticity. This unique synthesis of a rich and diverse cultural heritage combined with the extraordinary flora and fauna of the region, gave the new cities their own unique identity. The cultural and ideological components inherited from the Middle East were adapted; some important changes were made and then synthesized with a partially new essence. Thus, their inventions and innovations encompassed (and excelled) those of the Neolithic, Sumerian, Egyptian, Hittite, Urartu and Medo-Persian cultures.

The most important question here is: *Where was the center of this, the biggest intellectual revolution in history?* The initial city of the region was destroyed around 1,200 BCE and a period of chaos—the so-called Greek Dark Ages—followed.[45] In this period, the only settlements were a few Phoenician trade colonies. Thus, until around 700 BCE, there was no civilization in continental Greece or the Greek peninsula. The Achaeans leaders of the time were not called kings (that would require a city-state) but tribal chiefs—they were clearly still in a phase of barbarism. Although Athens was already well known in the 7th century BCE, it was still far from being a center of civilization. The cities formed by the tribes on the eastern shores of the Aegean played a more central role.

The most famous names of the Greek intelligentsia of the time (for instance Homer, most of the Seven Sages, Thales, Heraclitus, Democritus and Pythagoras) were all from the cities on the east Aegean shores and islands. Many of the famous gods (including Apollo) were from this or nearby regions. The most famous temples and centers of prophecy were also in this region. At the time, the material civilization here was much more advanced than in Continental Greece and on the Peninsula.

Other evidence may include the existence of the Ionian cities—as the new Aegean centers of civilization—at the same time as, or just after, the Hittites, Phrygians and Lydians.

Thus, continental Greece and the peninsula have the attributes of being sequels to the cities of the eastern Aegean. The invasion of this region by the Medo-Persian Empire around 545 BCE resulted in the center of Greek civilization shifting to Athens. All the ideological and material achievements of the civilization on the Aegean shore were moved to Athens. Most of the intellectuals took refuge in Athens or southern Italy. Under Persian rule, the region slowly lost its importance and Athens had a period of glory.

Undoubtedly, the Persian civilization was the most magnificent civilizations of its time. It not only *took* from the Greek regions, it also contributed in many ways. However, because the region on the eastern shore of the Aegean lost its independence, it lost its first and last chance to establish a great civilization. If this had not happened, I believe that they would have spread all over Anatolia, establishing a magnificent civilization, larger than that of the Sumerians, Egyptians, Chinese, Hittites, Persians and even the Byzantines. Then the Greek and the Italian Peninsulas probably would have been states dependent to them. The presence of the Persians in the Aegean not only caused the end of the Persian Empire itself, but also prevented the Aegean from leading a great system of civilization. We can but lament this. Alexander tried to establish such a center in the name of Macedonia, but all he achieved was a complex, poly-centric culture that was a synthesis between the East and the West. Although it is called the Hellenic "culture," it did not progress beyond being an eclectic synthesis; it is by no means an authentic creation. Later, under the Roman Empire, the Aegean had no opportunity to develop apart from it being a state with Pergamum as its center. Thus, again development in the eastern Aegean was stunted.

Indeed, in terms of expansion in size and increase in the number of cities, the Athens-centered civilization should be viewed as a true civilization. It left its mark on the era in terms of ideological and material civilization. When analyzing Athens, we should view it as a new compound formed out of all the previous civilizations. All the progress of the Neolithic culture, the ideological and material inventions gained during the long history of civilization, were integrated with the local influences, realizing the biggest revolution of civilization. The most important characteristic of the Athenian revolution was the embracing of philosophy as ideology and as an alternative form of belief to paganism. Philosophy paved the way for a blossoming of knowledge and understanding. This is the era when the seeds of all the different philosophical branches were sown: idealism, materialism, and dialectics. Before Socrates, natural philosophy was the priority; with Socrates, social philosophy became more influential. The growth of the social question as a result of suppression and exploitation played a role in this development. (With "social question" I mean the establishment of the city-trade-state-administrational chain of events.) Furthermore, the city as a material civilization more or less forced this philosophical thought: The city itself means a break with organic society; thus, a mentality removed from nature will easily be shaped in the city. The city civilization is established on the basis of betrayal of the environment and is the root of all abstract, vulgar metaphysic and materialistic thought.

Therefore, although philosophy is on the one hand a breakthrough in thinking, on the other it creates alienation from the environment. The sages who spread philosophy and knowledge were the intellectuals of their era—just like the 18th century European intellectuals. They taught the children of the well-off families in return for money. The philosophers established their own schools just as the priests of Sumer used religious inventions and temples. In a way, they established their own churches (or assemblies). Just like polytheistic religions, they formed multiple philosophical schools. Each of the schools may be viewed as a religion or a denomination. Religions, since they are forms of thought, may also be seen as philosophies that had become traditional, institutionalized and then took the form of a belief system. We should not think that the difference between religion and philosophy makes them complete opposites. Where religion is more the ideological nourishment of the ruled classes, philosophy is more nourishment for the youth and intellectuals of the privileged classes. Plato and Aristotle attempted to succeed in the priests' duty to construct, defend and liberate the city-state through the use of philosophy. The main task of the philosophers was to determine how the city-state and society would be administered and defended and, more importantly, how it should be constituted.

The second important characteristic of the Athenian civilization was the emphasis it put on the theoretical and practical aspects of what democracy and republic meant. Although this was a democracy only for the aristocracy, it was an important phase in the history of civilization in general. Citizenship of the city was restricted to a small number of people—likely not even ten percent of society. Still, it was a critical innovation. It also played an important role in shaping philosophy and the art of politics. Democracy would entail that the people deal with politics themselves—they handled their own administrational work. The essence of democracy is that people think, discuss and decide on critical social issues. Thus, the democratic politics of the Athenian civilization is a vital contribution to civilization.

In the Athenian Parthenon, the Greek gods proclaimed themselves through a brand new form of architecture. Here, it was far more obvious that the gods were products of human invention than it was in the sacred houses of the Sumerian civilizations. The traditional religious belief was gradually losing its value—almost as if the Sumerian founders of cities and gods were living their last days in the civilizations of Athens and Rome. Athens, the founding city of the Greco-Roman civilization, received its name from the goddess Athena—the founder and protector of Athens. This is reminiscent of the goddess of Uruk, Inanna and, once again, we see the similarities and consecutiveness between civilizations. Other parts of the cities included the *agora* (the town's civic and market center), theatre, *stoa* (a covered walkway), and arenas. The Greek cities attained more advanced institutional structures than those of the other civilizations. There were many palaces—some with, others without, the city having walled fortifications. These structures are reminiscent of those of the Hittites but they were more advanced and could accommodate bigger crowds.

Greek literature developed far beyond anything the world had seen before. It may even be the greatest recorded literary culture of all times. Theatre lived through its most revolutionary phase. The many historical works of art included written legends and tragedies. Often important events were the subject of the plays—heralding the formation of cinema. The remnants of the magnificent buildings indicate how highly developed the architecture was. Sculpture attained a level of near perfection. Impressive reliefs reflected scenes from mythology. Their strong mythological literature was a synthesis of all the mythologies of the ancient civilizations.

Music progressed in terms of variety of instruments as well as in variety of themes—ballads of the divine and the profane, of love and legend. The lyre was the outstanding instrument of this period. Poetic expression, although no longer as prominent as in the heroic era, continued its existence.

The arts of navigation and trade progressed as well. As far as navigation is concerned, the Athenians were second only to the Phoenicians.

Although trade was not a favorite occupation in Athenian society, the early seeds of capitalism existed there—albeit at a marginal level.

After Athens, Sparta was the most important of the Greek city-states. Its most important characteristic was that it continued the ancient traditions of the kingdoms. Although there always were rivalry and war amongst the Greek city-states, Athens and Sparta became the models for the entire Continental Greece, the Peninsula, the islands and Asia Minor. Even the regions around the Black Sea and the shores of Marmara made the transition to the city-state. The increase in population and trade initiated an advanced era of new colonization. On nearly all the Mediterranean shores and islands Greek colonies were established—in Egypt we can still see the remnants of Greek cities of this time. Trade houses were established from Marseille to the south of France and on the Mediterranean shores of Spain. Even the south of Italy was colonized to a degree. Despite all these major developments, the Greeks were not able to attain the imperial power of the Persians or the Romans. The spirit of the time demanded becoming an empire or being swallowed up by another empire. Around 340 BCE the Greek civilization, led by Athens, faced the threat posed by the Macedonians, who had risen as a new kingdom in the north. The Greek civilization was not able to transform its extraordinary ideological and material power into a central political system surpassing that of the city-states. After a few battles of resistance, the Greek civilization lost its independence once and for all. But, just like Babylonia, it continued its existence for a long time as the new cultural center. The final blow to the democracy of Athens came from Macedonia when Philip, who wished to unite in a tight alliance all the tribes that, although from different language groups, belonged to the Greek culture, succeeded in taking Athens in 347 BCE.

Philip's son Alexander was educated by Aristotle and was thus well equipped with knowledge of all the Greek cultural values and its mythology. Like all other Greek politicians, Alexander was well aware of the riches of the Persian Empire and it became an obsession of the Greeks to conquer the Persians (very similar to the desire of Islam to conquer the Byzantines). Alexander was better equipped than the rest to achieve this, partly because his army was not the traditional army of slaves. But it should be well understood that Alexander longed to possess not only the riches of the

East but also this successful culture. He moved with his voluntary military units, organized into a new military formation called the *phalanx,* led by the chiefs of those tribes that newly left barbarism behind. He conquered everything from Egypt up to the Indus. When he mysteriously died at the age of thirty-three, he left a conquered area much larger than that of the Persian Empire, an area opened up for the Greek culture.

Although this area had been civilized before Alexander's conquest, its ideological and material base was that of the first generation, slave-owning civilization. The Greek culture, on the other hand, had surpassed this culture long before this time and had a promising future. Hence, it had the ability to inculcate the area with new ideas. Just as the Sumerian priests inculcated the Neolithic culture to form the initial classed city and state culture, the Greek culture inculcated youth into the ancient areas of civilization; thus, during the Hellenistic period (323 BCE to 34 BCE), many kingdoms were established. The most important kingdoms at the time were those of the Ptolemies in Egypt, Pergamum in Anatolia and the Seleucid Empire in Syria and Mesopotamia. The Parthians, who formed a new empire after the defeat of the Achaemenid Empire, tried to restore the Persian Empire but they did not fully succeed. These approximately three hundred years of Hellenistic culture brought the construction of new cities and pantheons that represented a mixed culture of Greek and Persian gods. In addition, the fact that the Greek language and culture became the official language and culture of such a vast area led to the formation of an important synthesis. Not only was Alexander's life itself a synthesis of the East and the West, but so were all the dominant cultures of the time. History has never again witnessed such a grand synthesis of cultures. A vivid example of this can be seen in the ruins of Antiochus' tomb in Mount Nemrut.[46] This tomb is flanked by statues of the fully syncretized deities Zeus-Oromasdes, Apollo-Mithra-Helios-Hermes and Artagnes-Herakles-Ares, symbolizing the East-West synthesis.

What is importance for the issue at hand is not the fact that the slave-owning society of Sumer civilized the empty regions or the Neolithic cultures, but that a new slave-owning society, the Greek-Hellenic civilization, which had progressed to a higher level, attempted to re-civilize, under their new cultural domination, the whole area from India to Rome, from the northern Black Sea to the Red Sea and from there to the Iranian Gulf. The younger and more militant representative of the new culture that was rising in Rome would develop the same policy and construct the biggest slave-owning empire of its time.

Defining the Roman culture is no less important than defining the Athenian culture. One important reason is the fact that this was the flowering period of the slave-owning society—with its fall, the slave-owning society declined rapidly. Secondly, it was the biggest representative of the imperial culture. No other empire in history has ever been as glorious as the Roman Empire. Thirdly, Rome was the last and the strongest representative of the masked god-king civilization. The Roman emperors considered themselves both human and god, saw no need to give account of their own actions but everybody else was forced to account to them. Fourthly, this was the state that introduced law and citizenship to many other communities. Fifthly, it was this empire that developed the concepts of *world citizenship, cosmopolitanism* and *world religion* (Catholicism). Sixthly, the Roman Empire was the dawn and foothold of the European civilization. Seventhly, it existed as a republic for a long time.

The city of Rome did not miraculously attain these big developments. It obtained the latent power from the four important cultures that preceded it. Firstly, there was the Neolithic revolutionary culture. Around 4,000 BCE this culture not only influenced the whole of Europe but also the Italian Peninsula and the last representatives of this culture were the Italic tribes. It is probably correct to assume that these tribes began to define the ethnic identity of the present day Italy around 1,000 BCE. It can thus be said that it is this identity that would have been influenced by the Neolithic institutions and mentalities. They are probably of European roots. The second group that served as a channel for cultural identity was the Etruscan civilization. This civilization with its Mesopotamian roots was half-Neolithic, half slave-owning; they brought the Aryan language and culture to Italy via Anatolia. They probably settled in the North of Italy around 800 BCE and spread from there. They are the ones that should get the honor for bringing the first scatterings of civilization to Italy and the city of Rome. Thirdly, the Greek culture, centered in Athens, had one of its branches as a colony in southern Italy in the early days of Rome's formation.[47] Fourthly, Carthage and the colonies established by the Phoenicians channeled the eastern Mediterranean culture of Egyptian and Semitic origins to the Italian Peninsula.

The essence of Rome's success lies in this mixture of all (with the exception of the Chinese) cultures. A synthesis far superior to that of Athens and the eastern Aegean resulted from the unity of the latent powers inherent in these four cultures. The mythological construction of Rome by the twins Romulus and Remus, who were abandoned by their parents and raised by a she-wolf, is a tale that was used to explain the origin of many similar cultures—it is an interesting way of explaining an external source and a culture of mixed origins.

The mythological story of the construction of the Roman Empire after the fall of Troy by Aeneas, fellow warrior of Paris, is quite instructive in terms of its Anatolian characteristics; it is an epic expression of my own approach. The story of construction by the priest-kings around 700 BCE would have been suitable for the construction of any of the similar main city-civilizations. The many conflicts with the surrounding tribal clans explain the relationship between class and statehood in the construction of the cities. The rivalry and battle between the Etruscan and Latin tribes exemplifies all conflicts between a local Neolithic culture and the cultures of a civilization that were seen as external.

Rome had the luck that it was located at the western end of all the other civilizations, that it was on a peninsula, and that there was no strong civilization with European roots on its northern boundaries. All of this allowed the rise of the Roman city-state. It could have been threatened by either the Athens-centered civilization in Greece or Carthage, the strongest colony of the Phoenicians in North Africa, that later became an independent city-state. But it soon became clear that the Greeks would not become a serious threat for the Romans. The Greek civilization was prevented from turning itself into an empire or centralized monarchy by the continuous pressure of the Persians from the east and by the severe rivalry between the city-states. The result was that the Greeks were soon ruled by the Macedonian Kingdom.

Carthage was a more serious rival. Rome and Carthage were geographically not far from each other and thus expanded into the same regions. The fact that they both had the civilizational characteristic of prospective domination would sooner or later have them fighting. A century of battles finally removed the only real obstacle in the way of Rome's success. The biggest threat could have been Alexander, as he identified Rome as his next target just before his death. Instead of Rome, the Alexandrian empire could have easily become the strongest power in the world. Alexander had all the requirements. But his early death allowed for the rise of Rome. Except for the Parthians far to the east and the Iranian-Sassanid Empire, from 150 BCE onward, all the ancient civilizations and the world of the Neolithic culture lay open to Roman conquest.

Rome's establishment of a republic in 508 BCE can be attributed to it being an institutional continuation of Athenian democracy. Although the new cultural basis played a role in this, the strength of the aristocracy was the determining factor. Monarchies are usually conservative and do not allow aristocracies to grow.

The Republic raised the self-awareness of the Roman people and gave them the will to stand up for their own interests. The Roman Republic's two assemblies (one for the aristocracy and the other for the citizens), the consul, the development of the judiciary as a separate institution and the institutionalization of the city guard made the democracy of Athens look amateurish. The governance of the Republic became the main resource for the development of the art of politics. It not only illustrates the connection between politics and law, it also illustrates that law is indeed negotiated and institutionalized politics. As a republic, Rome attained a splendid cultural development internally and glorious conquests externally. Becoming a republic allowed the Roman civilization to reach its natural potential. The transition from republic to empire was the result of growing conflicts and of both internal and external threats. The conflict between Julius Caesar and his rivals can be viewed as a conflict between the center and periphery and between the aristocracy and the plebeians. This evaluation seems to be substantiated by the fact that Brutus justified his treason by claiming that under Caesar, the glorious dignity of Rome was sacrificed for the provinces, that the plebeians mostly took sides with Caesar, that the distinguished representatives of the city aristocracy took part in the conspiracy, and that the provinces mostly supported Caesar.

Externally, the rebellions continued and the Persians arrived at the Euphrates. The enormity of the threat can be seen from Caesar's expeditions to Gaul, Britain and Germania, the rebellions in Anatolia, the death of Crassus—the third most powerful person in Rome—during a battle with the Persians, the rebellion of the Jews in the eastern Mediterranean, the never ending fights in Greece and the Balkans, the emerging attacks by the Goths, Scythians and the Huns, the looting expeditions of the Arabic tribes at the far south and the continuing existence of the strong monarchic remnants in Egypt. The republic's never ending senate discussions, rival factions' disputes over consul nominees, and the fact that people had become accustomed to external looting complicated things for the republican regime when fighting off the external threats and making historical decisions.

This formed the basis for the policies of Augustus, the great-nephew of Julius Caesar, who led the transition from republic to empire. Rome required policies that would bring stability on the inside and reliability on the outside. Thanks to these policies, the glorious period of the *Pax Romana* lasted until 250 CE. Thanks to Augustus's policies, the senate was reduced to an assembly of consultation; the institutions were no longer administered by those elected but by those appointed; the people were entertained every day and hence kept busy; strong security stations were formed, reinforced by walls; and the transition to defensive wars was made. Augustus was the first in a list of very famous emperors—the last of the half-god and half-human kings! What is interesting is that the Roman emperors were also becoming aware that the classical pantheon of gods was meaningless. They could see that legitimacy could not be obtained through the masks of gods.

The great turmoil following the invasions of the Franks, Alamanni, and Goths around 250 CE and the inability to centralize the empire signaled its disintegration and collapse. Even Zenobia, the famous queen of Palmyra, pursued an empire encompassing what we today call Egypt, Syria, Anatolia and Iraq. In the East first Ardashid I, the founder of the Sassanid dynasty, and then the great emperor Shapur I, who can be seen as equal to Augustus, defeated the Roman armies. They proceeded all the way to the Eastern Mediterranean and the Taurus mountains. In the meantime, the famous garrison city of Zeugma, close to today's Birecik, was destroyed, never to revive again.[48] Upper Mesopotamia became a region of battle and continuously changed hands between the Roman Empire and the two Persian Iranian Empires of the Parths and the Sassanids. It thus became a region that was no longer a source of civilizations, but a region of destruction. After Urartu, this region has never been able to procure its own central formation. It is one of the most tragic developments of history that it has always been subjected to incursion, occupation, annexation and exploitation by other forces. It is like the fate suffered by women: although she has achieved the biggest cultural revolution, she has been violated the most.

The end of the era of the big Roman emperors arrived with Emperor Julian's tragic death during a fierce battle at the shores of the Tigris in 363. It was clear from these battles in the East and on the European continent that the empire could not be ruled from Rome. After the abdication of the famous Emperor Diocletian in 305 CE, six other emperors ruled simultaneously. Constantine I rose above the rest and changed the religion of the empire in 313 and moved its capital in 325. After the death of Julian, the last emperor in Constantine's line, the empire was officially split in 395. The Western Roman emperors were at the mercy of the Gothic chiefs. Even the chief of the Huns, Attila, could have invaded Rome in 451 if he had wished. In 476 the last Roman Empire was killed by King Odoacer of the Goths. But its culture lied beneath the earth, alive, waiting to resurface.

Although the story of the Second Rome, Byzantium, continued for a long time, this story was both insignificant and an imitation. The efforts of Justinian between 527 and 565 to hold together all the regions of the empire were effective but the provinces were all slowly detaching themselves. Byzantium defined itself as the Second Rome, but I think the claim that Constantinople is the Second Rome is an exaggeration. Constantinople was just an ineffective replication of the old Rome. Its Christian aspects will be handled under another topic. The Ottomans (and also the Moscow-centered Russian Slavs) like to see themselves as the Third Age of Rome. Their claim to be the third Rome is not only an exaggeration, it also leads to great confusion because it mixes different periods and cultures. I will try to interpret problematic concepts such as the *Christian civilization, Islamic civilization* and *Hebrew civilization* in the following section.

From England to the Black Sea, many new empires appeared after the fall of Rome. With the collapse of the belief in paganism there was an enormous religious vacuum. European paganism and mythology could not provide what was needed. The new age not only demanded a material, political and economic revolution, but one that was moral and religious.

But before I discuss the rise and meaning of the Christian and Islamic revolutions, I must give a rough overview of the cultural and monetary situation of Rome.

Under the imperial umbrella, agricultural production, mining, craftsmanship and trade grew considerably. The saying "All roads lead to Rome" signifies where the economic resources flowed. The whole world was nurturing Rome. Besides keeping Rome, these revenues built other magnificent cities. In the east, Hellenistic cities such as Antioch (Antakya), Alexandria, Pergamum (Bergama), Palmyra, Samosata, Edessa (Urfa), Amida (Diyarbakir), Erzen-i Rum (Erzurum), Kaisariyah (Caesarea, Kayseri), Tarsus and Trapezus flourished. The European architecture did not vary much from the Greek city architecture, but buildings were larger and even more magnificent. Splendid aqueducts, waterwheels and channels were built—a tremendous improvement on previous structures. The road network was enlarged enormously. Security was ensured— the *Pax Romana* really existed. Mines and architectural tools were also improved. Quarry works and stone carvings were incomparable, except for that of Egypt. Metallic armor coating and weapons were the products of a highly developed craftsmanship. Trade became totally institutionalized. In contrast to the Greek culture, under the Romans trade gained in reputation and was in high demand. It was a flowering period for trade.

Never before in history was law so developed and institutionalized. A natural result of law is the institution of strong citizenship. Being a Roman citizen was a great privilege. All of the aristocracy and merchants considered it a privilege to be a Roman citizen. Somewhat similar to today's obsession with life in the states of capitalist modernity, the Roman life style was desired by everyone.

Pantheons and the temples built in the name of gods lost most of their importance. Roman theology embraced the Greek theology but changed the names of the gods. Virgil used the poetry of Homer—especially the epic poems the *Odyssey* and *Iliad*—as a model to write the *Aeneid*, the epic poem about the establishment of Rome. All elements of the Greek culture, including Greek literature, theatre, history and philosophy were Latinized and embraced. Still, important original work was produced in Rome as well. Oratory was an important form of art and the Roman language became the standard to which people aspired. Latin gradually became the standard diplomatic and international official language, replacing Greek. If the classical work of the Greeks had not been translated to Latin, they would have been lost by now. Although clothing still showed Eastern influences, it acquired a unique Roman style.

However, some Roman sporting events were quite barbaric. The gladiator fights, the fights with lions and other wild animals, the offering of imprisoned people to hungry lions—these practices were appalling. A decline in morals was achieved by accustoming people to such entertainment.

When comparing the Roman and Athenian cultures, it can be seen that the ideological aspect dominated the Athenian culture, whereas the Roman culture was dominated by its material and political aspects—in Rome, politics was turned into a form of art. However, it is important to see that the two cultures form a unit. It is as if Alexander first, then the kings of the Hellenistic period, and then later the Romans, harvested the cultural foundations that Athens sowed. It is impossible to think of Rome becoming a world empire without cherishing the Athenian culture. But what is more important is that these two cultures represent the final evolution of the Eastern culture. Despite contrary belief, it is not a culture or an empire of pure Athenian and Roman origin. They are syntheses resulting from local elements being nurtured by Eastern cultural sources. Even Europe was able to achieve its own cultural revolution by the re-fusion of these cultural sources with that of the Roman and Athenian synthesis. Without the East and the main cradles, Mesopotamia and Egypt, one cannot even imagine a European culture. If developments are considered from a material point of view, it will be seen that history is a whole. The formation and multiplication of cities are connected like a chain, beginning in Uruk. It is not a coincidence that nearly all civilizations have an Uruk of their own. It is the dialectic of urbanization. The same dialectic was present at the birth and expansion of the Neolithic culture. Thus, this discussion of the expansion of civilization illustrates that no societal development can be understood if we study the society detached from its historical and geographical contexts.

With the Romans, the conquest of our world by the systems of civilization was largely completed. Indeed, it had even entered the vicious circle of re-conquering the old regions. The act of re-conquering between civilizations has the characteristic of seizure and looting, because the civilizations share similar characteristics. The only purpose is to loot the accumulated property income and to appropriate it for yourself.[49] Expansion based on clashes and change of hands between civilizations does not create new values but damages them.

When the monotheist religions are discussed, it will be seen that one of the most meaningful developments in history is their opposition to the regimes of civilization, which were polytheist and pagan, on the basis of a new mentality and new practices. Although some of the civilizations expanded on the basis of these religions, it is clear we face a new development. I will try to interpret these in the next section.

Stages of Civilization and Problems Associated with Resistance

When Rome collapsed toward the end of the fourth century, it was not just a city and civilization that collapsed—the longest period for all the civilizations of antiquity and the classical age ended. The following centuries, also remembered as the Dark Ages, are customarily called the Middle Ages due to the way history has been classified. This classification does not add value to our understanding of history—on the contrary, it spoils it. In the Marxist historical perspective, due to its classificatory method of history, this period is also called the Feudal Period. But calling it "feudalist" does not explain the full significance of this era. It can even be said that it serves to confound our understanding.

It may be more meaningful to interpret the disintegration of Rome as the disintegration of antiquity and the classical age. The fact that Christianity took the Bible, whose roots can be traced back to the Sumerian and Egyptian periods, as its manifesto, can only be viewed as this era's expression of unity in opposition to civilization.

I believe that the period after the fall of Rome requires a different interpretation. We can label this new period the "Dark Ages," the "Radiant Christian Age" or the "Radiant Muslim Age," but these labels do not explain what happened—they actually distort the significance of this era. Throughout my analysis of civilization, I have pointed out the importance of the construction done by the priests. When they had served their purpose, those who had the political and military power ended the rule of the priests and left their own, overwhelming mark on all phases of civilization. For me, the most important theme is the conflict between the civilizational culture as a whole and the Neolithic culture. The former has continuously tried to constrict, colonize, assimilate and eliminate the Neolithic culture. I believe that the conflict between the cultures goes beyond the narrow class struggles and is more important than class struggle. Class struggle should be seen as a *part* of this conflict. Conflict between civilizations has always been a "bloody slaughterhouse."

I think it will be more instructive to interpret all these struggles together in terms of the following two concepts: *ideological culture* and *material culture*. Fernand Braudel's description of the capitalist culture as "material culture" is important, and I would argue that this expression should not be used for capitalist civilization alone, but for all the classed, city, and state civilizations, as this might increase our chances of meaningful analysis.[50] The distinction between material culture and moral culture has always been present, from the establishment phases of civilization to the era of capitalism—capitalism only represents the latest phase and the peak of material culture. So, ideological culture (or moral, immaterial culture), which has also existed since the beginning, must now reach its peak with the sociology of freedom and its science of knowledge. Developing our investigation in this direction will improve our understanding of the relationship between the material and the ideological cultures of both the civilization and of the resistance to it—a resistance that has existed throughout the history of civilization. It will also help to establish the connection between the "Middle Ages" and "capitalist modernity" with the sociology of freedom, and to prepare a strong basis for the evaluation of the meaning of free life in terms of ideological culture.

The comments below should be seen as an experimental attempt to set out the sociology of freedom of the Neolithic and civilizational cultures. At a later stage, once I have made my observations regarding capitalist civilization, I will present a more comprehensive analysis.

a. Ideological and material cultures in Neolithic society

It seems that the coexistence of the ideological and material cultures in Neolithic society posed no serious problems as long as the two could be clearly differentiated. The problems began when the two cultures conjoined, as if in a bottleneck, and the Neolithic culture could not adapt as civilized society started to develop.

At this point, I must explain in more detail what I mean by the term *problem* that I so often use in my subheadings. As I use it, it denotes the chaotic situation when the ideological and material cultures can no longer be sustained by the individual and society. To resolve these problems, the new society must achieve meaningful structures. *Ideological culture* refers to the function, meaning, and mentality of the institutions and structures, whereas *material culture* refers to the visual aspects of the function and meaning of these institutions, as explained above.

Viewed in these terms, it appears there was no friction between the ideological and material cultures of the Neolithic society that would have threatened its existence or caused conflict, especially during its establishment and institutionalization phases. Social morality did not provide an opportunity for this to happen. Private property, the fundamental factor that leads to social cracks, did not have the opportunity to develop for two reasons: Division of labor between sexes had not yet led to the development of possessive and coercive relations. Because food was obtained collectively, there were no private property rights related to food. All communities—that had not yet grown in numbers or in size—had a firm, common ideological and material culture. Private property and coercion were seen as life-threatening, since it would have ruined the structure of society. Sharing and solidarity amongst themselves were the fundamental principle of their morality—a morality that sustained the society. It seems that as a result of this principle, the inner structure of the Neolithic society was quite strong. We can assume that this principle was the reason why Neolithic society lasted for thousands of years. Regarding the relationship between society and nature, specifically in comparison with the civilized society, both the ideological and material cultures seem to have been in harmony with nature. They saw nature as filled with sacredness and divinity, and nature was believed to be as alive as they were themselves. It was considered the strongest element of divinity as it provided them with air, water, fire and all varieties of plants and animals. One of the strongest reasons for the development of the notions of *god* and *divinity* can be found in this reality.

I will elaborate on civilized society's concept of *god* later, but for now it is important to note that for Neolithic society *divinity* had nothing to do with coercion, exploitation, or tyranny. It had more to do with mercy, gratitude, abundance, affection, excitement and, when things went wrong, fear and light. It was important to be in harmony with nature. They even went to the extreme of sacrificing their children. The social aspect of their reverence for the divine can be seen as an expression of the society's ancestral existence, through concepts such as *totem, taboo* and *meaning*. This social aspect was partly expressed as the ancestral mother-goddess religion. Although sacredness and concepts such as *totem, taboo* and *meaning* didn't exactly mean "divinity," they always had a prominent place in the mindset of Neolithic society. Attributing the quality of sacredness to an object or being is, essentially, the showing of submission or exultation, sometimes of fear or concern, at times affection and respect, and at times even pain and lamentation in reaction to everything that has an effect on people's lives. This is the value people give to the effects of objects and the meanings they have on their lives. We can also describe this value as morals. Indeed, the gods and sacred beings play a fundamental role in forming such communities' morals as they sincerely believe that this is how their society is sustained. They believe that if any of the rules were violated or disrespected, or a sacrifice not offered, disaster would follow. Such communities are completely moral societies.

Although there was a state of belonging between Neolithic man and the plants and animals that they domesticated, this could not be called "ownership" even though this state had become their true culture. Ownership entails owning objects, but at this stage the mentality that distinguishes between object and subject had not yet developed. People of the Neolithic did not see themselves as being on a higher level than the objects around them (thus, preventing any serious violation of the ecology). This state of belonging does, however, indicate a movement in the direction of ownership. The final transformation into ownership was realized only after a long time and under different conditions. It is important that we do not conclude from this that the Neolithic society was a "paradise." The society was still very young and its future was uncertain because of the often-changing conditions of nature. But they were aware of the fact that they were at the mercy of the elements and, in fact, it was this awareness that formed their mentality. It was inevitable that they developed a metaphysical system with mythological and religious dimensions.

This perspective may help us to understand the essence of the collective life that centered on woman, and the metaphysics of sacredness and divinity growing from this collective life. Woman's fertility and the nourishment and affection she bestowed made her the most important element of both the material and the moral culture. The man, even as husband, did not pose a threat to society's collectivism. Society's way of life did not allow it. Thus, it is clear that male attributes such as "the dominant gender," "the husband," "the owner of the property" and "the owner of the state" do not reflect any inherent male characteristics but are social constructs developed at a later stage. Neolithic society meant woman, her children, her sisters and her brothers. A prospective male candidate had to prove himself through hunting, plant cultivation and animal husbandry if he were to be accepted as a member. At this stage, the social institution giving a male the right to—and engendering the emotions relating to—say, "I am the man of my wife or the father of my children" had not yet developed. I am not saying that there are no psychological aspects connected to fatherhood—or even motherhood—but let us not forget that in essence *fatherhood* and *motherhood* are sociological concepts, phenomena and perceptions.

169

When did the Neolithic society enter its bottleneck or reached the point where it desired to transcend the society of collective life? We can establish possible internal and external factors that led to this point. It is possible that the male acquired the strength to threaten the matrilineal order by overcoming his weak position and attaining a stronger status through successful hunting and the gathering of subordinates. Agriculture and animal husbandry could have also given him the required strength. However, our observations suggest that Neolithic society was dissolved largely due to external factors. Undoubtedly, the most important external factor was the priest's sacred state-society. The oldest stories of the civilized society of Lower Mesopotamia and the Nile largely confirm this. As previously explained, the culture of the Neolithic society and the new artificial irrigation techniques led to surplus production, a prerequisite for the development of the new society. The new society, which became urbanized around this surplus production, organized itself as a city-state and its character changed as male power rose. The increase in urbanization meant commodification. This, in turn, led to the development of trade. Trade, on the other hand, infiltrated into the Neolithic society through colonies and accelerated the disintegration of the Neolithic society by causing commodification, exchange value, and ownership to become widespread. The Uruk, Ur and Assur colonies are clear evidence of this. The main region of the Neolithic (the Mid and Upper Euphrates and Tigris river basins) joined the civilization society on this basis. All the other clan communities that had or had not reached the Neolithic level, faced civilized society's attacks, occupation, invasion, colonialism, assimilation and annihilation.

My observations lead me to believe that developments such as these were experienced in all regions inhabited by human communities. The Neolithic society (and similar societal forms from different periods) which we can regard as the stem cell of society, started to disintegrate as a result of civilized society's attacks, but has continued to maintain remnants of its previous existence until today. My personal view is that the societies that preceded civilization can never be annihilated. This is not because they were exceptionally strong but, just as with stem cells, because social existence is not possible without them. Civilized society can only exist in co-existence with the society that preceded it. (A paradoxical situation similar to the one that there can be no capitalism if there are no workers.) Furthermore, maintaining civilized society is only possible if it is based on uncivilized or partially civilized societies. It is possible that partial annihilation and elimination of pre-civilized societies did occur, but they could not have been complete.

We should not belittle the ideological culture of Neolithic society that existed for such a long time. Timeless values such as maternal laws, social solidarity, fraternity, affection, respect, doing good not for personal gain but for the good of the community, morality, voluntarily helping one another, devotion to the undistorted essence of what is sacred and divine, respect for the neighbors, and the desire for equality and free life were the fundamental reasons why this society existed for such a long time. Furthermore, these values will not cease to exist as long as social life continues to exist. Since the values of civilized society are burdened with unnecessary material and moral cultural elements—such as oppression, exploitation, seizure, looting, rape, massacre, immorality, annihilation and dissolution—their existence within society is temporary. They are mainly the features of a society with problems. In *The Sociology of Freedom*, I will investigate how the unsound and distorted values of civilized society can be transcended and how the permanent values of society can become an integral part of a free, equal, and democratic society.[51]

b. Material and ideological cultures in civilized society

It may be instructive to interpret the civilized society as having three phases: he initial or constructing phase, the middle or maturity phase, and the final phase. However, one should keep in mind that civilized society is a whole and, although such divisions may be handy for analyses, in the long term, it will preserve its wholeness.

Attributes such as refinement, politeness, genteelness, respect for rules, moderation, systematic thinking, intelligence, devotion to rights and peacefulness are ascribed to civilized society. However, these are fabrications with only propagandistic value. The real face of civilized society is one of violence, lies, deception, vulgarity, conspiracy, wars, enslavement, annihilation, servitude, treachery, seizure, looting, immorality, disrespect for the law, adoration of power, distortion and abuse of what is sacred and divine—all for the benefit of a rapist and gender discriminatory elite. It is a society where some have access to everything while others are hungry and poor. The result is that society is brimming with slaves, strayed villagers and unemployed workers. With the might of propaganda and a false, harmful metaphysical approach, it endeavors to continuously hide its real self.

We can define civilized society as the society ruled by an organization called the state, which is based on urbanization and class division. Kinship and solidarity in ethnic and tribal structures will at most lead to hierarchy as a form of social diversification—class division and attainment of statehood are not compatible with its nature, and tribal culture is not compatible with the culture of classed-state. The essence of class division is for one class to have the surplus product at their disposal. It is also the seizure or possession of the land and production tools that lead to surplus production. The common saying that property is theft from society holds true; surplus production is of course the return on that theft. The state organization is, at its heart, the collective means of protection of this stolen property and the distribution of the total surplus product to its owners. Organized property is actually the ownership of surplus production and surplus value. Of course there was always a need for tremendous armies, bureaucracies and weapons. And, as the society needed to establish itself, there was an enormous need for the tools of legitimization. Thus, they had to invent a science, utopia, philosophy, art, law, morals and religion that would bind society to themselves. Meaningless metaphysics has distorted the social roles of these institutions and the society's links to free life.

The relationships between civilized society and the ideological and material cultures are rife with complexities and distortions, but of crucial importance is the structuredness of this society. This characteristic, in turn, increases the extent of the material culture. I am not saying that ideological culture ceases to exist at this point but that it becomes secondary and distorted.

This issue needs to be understood. Now, *structure* and *functionality* are two concepts from epistemology, the science of knowledge. Each structure has a function and each function has a structure. When in a state of chaos, both the structure and the function enter a crisis and face disintegration and dissolution. At this point, temporary, mixed structures and contradictory functions step in. This is a universal phenomenon.

Every organic and every inorganic form in the universe contains inherent structure and functionality. In general, if matter is structured, then, in order to sustain this structure, there is a need for energy. For matter, energy is functionality. As we know from science, energy is fundamental and material structures cannot exist without energy—but energy can exist without material structure. Matter as a structure can cease to exist, but energy cannot be destroyed. As far as we know, for energy to develop its functionality material structure is needed. Even the phenomenon of life is linked to highly developed material structures and environments. Aliveness without material structure is inconceivable. If it does exist, then we are not aware of it. To draw a generalization: the counterpart of highly developed material structures is highly developed functionality.

The societal equivalent of material structure and functionality is material and ideological culture. Although the material structure in civilized society is excessively developed, it has not fully developed its functionality. On the contrary material structure has lost its functionality and in return it has also ruined its own structures. The fundamental reason for this is that civilized society does not abide by the main structural and ideological cultures that enable sociality. In fact, it places too big a strain on them. Had the development of the material culture been equivalent to and consistent with the development of the ideological culture, we would not have been talking about the drawbacks of material culture and its damage to society. All that could have been said would have been that it was normal. However, in cases where the material culture is developed and accumulated in the hands of an elite social group, it means, in a broad sense, a structural and functional deterioration of society and, in a narrow sense, expansion of the material culture and dissolution of the ideological culture.

Let me explain this with an example. The Egyptian Pyramids are very large material structures. But their counterpart is the millions of people who lost their functionality—that is a meaningful life and freedom, i.e. the ideological culture. This is what civilization is. It constructs huge structures (temples, cities, walls, bridges, fields, depots) and through its constructions, reflects its magnitude. Such societies have been made possible by civilization. However, when one searches for functionality or ideological cultural value in the same society, we find that it is either absent or we find a distorted version. An elite had broken away from society and gained control over society through merciless oppression and exploitation. It had either torn society away from its ideological culture or had presented a distorted version that deprived society of its fundamental values of ideological culture.

The ideological and material cultures that nourish the minority result in an unsound society—a society suffocating in matter and totally detached from an ideology of free life and concern with ecology. This is what I mean by the state of "social problems"—a state that resulted from the dialectical development described above. This is exactly why civilized society is detached from the environment. The existence of civilized society necessarily means a break with the environment. It is immaterial how we define the environment and ecology (whether we describe it in broad terms as "the unity of nature and society" or, in the most scientific terms, as "the integration of nature and society"), but a healthy environment and ecology needs a society that transcends the fundamental elements that constitute civilization: class, city, and state. I am not pleading for a vulgar elimination. The new society can only be achieved if material and ideological cultures are balanced and consistent. The synthesis of society's internally balanced and harmonious material and ideological culture with that of nature will result in free nature (or, as Murray Bookchin puts it in *The Ecology of Freedom*, "third nature").[52] This will also serve as a means to overcome the contradiction of civilized society's imbalance between nature and society.

Looking at the initial construction period of civilized societies from this perspective reveals in nearly all of them a significant material culture. The huge pyramids of Egypt, the ziggurats of Sumer, the underground city of China, the temples of India, and the cities and temples of Latin America clearly show the existence of the material culture. The inner meaning or ideological culture of these places lies in the mummified bodies, statues of gods, and the march of the statue-king and his army in the nether world. But it is a meaning that has been severely distorted. One could try to find sense in such grandeur by emphasizing the concept of *I*, but it is clear that what these structures really signify is the transformation of sociality. It is quite clear that without society—or, rather, without its transformation—such structures cannot even be conceived. Even the act of deifying the king is itself a work of mentality, of a mindset. But it is a distorted mentality and one that destroys the ideological culture. It is in vehement opposition to this mentality that the monotheist religions were founded—even though they risked demolishing the ideological culture. Thus, this society, which has established itself in cities and has organized itself as classed-state, presents its grand accumulation as material culture. In reality, its grandeur signifies a distorted mentality, a harmful metaphysical framework, alienation from nature, subjugation of nature, and the pretense that it possesses a creativity that can entirely be separated from nature. This entails the distortion of ideological culture and relegating it to a position of secondary importance.

Of course these changes were not always met with joy; naturally, they were met with opposition. It is important to understand that the early resistance to civilized society was a rebellion of the ideological culture and that it was multi-dimensional. The fact that the cities were enclosed with fortified walls as soon as they were built denotes a rebellion of the ideological culture of ethnic groups from outside. Mythological narration, the well-disguised expression of reality, and sacred religious texts also tell the stories of resistance. The fierce resistance against women's imprisonment in the house and her subjugation to male domination is clearly reflected in the persona of Inanna.[53] In-depth analyses of the personas of the creator-god and the subject-human will show that an intense class struggle raged. The manufacturing of the creator-god replaced the nature-god, whose essence was destroyed. In fact, the ruling class, who had nothing to do with creativity, declared itself the creative and masked gods. On the other hand, the members of society who were the real creators and had a meaningful system of sacredness and divinity were described as having been created from the self-proclaimed gods' excrement. This is indeed the mythical expression of an immense class struggle.

The fall of the ideological culture is also disguised in these narratives. The myths dealing with the early construction of civilization, especially the proficiency of the god's construction, can be seen as the ideological form of the class struggle. What happened could only have been explained through mythology. The rivalry and wars between cities indicate an intensive social struggle. The epic poems, the arrangement of the pantheons, the architecture of the cities, and the construction of their tombs clearly reflect the gap between classes and between city and the rural society. The stories of the Pharaohs and Nimrods document the deep cleavage within society. Tribal tunes, on the other hand, tell of despair and hardship in the face of attacks by civilized society.

The most significant resistance to civilized society that we know of is that of the prophetic tradition. Their story starts with Adam and Eve, the first two people. All the characteristics of this story carry the mark of ideological culture. If viewed as the personification of civilization's mentality, Adam and Eve provide the clues to the initial master-servant conflict. The dialogue between Adam and god and his relationship with Eve symbolize not only the distinction between master and slave but also the relegation of women to secondary importance. Noah's exodus is reminiscent of Neolithic society's departure to a mountainous region beyond civilization's reach where they attempted to reconstruct society. It is indeed the story of the Sumerian society and the resistance of the Neolithic society in an attempt to survive. Adam and Noah show that resistance has existed since the beginning of civilization and that it will continue as long as civilization continues to exist. The history of dynasties is the history of the ruling class, whereas the history of the prophets is essentially the history of cultures, tribes, heroines and heroes that resisted. The feature they share is their opposition to paganism.

We should of course distinguish between the paganism of civilized society and the tribal symbols such as totems. The gods gathered in the pantheons of civilized society all had human shape, looking like copies of the rulers of the specific period—in fact, they *were* the rulers of the time. So, when the prophets attacked these figures, it was seen as an attack on the ruler. And indeed it was, for at the time anti-paganism was synonymous with being anti-state. It was an opposition to all the notions and icons that symbolized institutionalized society. It was resistance. The struggle between the priests and the rulers of the political kingdoms had different characteristics. It was a struggle that took place within the upper class. It was a struggle internal to the state. The priest was essentially the state's clergyman: he was not concerned with society. The prophets, on the other hand, were the spokespersons of a society that had been excluded by the state. But, of course, since they were the ones that had manufactured the ideological culture, the priests had some influence on the prophets, albeit indirectly.

The unique aspect of the tradition initiated by the prophet Abraham and institutionalized by Moses, was the courage to completely break away from the Egyptian and Sumerian society and the willpower to construct their own society. This was an ideological culture revolution. "Nimrod" and "Pharaoh" are the symbolic titles given to the rulers of the two state-societies. They had fixed characteristics and denoted total domination. Abraham and Moses renounced this domination by announcing their own ideological culture and mental resistance. We should not underestimate the significance of such a declaration during such an age. Comparatively, the declaration that another world besides the official world of the Pharaohs and Nimrods existed is as significant as admitting the possible existence of other worlds would be today. To this end, they had intense discussions with their own community; thus, the prophetic resistance was a communal movement. But above all else, it was a movement of hope. I believe that a significant part of the strength of the modern Israel (or, at least, the strength of its ideological culture) derives from the narratives of Abraham and Moses. All the stories and the utopia of the Abrahamic tradition are about the struggle and yearning for a tribal order that was prevented by civilization. Although they had been influenced by both civilizations, they rejected the essence of civilization and their aim was not to build a similar civilization. This ideal played an important part in the conflict between the prophets and the priests of the kings of Israel. (I believe the strong discord that exists today between the Israeli state and society is a continuation of this ancient conflict.) The Hebrews and the prophets were the historical witnesses of the Hittites, Mitannis, Assyrians, Medo-Persians and finally the Greco-Romans and the residuals of these civilizations had accumulated in their memories. The period between 1,600 and 1,200 BCE was a golden period for the material culture. The relationship between the Hittites,

Egyptians and Mitannis presents us with the initial examples of international diplomacy. The Hebrews followed these developments from close by. Thus, we will not understand Abraham and Moses, nor any of the other prophets, if we attempt to analyze them without taking the developments of that period into consideration. Their response to these developments was that of ideological culture. I will later discuss the role of Jesus and Mohammed, the two major reformers within this tradition, in the rise of ideological culture.

Babylonia and Assur are the two important links in connecting the rise of material culture. In the time of these two kingdoms, the enlarged city and trade developed significantly. Babylonia was what Paris is today. The Assyrians were the most brutal representatives of the merchant-kingdom and, later, the empire. This is the management tradition that best represents the material society in the Middle East. They played no small part in reducing the ideological culture to secondary importance and in distorting it.

The Zoroastrian culture, which the Medo-Persian tradition is based on, waged an important struggle to regain the dominance of the ideological culture. Zoroaster, Buddha and Socrates, who lived at more or less the same time, were great moral philosophers and sages who represented the superiority of ideological culture over that of material culture. They provided the great stimulus and voice of human conscience that had been degraded by civilization. Through their own life styles they were able to show, at a time when material culture had a vastly superior position, that another world was possible and that they were seeking it. During this time, the resistance and offensive of peripheral cultures, primarily the Scythians, provide ongoing evidence that ideological culture cannot be destroyed that easily.

During the initial phase of civilization, the Semitic culture of the Amorites, the Aryan culture of the Hurrites, and the north Caucasian culture of the Scythians all resisted civilization. We cannot wish for clearer evidence that resistance to civilization has been as sustained and as strong as civilization itself. What the Goths meant to Rome, the Amorites-Arabs, Hurrites-Medes, and Scythians meant to the Middle Eastern empires. And, like Christianity later, religious movements have always played a significant part in the social resistances of the Middle East.

c. Greco-Roman civilization

The Greco-Roman civilized society represents the middle or maturity phase in civilization's history. It can also be called the civilization of the Classical Age. They developed the best of civilization's potential and the most magnificent age of material culture. This civilization managed most successfully to synthesize the material cultures of all its predecessors. It was the apogee of this civilization; it was also the last of its kind. (Finding anything today comparable to the material culture that they attained is quite difficult—capitalist industrialism is not a civilization but a disease attacking civilization.) The Athenian period also meant the end of antiquity's ideological culture. The Athenian pantheon was like a graveyard for the gods who had lost their aliveness, or, indeed, their ideological cultural worth; the birth of philosophy was the end result of this process. It is understandable that such a situation arises when societies are at their peak—all peaks end in decline.

It is clear that a slave-owning society amounts to a system of a completely material culture. The primary characteristic of this system is the profound degradation of humanity, a degradation not seen in any other species. This capacity for the collapse of conscience is closely linked to the attractiveness and magnificence of the material culture. Even today, it is nearly impossible not to be filled with awe and admiration for the monuments and structures created by this culture. This is the closest the human being can get to being divine. However, when divinity targets humans themselves, it turns into a catastrophe. For the gods everyone else is servant. None of the other contradictions and struggles was so openly displayed as that of the god and the servant. The degradation can be best understood if the pederasty in ancient Greek culture is analyzed properly. Its connection to the enslavement of women goes deeper than just that of sexuality; in essence, the enslavement of women and the sexual bondage of boys are the same social phenomenon.

Two of the most striking features of woman's enslavement are the oppression and dehumanization. Being confined to the house is not just spatial imprisonment. It is worse than being in a prison: it is being kept in a state of continuous and profound rape. No matter how hard one tries to disguise this reality with engagement and wedding ceremonies, even one day of a practice of this kind signals the end of humanity's honor, especially for those who have self-respect. With the rise of male dominated society, woman was systematically removed from the values of production, education, administration and freedom through various forms of violence. Her violation through ideological degradation—including appraisals of love—was so extreme that the result was worse than submission. She completely lost her identity and was recreated as something else: a wife. Even in the eyes of an ordinary man a woman could be nothing but a wife. And her being a wife permitted the rise of all sorts of disposition rights—including murder. She was not just property but private property. For her owner, it denoted the potential of being a small emperor—as long as he knew how to make use of it! The principle pillar that prepared the ground for civilization was this very reality. This reality is also one of the main reasons why the material culture has no boundaries. The success of the experiment with women meant that it could be tried on the whole of society—this was the second, grave infliction. Society was to function as wife to its master. As I will argue later, the process of housewifization of society was completed by the capitalist system. However, the foundation for this had been laid during the initial phase of civilization, and during the Greco-Roman period there was an attempt to attain the housewifization by presenting pederasty as an example of a successful society. Society can only be turned into a wife if man too were turned into a wife. The Greco-Roman society realized this and took its own precautions. It was widely accepted that the situation of a slave was much worse than that of a wife. The problem was to turn those men who were *not* slaves into wives. The Greeks' solution was pederasty. I am not referring to homosexuality—a phenomenon that has biological and psychological dimensions. In ancient Greek society it was fashionable for every free adolescent boy to have an adult man as a partner. The boy had to be the lover of his partner at least until he was experienced. Even the great sage Socrates took part in this practice. What was important was not how much one took advantage of the boy, but that the boy had to learn the soul of submission. The mentality underlying this practice is clear. Since attributes such as freedom and honor are incompatible with an enslaved society, they must be wiped from society's memory. And indeed, in an environment of human freedom and honor, enslavement cannot flourish. The system understood this and strove to implement the required mental attitude. However the Greco-Roman culture was prevented from completing this mission. Internally, Christianity developed through free philosophical schools and externally the continuous offensives and rebellions of the different ethnic groups presented other problems for society. At the same time, there were indications that material culture did not have the strength to overcome everything. Later, however, society would be turned into a wife without the need for pederasty.

Essentially, the resistance of tribal forces and the Christians—paying a painful price in the process—was to end this type of society that meant the destruction of humanity. Their later reconciliation with the system does not negate the value and aim of the ideological culture of these resistance movements. These movements had no significance in terms of material culture, and their later advances should be seen as the rise of the ideological culture. A similar example would be the relationship between the Sassanids, Islam, and the migrating Turanians. The profoundness of the rise and fall of societies cannot be explained simply in terms of oppression and exploitation; it is vastly more comprehensive. Capitalism has not yet been resolved and dissolved because we have not been able to make an appropriate analysis of civilized society. The analyses of capitalism that have been done are like the small part of the iceberg above the water. The essential bulk is the civilized society and that is still below the water.

d. Christianity and Islam

It is not clear whether Christianity and Islam should be seen as civilizations or as moral systems (Christian and Islamic theologians and believers are themselves not clear about this). Although there is no easy answer to this question, it remains an important one. But even if they started off as belief and moral systems, it has not been explored sufficiently where and until when they remained like that, what their relationships with the civilized and the excluded societies were, and to what degree they formed or opposed civilizations.

In my opinion, these two important belief and moral systems, formed during the Sassanid and Greco-Roman empires, represent a great offensive by the ideological culture against the deterioration of ideological culture, and against the vast proportions that the material culture had reached. If the intention was to construct a new civilized society, they would have based themselves on city and class formations, as happened in the construction of all classic civilizations. To the extent that they intended to established cities and classes, this was only because they wanted everyone to adopt their belief and moral values and not because they wished to become civilized societies themselves. Their most important objective was not to achieve power or to take possession of the material culture. On the contrary, they wished to attain the hegemony of a new ideological culture that would protect humanity against a meaningless material culture that was no longer on equal footing with ideological culture. Therefore, simply defining the age of Christianity and Islam as civilized systems is insufficient and may lead to misconceptions.

The collapse of Rome was not an ordinary event nor was it the collapse of an ordinary civilization. Indeed, with its collapse a tradition of civilized society at least four thousand years old also collapsed. The details of the internal and external reasons for its collapse do not concern us here. What *does* concern us is whether or not there was a connection between the values of civilized society and the general collapse, and if so, what role these values played in the collapse.

Rome can be seen as representative of all the initial and classical civilizations (with the exception of China). Not only because it too institutionalized slavery, but because it shared all the material and moral cultures of these civilizations. The fundamental reason for our inability to understand this reality is because these societies are analyzed on the basis of their daily oppression and exploitation. This flawed approach is one of the most significant distortions caused by positivism—the school of thought that, arguably, underlies the most pernicious aspects of European thinking. If a society is not analyzed on the basis of its material and ideological cultures, the conflicts and contradictions, the harmony or incompatibility between these two cultures of the society, a meaningful interpretation cannot be reached. Consequently, new paradigms for a freer life cannot be constructed.

It should now be clear that the collapse of Rome also meant the collapse of the preponderant material culture of civilized society and its ideological culture, an ideological culture that had no bearing on a meaningful life. Even Rome's architecture was the crowning of a four thousand year old architectural tradition, which included that of Egypt. The Roman pantheon was the final, most magnificent, stage of the top level of the four thousand year old Sumerian priests' ziggurats. Thus, the material and ideological cultures that concomitantly collapsed with Rome were at least four thousand years old. Similarly, an analysis of how and by whom this demolition was brought about indicates a history of resistance that forms one continuous whole. The history of external resistance to and attacks on civilization, starting with the early Amorites and Hurrites and ending, finally, with the Goths, dates back four thousand years. The long history of internal resistance began with Noah and continued until Mohammed. The story of every prophet indicates the length to which they went to gather the communities around them. What is important is not only that the history of resistance stretched over millennia, but also the vast area over which it occurred. From the Arabian deserts to the Taurus and Zagros skirts, from the Central Asian deserts to the deep European forests, it left profound marks on both the material and the moral cultures of the nomadic tribes.

The Eurocentric structures of knowledge are not interested in investigating these matters (and this is precisely why *"Eurocentric"* is an appropriate description). But, without a meaningful interpretation of the historic civilizational sources of Rome's material and ideological cultures, and without the real history of Rome, we will not be able to identify the roots of Europe's material and ideological cultures.

The two hundred years prior to the collapse of Rome were described as centuries of darkness and complexities—no societal collapse is simply a matter of the events occurring in its few final years. This also applies to the collapse of the Sassanid Empire—the Eastern version of how the Sumerian priest-state came to its end. Although the Zoroastrian influence had strengthened its moral character, this influence was not strong enough to prevent Sassanid Iran's moral collapse. Just as Buddha could not prevent the Rajahs from constructing civilized society based on material culture, and as Socrates could not cure the moral decay of the Athenian culture, so Zoroaster could not prevent the excessive luxuries of the huge Persian and Sassanid material cultures. History shows us that the final period of the Iranian Sassanid Empire was no different from that of Rome. The Turanian attacks from outside and the religious and sectarian conflicts on the inside, slowly brought about its end. When the Mani movement, a strong offensive of ideological culture, was eliminated around 250 CE, it was left destitute, unable to renew itself. If not for the wars waged by Islam, the Nasturi priests, just like the Catholic priests in the West, might have ideologically conquered Iran. Islamic occupation prevented this.

Now that we understand what the collapse of the two big slave-owning civilizations entails, we can define the two famous movements that call themselves ideological alternatives: Islam and Christianity.

The constructing of an own official society in Rome led to many marginal sections within the society. These were not traditional migrating tribal groups with their own ethnic characteristics. They were the newly formed group of the déclassé, the rabble, or, as the Romans put it, the "proletariat." They did not start off as identifiable groups with their own ideologies; rather, they were the unemployed of the slave-owning society. For the first time in history a new social stratum was formed and gradually new cults such as the Essenes in Roman Judaea developed around them.

We do not need to concern ourselves with the ongoing debate whether Jesus was an historic person or a symbolic persona created by the conditions of the time. With the Siege of Jerusalem in 63 BCE, despite great resistance, the small Hebrew kingdom was conquered by the Romans and administered through governors. At the time of Jesus's birth, Rome was at its peak under Emperor Augustus. The Jewish upper classes had become professional collaborators—their long history of collaboration with the Nimrods and Pharaohs prepared them well for collaboration with Rome. On the other hand, since the time of Abraham and Moses, the Hebrews always had a strong leaning toward freedom. Jesus was the continuation of this tradition. We can deduce from his last actions that Jesus had an ideological interest in Jerusalem—the reason for his crucifixion.

Initially, Christianity was not an organized movement nor did it have an ideological manifest. There was only a small group of followers loosely attached to Jesus. These early leaders of Christianity, the so-called disciples and later the apostles, had no hierarchic, ethical or official status in society. For such a group, life in Roman Judaea could not have been easy. Crucifixion, an often-used method of punishment in this region, was but one of Rome's terrible inventions that drove many groups deeper into the interior or to the shores of Syria (the opposite direction of Abraham's flight to the region where Jerusalem would later be built).

A century after Christ's death the first drafts of the Bible were compiled. One of the earliest was that of Marcion.[54] The early saints within the Roman Empire surfaced in the 1st century and increased in the 2nd and 3rd centuries. The 4th century is the century of Christianity. After Emperor Constantine paved the way for Christianity to become the state religion, there was a huge increase in the number of saints and in the number of believers.[55] During these centuries, Christianity began to divide into various denominations and state Christianity developed.

A central doctrine of Christianity is that of the Trinity, the expression of God in three personae: God the Father, God the Son, and the Holy Spirit. Mary, the mother of Jesus, is not one of the Holy Trinity and not seen as divine, but veneration for Mary has been high ever since the first century, so that one could interpret the Father, the Mother and the Son as a trinity of god figures. I am not going to embark on a theological discussion, but I must indicate that the roots of the belief in the Divine Family can be traced back to our earliest history. The Sumerians were the first society to channel this belief into the ziggurats, the official temples. The initial pantheon trilogy consisted of the goddess Inanna (the Mother), the god An (the Father), and the god Enki (the Son). Thus, the often heard claim that Christianity has been strongly influenced by paganism is not something that should be brushed aside. What is of more interest to us, is that Christ came from the Abrahamic tradition, a tradition strongly opposed to paganism. The religious movement resisting in the name of Christ seems to have reconciled these two traditions.

This matter has confused people over the ages and has led to discussions, divisions, and conflicts between denominations. At the heart of the discussion is the question whether Christ is of divine or mortal essence. Mostly, those who accept Christ's divine essence are those who align themselves with official Christianity. In 325 CE, the Christian bishops convened for the First Council of Nicaea declared that the Son was of the same divine essence as the Father; thus, that Christ was truly human, but at the same time, *truly God*. Constantine (the convener of the council) himself accepted this interpretation. Thus, the state's concept of divinity is the concept that has been officially accepted. Those who claim that Christ is only of human nature mostly were those who have not been integrated into the state.[56] (A parallel can be drawn with the division between the Sunni sect, being the state religion, and the Alevi sect, whose members have not been integrated into the state.) The foundation for this was laid by the Sumerian priests. The initial separation of religion based on two different social strata began with the Sumerians, whereas the concept of the divinity of humans was handed down from the Neolithic culture. Or, rather, the concept carries some important remnants from that culture (paganism too has retained some of these aspects).

Christianity underwent two important changes in the fourth century. The first was that it became a state religion. In this form it also became the religion of civilization. This was Rome's attempt to overcome the moral crisis, or the crisis of legitimacy, experienced by the Roman material culture. The second change was that it became the religion of the masses. It was no longer the belief of small groups of saints but the official or unofficial religion of large numbers of peoples, amongst the Armenians, Assyrians, Greeks, Latins, and others.

This is how we entered the infamous Middle Ages—the so-called Dark Ages. On the one hand, based on the legitimacy of Christianity we had the original, collapsed Rome replaced by the Rome of Constantine. On the other hand, there was the incredible development of Christianity as a large offensive of the ideological culture. The two main actors of this period— Christianity of Constantine's Rome of and the Christianity adopted by the masses—acted according to the division around the doctrine of the Trinity: the religion with an official god and the religion of unofficial gods. The historical division continues, although in changed form, and conflict between them has caused much bloodshed. The previous conflict between Christianity and paganism has become the conflict between the Divine Christ and the Human Christ. Ultimately, though, this division is but the continuation of the ancient struggle between the civilizations, various classes and ethnic forces under new conditions and masks. A clearer interpretation of this division is that part of this new offensive of the ideological culture, with its profound historic roots, had become part of civilization by reconciling with the material culture and therefore corrupted. Another part had refrained from reconciliation and continued to pursue ideological and cultural hegemony.

The thousand years after the fall of Rome (more or less from 500 CE to 1,500 CE) can be seen as a period of rivalry, conflict, and reconciliation between those who struggled for the supremacy of the material culture and those who struggled for the supremacy of the ideological culture. Calling the Middle Ages "dark" or "feudal" can only partially explain what it was that really happened during this time. If we can answer the question of what filled the vacuum left by Rome's collapse, we may arrive at a better understanding of the forces that caused the collapse of the Roman material culture. Elements of the material culture continued in the East in the Byzantine cities. In Europe, it reappeared in the newly constructed cities. Indeed, the history of modern Europe's material culture can be attributed to this new movement of urbanization. If cities such as Paris were mere continuations of the 4th century Roman settlements, then the domination of the material culture around 1,500 CE would not have been possible. Not only could the medieval cities not be compared to Rome, they did not even surpass the Mesopotamian cities of 3,000-2,000 BCE or the Aegean cities of 600-300 BCE. Even the medieval European castles did not surpass the castles of Taurus and Zagros of 2,000-1,500 BCE. In short, the urbanization of Europe between 500 and 1,500 CE could not have provided the necessary power to surpass the "dark" ages. But the new moral culture, the hegemonic ideological culture of Christianity, did have this ability. For European history, Christianity's superiority undoubtedly has had important consequences. Historians interpret this period to be the conquest of Europe by the moral culture of Christian belief and values rather than material culture, and I agree.

The really important question is why Rome remained at the level of a material culture of two thousand years ago. And even more importantly, how was it possible for a system of beliefs and moral values such as Christianity, which was not really in a position to satisfy the present need for ideological culture, to conquer Europe. I believe an important reason is the fact that Europe had only experienced the Neolithic culture at the time and was, so to speak, virgin soil. As a result you can reap what you sow and its one thousand year old history has proven this reality. The second reason could be external factors: the threat of the Turks (both as Muslims and as pagans) and of the Arabs coming from Sicily and Spain. When seeing these two factors in combination, it is possible to understand the long duration of the "darkness" of medieval Europe. There was a need for Christianity because paganism collapsed with the collapse of Rome. Even before Christianity, the belief and moral system of European paganism had proven to be insufficient. As a result, the conditions for the hegemony of Christianity, ideologically and culturally, were ripe. However, its material culture had always been weak compared to that of Rome and the East. Obviously, it was impossible to establish magnificent cities like Paris from communities who had just left the Neolithic period. As a result of this double incompetence (the inability of Christianity to overcome the need for ideological culture, and the structure of cities that had not surpassed those of thousands of years ago) it was possible for Europe to launch its grand material offensive in the 16th century.

There is, however, a close relationship between the grand offensive of the material culture and the hegemony of Christianity as the ideological culture. (Indeed, the fact that major religions have always been in conflict with sectarian splinter groups proves that this is a universal reality.) European capitalism, as the offensive of a splendid material culture, used the weaknesses of Christianity—such as its lack of strong ideological content—to construct a new age by transforming the merchant and profit cult into the new official power of civilization. No previous civilization had dared to do this. This is how the transition from the middle stage to the final stage of the material culture came about in the West. I will discuss later whether this age, capitalist modernity, should be seen as the crisis of the civilization, whether it had become a cancerous disease, or whether it is the final stage of old age.

The story of Islam is more complicated, as Islam became rapidly civilized and has been involved in serious conflicts with Judaism and Christianity since its inception and, internally, with itself. I see the two hundred years before Mohammed as the crisis of the last phase of the slave-owning civilization. Christianity came out of this crisis as the stronger side. It succeeded in becoming the first organization for the poor and un-influential of society. It succeeded as an alternative power. Although there are problems associated with Christianity, I shall evaluate these problems under Islam (since they arose from the same roots). This section shall be finalized with a look at other possible alternatives and the rise of Islam.

Before I proceed, I need to raise several points. Firstly, Islam is the final religion in the Abrahamic tradition and this is how it constructs itself. Hence, its roots include the Abrahamic tradition that is at least two thousand years old. We can conclude from this that the conflict between the Arabs and the Jews is in a way the conflict between two sects of the same religion. Secondly, Mohammed viewed the mentality of Mecca, his hometown, as ignorance. It is indeed a way of criticizing the paganism of Mecca. Thirdly, Mohammed's dialogues with the Nestorian priests could be seen as a link to Christianity. Fourthly, his involvement with trade is due to his being employed by the merchant Khadijah, whom he later married. Fifthly, he was severely influenced by the tribalism that reigned amongst Arabs for thousands of years. Sixthly, he lived during the last magnificent stages of both the Byzantine and the Sassanid Empires.

Although these are the main factors that ensured the birth of Islam, there are of course other factors. What I am trying to point out, once again, is that the birth of Islam was also not a "miracle in the desert" but the product of strong material and historical circumstances. Not only are its strengths linked to these circumstances, but so are its weaknesses. Islam is not a synthesis of civilizations, like early Sumer or late Rome, but predominantly a movement of beliefs and morals.

Mohammed's life is much better known than that of Abraham, Moses, or Jesus. Many of his characteristics are also known. His message, the Qur'an, does not target a single nation, tribe or class but the whole of humanity. I believe that the concept of Allah, the most used in the Qur'an, should be the main topic of Islamic theology. Mohammed was deeply influenced by this. He viewed Allah as the Lord of all worlds. The term "Allah" is conceptually so wide that sociologically speaking it has the capacity to integrate the divine in nature with that in society. The ninety-nine attributes it contains define the combined effects of the forces of society and the forces of nature. However, the issues its followers would like to understand as "perpetual laws and orders" are extremely unclear. This is because no attributes with social roots, which are necessarily transitory, and not even all aspects of nature, can have the value of a law. The concept of the immutability of law itself resulted from the extreme formalism of Hebrew tribalism. This understanding of law as changeless might have been useful in overcoming tribal anarchy, but in later centuries it led to great conservatism in the Islamic society. In any case, if we consider the rapid nature of social development, it is clear that there are potential dangers contained in the *ummah* concept.[57]

Mohammed's strong belief in Allah determined his metaphysical strength. At least, by accepting the existence of a superior power, he escaped contracting the familiar disease of being the god. Keeping in mind the big dispute over the divinity of Christ, Mohammed's approach clearly was more productive. But one of his failings was his inability to overcome the Judaic rigorousness. The heavy bill is now being settled in the Arab-Israeli conflict.

It is worth discussing whether Mohammed intended a society with a predominantly material or a predominantly ideological culture. In Christianity, the moral aspect is prevalent, but Islam appears to have established a strong equilibrium between the material and the ideological culture. Despite its insufficient and controversial content, I see this equilibrium as the strongest feature of Islam. One of Mohammed's *hadiths*, "work for this world as if thou will never die and work for the afterlife as if thou will die tomorrow," explains this structure well. It is known that he was not in favor of the classical Roman, Byzantine, Sassanid or the more ancient Pharaoh and Nimrod systems and that he vehemently criticized them. Thus, from this perspective, he was a strong critic of civilization. However, neither the material circumstances nor the ideological capacity of his time sufficiently explains his ideal of a city-state. (It is similar to the socialists of today not being able to find an alternative system to the modern state.) But his emphasis on morals indicates that he was aware of the problems inherent in civilized society. This made him a great reformer, even a revolutionary: he refused to acknowledge any society where morality was not prevalent. His rules about interest prevented the development of the capitalist society in the Middle East. In this regard, he was ahead of both Christianity and Judaism. He had well-known abolitionist tendencies, was quite affectionate and favored freedom. Although he was by no means desirous of equality and freedom for women, he did despise the profound slavery of women. He recognized the differences in class and ownership in society but, like a social democrat, he tried to prevent the forming of monopolies and their social hegemony by using excessive taxation.

This short summary shows us that Mohammed and Islam neither wanted an unbalanced material culture, nor wanted to remain a purely ideological culture. It is this aspect that strengthened Islam both against civilizational powers and against other ideological and cultural formations. As far as I can see, no other social movement, apart from those of the Sumerian and Egyptian priests, was able to maintain the unity of material and ideological culture as Islam did. If radical or political Islam is still growing strong today, we need to understand the structural aspects of this religious movement.

It may be worthwhile to reexamine the development and changes the material and ideological cultures went through at the end of the Roman and Sassanid civilizations. The four thousand year old slave-owning system had deeply damaged humanity's conscience and morality and created a big moral vacuum. Rome's attempts to fill the vacuum failed, as evidenced by its own collapse. There clearly was also a big vacuum in the world of belief. People now realized that the gods they had been made to believe in for the past four thousand years were not what they were said to be. Paganism had lost the element of sacredness; the huge material structures left a ruined humanity behind.

We could call this period a state of crisis and chaos. Continuous wars turned the idea of peace into a mere utopian ideal. Old laws and life styles lost their significance but there was nothing to fill the void. In the center, the threat coming from the movements of the unemployed masses and the vast number of abandoned slaves intensified; on the periphery, the threat coming from the nomadic tribes was as intense. It must have felt as if the foretold arrival of heaven and hell had dawned. All awaited a message of salvation. And, indeed, it was an ideal setting for this message to reverberate throughout society. Great movements *had* to be born; thus, there was an urgent need for a new utopia and new programs. This time, the structural and functional crisis of the system of slave-owning society was irreparably deep; society could no longer be ruled through (even newly constructed) slave-owning systems. Under circumstances like these, the human conscience and mentality desired something new. When the last material structures upholding the system could no longer be sustained, the circumstances for the world religions had been prepared.

Much has been said about the feudal society that existed in the aftermath of the old slave-owning society. It was, however, based on similar principalities that date back to 4,000 BCE. Stronger castles had been built around 2,000 BCE, and even at that time there were peasantry and servants around these castles. In the event of an empire disintegrating, anyone in any of the ethnic communities could easily have formed their own principality. After all, the empire was the unity—the federation or confederation—of such small states. The small states that were formed after the fall of Rome and the Sassanids came about in the same way. The villages and the mentality of the villagers were, in fact, not so different from the period of Neolithic institutionalization around 6,000 BCE. Nothing had changed in the relationship between woman and man, and nothing had changed in the relationship between serfs and seigniors. The essence of ownership remained unchanged and there was no revolutionary development in the means of production. Thus, the material order that formed around the 5th and the 6th centuries cannot really be called a new civilization.

As a matter of fact, the urban structures in Europe were not sufficient to form a new civilization. The empires that came about in the West were nothing but remnants of Rome. The same can be said about the East. Calling them the remnants of the system preceding capitalism is more meaningful; at best they can be called a revisal of the old. In other words, we should not deny the material structures preceding capitalism. Most probably, the period of chaos came about because in order to make the transition to capitalism different structures than those of the slave-owning systems were needed. The urbanization of Europe, especially after the 10th century, heralded capitalism. Thus, we should not take concepts such as *feudalism* and *Dark Ages* too seriously. A more realistic interpretation is that a four thousand year old social system of masked gods and enslavement had dissolved within the scope of the *longue durée*, the long term. The dissolution of the Neolithic system still continues today. Long-term systems may take hundreds of years to collapse or to be revised. If we need to give it a name, then the period after the 5th and 6th centuries can be called the Period of Late Systems.

So what does all this mean in terms of Islam and Christianity? Their utopia, like all utopias, makes promises of paradise or talks about millennia of happiness. The "promise for paradise" reminds me of the longing for an oasis. Its opposite is an infertile life. The prophets promised hope and a future for their communities; the quest for paradise is nothing but a promise of a future in a new world. We can also look at it as a harbor inevitably constructed by those who have lost hope. In this regard, Saddam Hussein's relationship with the Qur'an just before his execution is quite intriguing. The Qur'an provides exceptional power to construct the minds of those who have no hope left. One cannot properly understand the messages brought by the Holy Books without understanding the conditions of slavery. Given this and the metaphysical nature of the human, the construction of many a utopia, including heaven (and its counterpoint hell), was inevitable. This is what being human entails. Without striving for a better future life cannot really be lived. And there would have been no foundation for us to base our efforts for a better life upon.

Fear of death itself, I believe, is a social construct. In nature, death is experienced differently from the way it is experienced in human communities. The profound pain and grief caused by socially experienced death result from its contrast with the reality of natural death. If there were no death, we could not have talked about living. This is why the most precious part of life is becoming aware of death. The alternative is to strive for immortality.

The utopia of Islam and Christianity held an intriguing promise for ending slavery, even though it was not clear what outcome could be expected. The question of an alternative was evaded with the promise of a life that would be like living in paradise. The communities at the monasteries and madrasahs can be seen as examples of the new society to be constructed. Madrasahs, monastries, different orders and denominations are all attempts at construction programs for a new society. Christianity and Islam both have pursued this goal intensely—for two thousand and one thousand five hundred years respectively. On the other hand, the heads of the Christian churches as well as the conquest commanders of Islam easily created a late, revised slave-owning system. These late slave-owning societies are just interim societies following the conquest and do not represent permanent systems of living for the entire society. Calling them Islamic and Christian civilizations would be unjust. The aim of the utopia was not the creation of new civilizations but to salvage life and to turn it into something beautiful.

Thus, we see that the belief and moral systems of the two religions do not give us a consistent answer to the question as to whether or not they were civilizations. But their role in surpassing the four thousand year old system was significant. Although there were some revised slave-owning regimes, principalities, city-states and empires constructed in their names, none of these can be considered Islamic or Christian civilizations. If they are considered thus, one must put this down to ideological distortions. The priest cannot simply come out of the church and become an emperor, and neither can the imam become the head of state. These religions have always seen turning their structures and organization into states as a wrongdoing, and have warned those clerics who use the church to become heads of state to comply with the requirements of religion. Not that their warnings have had any effect or ever will.

We might now be in a better position to answer the question of why we ended up with capitalist civilization. The ground for capitalism might have been prepared, intentionally or unintentionally, by bringing the gigantic empires (which were in the way of capitalism's development) to collapse and by the monotheistic systems not turning their aims and structures into civilizational constructs. Wallerstein's argument that empires were in contradiction with capitalism is indeed a very strong one, whereas Max Weber clarifies this by showing how the spirit of the Reformation paved the way for capitalism.[58]

Max Weber calls the capitalist civilization "the elimination of magic from the world."[59] Of course, in a highly advanced system of material culture a magical life cannot exist. Such a life is only possible in the world of ideological culture. Islamic, Christian and similar cultures do not have the skill to enchant the world of capitalist life. This can only be procured by the power and skill of the sociology of freedom, which can utilize the entire inheritance of the ideological culture. I shall discuss this point in detail. I shall demonstrate that life itself is the most magical element there is. Therefore, our slogan should not be *Socialism, not capitalism*, but rather: *Free life, not capitalism!*

But could there have been a solution that did not include civilization? The only way in which this could have been accomplished would have been something like going back to the Neolithic society. Since the cities could not be removed, trade also could not be prevented. The male-dominated society could not have been abandoned. No matter how much it was criticized, the state could not have been removed under those circumstances. Indeed, monasteries, madrasahs, different denominations and the Sufi way of life grew from such despair. They saw the degenerative and damaging effect of all the mentioned classifications above and wanted to escape them. However, their remedies could never be anything but marginal. So, they always left the door open for the emergence of a new civilization.

Perhaps another glimpse of the Hebrew tribe's story will be instructive. During the Roman and Persian-Sassanid periods, the Jews spread throughout the known world. They were experts in matters of trade and money. They were the spirit of the material civilization (or rather, its filtered power). They also had a very strong tradition of literacy. Their authors took the position of the prophets. They were the leading proponents of a new system of civilization, i.e. capitalism. Furthermore, they were the experts on religion and god. Their mark on the utopias cannot be missed—the infiltration of the power of money and trade into the new belief systems was enormous.

Christianity conquered all of Europe in its own age of ideological culture. Its influence in Asia was limited, although traces of its influence were present in African civilizations. Islam rapidly conquered all of Arabia, North Africa, and Central Asia. Not only were all the old systems of civilization conquered, new regions were added to the empires of ideological culture. However, what happened was not an expansion of civilization. Rather, we can call it the development of the moral world. This is exactly what Christianity means with its "thousand year reign of peace" and Augustine with his "City of God."[60] Both the Christian and the Islamic utopias were influenced by classical Greek philosophy (and played a role in its revival). Their roots are partially in Aristotle and Plato, and partially in the Egyptian and Sumerian mythology. Both have weak scientific bases and as freedom utopia, they are unsophisticated. But the moral side of both is well developed. Let me repeat that for a religion morality is the essential aspect, not theology. Because morality does not lose its importance, similar moral doctrines have retained their importance in Christianity and in Islam. Utopias are not always faultless—they mostly serve contrary to their objectives. The Christian and Islamic utopias served the onset of capitalism, despite their objectives. It is also true that these utopias have been in severe conflict with each other. In addition, in the name of Islam, limitless and unjust seizure of land and culture took place for the benefit of barbaric and dominant tribal aristocracies. It is often said that Islam impeded the progress of Christians but this is a reality for all religions. Moreover, the conflict between those elements of Islam and Christianity that became the state itself cannot be called conflict between Islam and Christianity. These conflicts have their origins in civilization, and religion is only used as their disguise. I shall elaborate on these matters my forthcoming book, *The Sociology of Freedom*.

In conclusion, the ideological and material cultures are problematic matters but nevertheless they are realities and a study of these cultures is much needed. The role of the conflict between slave and master, serf and seignior, in the making of history is both limited and indirect—the wheels of history turn differently. It is this "different turning" that I am investigating. I know my attempt is amateurish and unpolished, but this work is necessary—not only so that we can understand history, but also so that today's problems can be resolved.

The subject matter will not be complete without an evaluation of the other branch of resistance, the migration of peoples. In the final stages of the slave-owning civilization, the migrating Goths and Huns in Europe and the Arab tribes in the Middle East progressed very quickly from resistance to taking the offensive. The migration, resistance, and offensives of these peoples with their advanced tribal hierarchies and their pre-civilizational patriarchal societies were very much alike to movements of the ideological culture. Although their communities were partially egalitarian and carried elements of the Neolithic culture, still, they were in admiration of the civilization. They did not have the ability to develop metaphysical systems that came close to that of a religion. Mostly, they were soldiers of fortune and willing to shed their blood for various empires. Yet, they must still be regarded as amongst the most important history-makers. If it were not for the Germanic, Turkic, Mongolian, Arabic, and before them the Hurrian, Amorite and Scythian assaults, the course of history might have been different. Whilst the Germanic peoples and Arabs destroyed both Roman Empires, the Turks and Mongols played their role in the destruction of the Iranian as well as the eastern Roman Empire. Afterwards, however, all the tribal chiefs either crowned themselves or took positions in the army or bureaucracy. The rest either formed new tribes or lived as the déclassé at the bottom of society. Although these forces played an indisputable role in the collapse of the slave-owning system, they were not able to present alternative systems and to construct something new. They were able to destroy and loot, but not to create and protect.

Final Remarks

Up to this point, this work researched how the ground was prepared for capitalist modernity. I have tried to show which historical developments led to the development of capitalism. One of the fundamental characteristics of the capitalist science and power structure is that it presents itself as having no history. In order to claim being the ultimate and final system, it is important to have no history and no location. But history cannot be evaded although capitalism may think it will last until the end of time—many other forces of civilization had also made similar claims. Let me just underline the main thesis of this section of my work: The state-civilization system, which came into existence on the basis of the intertwined formations of class, city and state, has multiplied itself up until the financial stage, the last phase of capitalism, basing itself mostly on the exploitation and oppression of agricultural and village communities and, later, urban workers. If the five thousand year old state-civilization is able to continue its existence in the face of democratic civilization, this will be essentially due to its ideological hegemony. Systems based on coercion and tyranny can only be successful if they have ideological hegemony. Thus, the main conflict is not only one of class division but also one at civilizational level. The historical struggle, that can be traced back to at least five thousand years, is essentially one between state-civilization and democratic civilization; the latter consisting of pre-state village and agricultural communities. All ideological, military, political and economic relationships, conflicts and struggles occur under these two main systems of civilization.

We are now ready to deal with capitalism as our next topic. In the upcoming sections of Book II, I will attempt an evaluation of my main thesis as set out above and how it is to be interpreted with regard to the Middle East and Kurdistan.

Introduction

1. "The main dimension of Turkish-Israeli relations is military. Landmark agreements on military cooperation in February 1996 and on military industrial cooperation in April 1996 have produced unprecedented military exercises and training, arms sales, and strategic talks." Carol Migdalovitz, *Israeli-Turkish Relations* (1998).

2. In September 1958 Syria accused Turkey of massing troops on the Syrian-Turkish border with the intent of executing a U.S.-backed attack on Syria.

3. As I said during my interrogation to the representatives of the four main institutions of Turkey (the Intelligence Service of the Chief of Staff, the National Intelligence Service, the Security General Directorate, and the Intelligenceof the gendarmerie) *they* had no reason to celebrate my capture. I told them they did not take part in a brave fight but in a conspiracy.

4. The Grand Chamber of the European Court of Human Rights (ECtHR) had deemed the 1999 trial on Imrali unfair and recommended a retrial.

5. All these titles are available at http://ocalan-books.com/english/

6. *In Defense of the People* has not yet been published in English.

7. Assize Courts are the remnant of the former State Security Courts.

8. Öcalan completed the work with a fifth volume, dealing broadly with the practical implementation of these concepts, especially that of *democratic nation*. The five volumes were published in Turkish between 2009 and 2012.

Section 1

1. His most famous statement, found in §7 of part I of *Principles of Philosophy* (1644) and in part IV of *Discourse on the Method* (1637).

2. Francis Bacon links knowledge and power in *The New Organon* (1620).

3. The Persian Sufi was tortured and publicly crucified in 922 CE by the Abbasid rulers for his alleged heresy. As for Giordano Bruno, it is not clear whether this Italian mathematician and astrologer was burned at the stake in 1600 for his pantheistic religious believes or for his cosmology.

4. Democritus was one of the two founders of the ancient atomist theory. He elaborated

a system originated by his teacher Leucippus into a materialist account of the natural world. The atomists held that there are miniscule, indivisible bodies from which everything else is composed, and that these move about in an infinite void.

5. These speculations are aimed at opening our horizons, at shedding the unsound aspects of a methodology and distorted knowledge and belief systems produced by powers of state and society. They formed our thought structure with their lies and tools of distortion and to a great extent destroyed our ability for sound reasoning.

6. An example of such a cell is seen in the Euglena, which is a present-day unicellular organism. It has properties both of animals—it does move and it takes food from the environment when there is not sufficient light around for it to photosynthesize but when there is sufficient light, it will photosynthesize and produce its own food.

7. I will go into more detail about sex and reproduction in the human society at a later stage, but for now, suffice it to say that the pleasure obtained from sexual activity should not be confused with love. On the contrary, pleasure based purely on physical sex is denial of love. Capitalist modernity is destroying society in the name of love by advocating physical, loveless sex. Sexual lust is related to the loss of freedom. Love can only be achieved in freedom and morality. Real love is the great excitement experienced from the universal creation. Mawlãnã's saying, "Love is all there is in the universe, the rest is frivolous" is the true interpretation of love: the awareness of the bond between all elements in the universe, delighting in the harmony of creation.

8. Once again, light comes into play here because sight is impossible without light.

9. Verse 56 in sura 51 in the Qur'an reads: "And I did not create the jinn and mankind except to worship Me." A common interpretation is that "to worship" here means "to know." A hadith reads: "I was a hidden treasure, and I wished to be known, so I created a creation (mankind), then made Myself known to them, and they recognized Me." (Keshfu'l-hafâ, II, 132, Hadis: 2016).

10. Nietzsche developed this concept in *Thus Spoke Zarathustra* (1883).

11. The French philosopher, mathematician, physicist and writer Descartes spent most of his adult life in the Dutch Republic.

12. This concept was developed by Fernand Braudel, which is "proportionate to individuals, to daily life, to our illusions, to our hasty awareness—above all the time of the chronicle and the journalist. Social science has almost what amounts to a horror of the event. And not without some justification for the short time span is the most capricious and the most delusive of all." *On History* (1980), p. 28.

13. Braudel used this concept to stress the slow, often imperceptible effects of space, climate, and technology on the actions of human beings.

14. See the works of Élisée Reclus and Murray Bookchin.

15. See Aristotle, *The Politics*, 1253a1-3.

16. Scientism claims that science alone can render truth about the world and reality. It deems it necessary to do away with most, if not all, metaphysical, philosophical, and religious claims, as the truths they proclaim cannot be apprehended by the scientific method. In essence, scientism sees science as the absolute and justifiable access to the truth.

17. See *Genealogy of Morality* (1887) Part I §11 and *Thus Spoke Zarathustra*.

18. Fernand Braudel, *The Mediterranean and The Mediterranean World in the Age of Phillip II* (1949).

19. Theodor Adorno, *Minima Moralia: Reflections From Damaged Life* (1951), p. 39. Adorno maintains that it is no longer possible to live a good, honest life because we live in an inhuman society.

20. Michel Foucault, *The Order of Things: An Archaeology of the Human Sciences* (1966).

21. We do not see resistance against capitalist modernity in any other cultural area besides the Middle East. Those that did resist could not escape elimination.

22. Coined and described by Maria Mies in *Patriarchy and Capital Accumulation on a World Scale* (1999), Chapter 3: "Housewifization means the externalization, or ex-territorialization of costs which otherwise would have to be covered by the capitalists. This means women's labor is considered a natural resource, freely available like air and water. Housewifization means at the same time the total atomization and disorganization of these hidden workers. This is not only the reason for the lack of women's political power, but also for their lack of bargaining power. As the housewife is linked to the wage-earning breadwinner, to the 'free' proletarian as a non-free worker, the 'freedom' of the proletarian to sell his labor power is based on the non-freedom of the housewife. Proletarianization of men is based on the housewifization of women." (p. 110).

23. Hitler likens the society to a wife.

24. In *Leviathan* (1651), Thomas Hobbes uses these words to denote pre-capitalist society.

Section 2

1. Editor's note: Genetic evidence that has come to light since the writing of this manuscript, indicates that all descendents of the humans who had left Africa during the first migratory wave, about 125,000 years ago, died out before the second migration out of Africa. The

evidence indicates that the second migration took place about 85,000 years ago, when one group of humans, consisting of a few hundred individuals, left East Africa in a single exodus. Their mitochondrial DNA shows that all non-Africans are descendent from one woman, the "Out-of-Africa Eve." See Stephen Oppenheimer, *Out of Eden* (2004).

2. Thousands of rock paintings and carved stones can be found at the Trişin alp, Gevaruk alp and Peştazare, all located in the Hakkari province.

3. There is a hypothesis that groups that acquired a symbolic, referential communication system, which united them through shared concepts, could not remain in constrictive clan groups for long and, furthermore, that they possessed the dynamics to transform themselves into a more advanced form of societal organization.

4. V. Gordon Childe hinted at the importance of this cultural era when he remarked that the Neolithic era in this region is no less important than the four hundred year old culture of Western Europe in his book called *The Dawn of European Civilization* (1925).

5. The Hyksos were a group of mixed Semitic-Asiatics who settled in northern Egypt during the 18th century BCE. In about 1630 they seized power and Hyksos kings ruled Egypt as the 15th dynasty (c. 1630-1521 BCE).

6. See "The Indian Stone Age Sequence" by Bridget Allchin in *The Journal of the Royal Anthropological Institute of Great Britain and Ireland*, Vol. 93, No. 2 (July-Dec. 1963).

7. Positivism can be defined as any philosophical system that confines itself to the data of experience, that excludes *a priori* or metaphysical speculations and emphasizes the achievements of science. See Section I of this book for Öcalan's critique of positivism.

8. Michel Foucault, *The Order of Things: An Archaeology of the Human Sciences* (1970).

9. It is an encompassing concept that refers to the very slow movement of historical time. Indeed, it represents a temporal rhythm so slow and stable that it approximates physical geography. It forms at the interface of the natural physical world and human social activity—of physical space and human space. The *longue durée* provides the unifying element of human history. The theoretical assumption supporting Braudel's concept is a human history formed through the "structures of the *longue durée*." Humans make their history in space and in time. Thus, Braudel's concept emphasizes the physical characteristics of the earth, geography, natural resources, material processes and culture as constitutive elements of human history.

10. Francis Fukuyama, *The End of History and the Last Man* (1992).

11. Fernand Braudel, *On History* (1982).

12. The medium is called conjuncture or medium term socio-economic cycles by Braudel.

See *The Mediterranean and the Mediterranean World in the Age of Philip II*. Braudel's own great contribution saw time as a social—more than as a physical—phenomenon, whence the idea of a plurality of social times. The great trinity that Braudel constructed and used as the framework for his book on the Mediterranean was structure, conjoncture, événement: long-term, very slowly evolving structures; medium-term, fluctuating cyclical processes; and short-term, ephemeral, highly visible events.

13. V. Gordon Childe coined the term "Neolithic revolution" in 1923 to denote a period of important innovations like agriculture.

14. When the possibilities of class division combined with that of urbanization, any one of the dynastic and hierarchic groups in the area could have made the transition to being a "state" organization through mobilising the resources of the "strong man." Not only Lower Mesopotamia, but also Upper and Middle Mesopotamia witnessed numerous such attempts. Although some of them have become permanent others have not due to the conditions of the time.

15. Karl Marx and Friedrich Engels quoted Charles Fourier like this in their work, *The Holy Family* (1844).

16. The Nur Mountains lie at the south-western end of the Taurus range.

Section 3

1. Any object that has an importance in the clan's life can be the totem. Usually it is based on an entity that also embodies power. To date we still come across tribes named after lions, snakes, falcons, wolfs, the sun, rain, wind and names of important plants and trees.

2. See Samuel Noah Kramer and John Maier, *Myths of Enki, the Crafty God* (1989).

3. As I have argued before, in my opinion this does not signify a backward mental state; on the contrary, it is probably more progressive and closer to the truth than the modernistic view of nature as being a lifeless object.

4. The woman figures of the mother-goddess period were much more modest, symbolizing the productive and fertile woman.

5. In Sumerian mythology the Mes are divine decrees underlying the social institutions, religious practices, technology, behavior, mores and human conditions that constituted civilization, as understood by the Sumerians. They are fundamental to the Sumerian understanding of the relationship between humanity and the gods.

6. Guenther Roth and Claus Wittich, *Max Weber: Economy and society*, Volume 1 (1978).

7. In Turkish, a common name for brothels is *public house*. Therefore, *public prostitute*

refers to prostitutes in a brothel and *private prostitute* to wives in a patriarchal marriage.

8. Although widely quoted as *slaughterhouse* Hegel actually used the word slaughter-bench or *Schlachtbank* in his *Lectures on the Philosophy of History* (1825–26).

9. Editor's note: The houri are dark-eyed virgins of perfect beauty believed to live in Paradise with the blessed.

10. Peter A. Kropotkin, *Selected Writings on Anarchism and Revolution*, edited and translated by Martin A. Miller (1970.)

11. It is difficult to draw the borders between science and philosophy. One can think of them as being theoretical and practical aspects of the same phenomenon.

12. Fernand Braudel's right and just interpretation.

13. Çatalhöyük, the largest and best preserved Neolithic site found to date, existed from approximately 7500 BCE to 5700 BCE.

14. The ethnic origins of the Urartu kings are not clear. This is true for all the dynasties, since they all used the dominant culture and language of the time. Hence, in Urartu and later in the Persian palaces, Assyrian and Aramaic were the official state languages.

15. In fact, the period of the Gutian invasions (2,150 to 2,050), the Kassit invasion (around 1,600 BCE) and the Median and Persian counter-expansions indeed point to this.

16. Archeological work began at the Kazane mound in 1992 by Patricia Wattenmaker; Timothy Matnet led the work at the mound Titriş between 1991–1999; Gre Virike was first discovered by Guillermo Algaze and his team 1989; and the mound of Zeytinlibahçe was discovered by Guillermo Algaze in 1998. Archeological work began in 1999 under the leadership of Marcella Frangipane for the Rescuing Archeologic and Cultural Assets Project as they would fall in the catchment area of the Ilısu and Karkamış Dams.

17. Editor's note: It seems that some of these sites originated in an even earlier time. Göbekli Tepe was erected by hunter-gatherers (who lived in villages for part of the year) about 11,500 years ago—before the advent of sedentism. Some scholars suggest that the Neolithic agricultural revolution took place here. They suggest that different nomadic groups cooperated to protect concentrations of wild cereals. See Klaus Schmidt: *Sie bauten die ersten Tempel. Das rätselhafte Heiligtum der Steinzeitjäger* (2006).

18. Editor's note: This seems to be the case indeed. It seems that the erection of monumental complexes was within the capacities of hunter-gatherers, and not only of sedentary farming communities as had been previously assumed. In this way, Göbekli Tepe profoundly changes our understanding of a crucial stage in the development of human societies:. As excavator Klaus Schmidt concludes: 'First came the temple, then the city.'"

19. The Kurdish equivalent to Washukanni, Bashkani, means "charming and beautiful fountain."

20. Proof of this may be the written treaty between the Hittite king Suppiluliuma I, who had conquered Aleppo and Carcemish, and the Mitanni prince Shattiwaza, his son-in-law.

21. Troy was either a Hittite establishment or a close ally and a unique city civilization from the same cultural group. The dwellers of Ahhiyawa can be seen as belonging to the Aryans who were influenced by Anatolia or who migrated around 1,800 BCE. I believe that it is a mistaken claim that they had European origins from the north. The same mistake is made with regards to the Hittites. The Cilician state was located south of the central Anatolian plateau in the time of the Hittites (bordering on the Taurus Mountains in the north and east and the Mediterranean in the west).

22. It also reflects an alliance amongst the governors.

23. After the battle of Kadesh near the river Orontes and the city of Hama.

24. It has been suggested that Nefertiti, the chief consort of Akhenaton, was the Mitanni princess Tadukhipa.

25. The Assyrian word *Nairdi* was used to refer to both the land and the people around Lake Van. It means "people of the rivers and streams."

26. Guda, Gudea and Got probably all originated from this god's name. What Allah means for the Semitics, Guda means for the Aryans. Literally it means "to come into being by itself." It is still used by the Kurds and Iranians rather than "Allah."

27. Probably located near modern Bradost region in South Kurdistan.

28. Similar to the culture of the god Dionysus in the ancient Greek culture.

29. The period from 521 to 506 BCE.

30. The Medes always had been second in power and a fundamental force in the army. Being relatives of the Persians may have had a role in this.

31. The initial longest road known in history, the King's Road, starting from the Aegean shores of Sard and ending in Persepolis.

32. *Serug* in Hebrew, the name of the great-grandfather of the prophet Abraham.

33. From 70 BCE to the year 70.

34. "Rabbi" means religious teacher, while "nabi" means "prophet" or "God's emissary."

35. With Jesus, Judas did the betraying; with me, this role was played by the alliance of MOSSAD and the CIA.

36. According to Oxford's *Dictionary of Sociology* (1998), the "center–periphery (or core–periphery) model is a spatial metaphor which describes and attempts to explain the structural relationship between the advanced or metropolitan 'center' and a less

developed 'periphery', either within a particular country, or (more commonly) as applied to the relationship between capitalist and developing societies. The former usage is common in political geography, political sociology, and studies of labor-markets." This model is important in the world system theory of Wallerstein and Andre Gunder Frank, to name but a few.

37. A kind of a version of the Hebrew's Sacred Book, the Torah, but much longer and more complex.

38. Confucius in China, Socrates in Greece, Zoroaster in the Medo-Persian Empire.

39. Although there are different historical interpretations, the most logical one would be right after a glacier period, which coincides with this date.

40. The sacrificing of humans to gods is not unique to these civilizations.

41. See David Wilkinson's idea of a "Central Civilization" in: Andre Gunder Frank and Barry K. Gills, eds., *The World System: Five Hundred Years or Five Thousand?* (1994).

42. 3,000 to 1,200 BCE.

43. This term refers to a confederacy of seafaring raiders of the second millennium BCE who sailed into the eastern Mediterranean and attempted to invade Egyptian territory as well.

44. The heroic wars of this long period of settlement—and especially the events around Troy—were told in Homer's great epics. The *Odyssey* tells the stories of island settlement.

45. Mycenae grew from a settlement started about 2,000 BCE.

46. Antiochus I was king of the Commagene Kingdom that had its capital at Samosata (modern day Samsat).

47. Pythagoras and his group, around 500 BCE.

48. A town and district of Urfa in Turkey on the river Euphrates.

49. Whether state or private property, all the values seized, after the people who work on the property are fed, are justified by the fact that property is owned.

50. For Fernand Braudel's analysis, see *The Wheels of Commerce* (1983).

51. *The Sociology of Freedom* is volume three of *The Manifesto for a Democratic Civilization*.

52. Murray Bookchin, *The Ecology of Freedom: The Emergence and Dissolution of Hierarchy* (1982).

53. Inanna is the Sumerian goddess of sexual love, fertility and warfare. This mythological tale from Sumer features the struggle of Inanna against the male god Enki, whom she accuses of having seized everything that has value to society and that is rightfully hers.

54. Marcion (65-160) was the first to introduce a Christian canon of books. The so-called Bible of Marcion excluded all the books of the Hebrew Bible on the grounds that the

"vengeful" god of Abraham and the Hebrew Bible could not have been the same as God the Father of Jesus.

55. Constantine's edict of tolerance was issued in 313, in 380 Emperor Theodosius I promulgated the Edict of Thessalonica, declaring Nicene Christianity the state's official religion.

56. Until the 7th century Arianism was widespread in central and south-eastern Europe, especially among Germanic tribes like the Goths. Arian Christians held that only the Father was God.

57. Before Islam Arabic communities were governed along tribal affiliations and kinship ties. Muhammed developed the ummah idea, which is not only for Arabs but universal. Accordingly, the purpose of the ummah was to be based on religion rather than kinship. Therefore it is like a commonwealth of believers.

58. Max Weber, *The Protestant Ethic and the Spirit of Capitalism* (1905).

59. Ibid., Chapter IV.

60. For the "thousand year reign of peace," see Revelations 20 in the Christian Bible.

Index

Aaron   141

Abraham   41, 137, 141-142, 177-178, 184-
185, 189, 205, 207

Abrahamic religions   98, 100, 137, 142,
177, 185, 189

Abyssinia   136

Achaemenid Empire   139, 157

action-reaction principle   46-47

Adorno, Theodor   61, 80, 90

Aegean   139-140, 151-153, 159, 187, 205

Aeneid   164

Aeolian tribes   151

aesthetics   57

Africa   70-71, 73, 77-79, 148, 150, 159,
195, 201

Ahhiyawa   134, 151, 205

Akhenaton   136, 205

Akkad, Curse of   131

al-Assad, Hafez   22

al-Hallaj, Mansur   41

Alevi   186

Alexander the Great   80, 146

Amenemhat I   135

America, North   147-148, 150

America, South   147-148, 150, 174

Amorite   76, 143, 178, 183, 197

Amun   136

analytical intelligence   41, 53-54

anarchist schools   63

Anatolia   25, 124, 159, 205

animal kingdom   47, 49, 50, 53

animate   32, 36, 45-47, 99

Apiru   143

Arabs   30, 148, 178, 188-189, 197, 207

Arameans   76, 133

Aras valleys   137

Aristotle   35, 58, 141, 154, 156, 196

armed struggle   23-24

Armenians   30, 186

arts   42, 56-57, 65, 72, 75, 85, 87, 95, 98,
111, 118, 121-122, 124, 125, 150, 155

Aryan   15-16, 73-79, 89, 106, 132, 134-135,
138, 140-141, 144-145, 158, 178, 205

Ashoka   146

Aşkava   134

Assize Court   26, 199

Assur   138, 140, 170, 178

Assyrians   76, 105, 131-134, 136-138, 140,
142, 149-150, 177-178, 186, 204-205

Astyages, King   139

Athens   19, 23, 123-124, 152-153, 155,
156, 158-160, 164

Atoms   44

Augustus, Emperor   161, 184

Babylon   76, 93, 103, 131-133, 137, 140-
142, 149, 150-151, 156, 178

Bacon, Francis   35-36, 44, 51, 66, 199

Bacon, Roger   35-36, 44, 51, 66,

Bakunin, Mikhail   117

Black Sea   73, 132, 156, 158, 163,

Bookchin, Murray   12, 62, 174

Brahmins   145, 146

Braudel, Fernand   12, 60-61, 81-83, 129, 166, 200-204

Bruno, Giordano   41, 199

Buddha   146, 178, 183

Byzantine Empire   143, 153, 156, 187, 189, 190

Caesar, Julius   160-161

Cairo   135

capitalism   13, 23, 28-29, 35-36, 39-40, 51, 62, 63, 66-67, 94-95, 117, 122, 126-128, 142, 144-145, 147-148, 150, 156, 166, 171, 181, 188, 192, 194-198

capitalist modernity   13, 23-27, 29-31, 37-43, 47, 50, 52, 59, 60, 62- 69, 74, 80-81, 88, 90, 93-94, 110, 112, 163, 167, 188, 197, 200-201

capitalist society   38, 190, 201

capitalist system   24-25, 38, 42, 51, 60, 128, 180

Cappadocia   132

Cartesian mechanism   38

Carthage   159

Çatalhöyük   130, 204

Caucasia   30, 76, 134, 137, 142, 178

Celtics   148

China   23, 105, 121, 140, 143-146, 174, 182, 206

Christianity   79, 103, 120, 125, 136, 148, 162-163, 166, 178, 181-182, 184-191, 193-196, 206-207

Cilicia   134, 205

citizen   36, 67, 134, 154, 158, 160, 163

civilisation   14

class   13, 15, 33-34, 37-38, 53, 83, 85, 95, 100-101, 108-110, 112-115, 117, 119-123, 125, 127, 145, 154, 157, 159, 166, 172, 174-177, 182, 184, 186, 189, 191, 197-198, 203

classless society   33

Cleopatra   136

commerce   64, 128, 131

Committee of Ministers of the Council of Europe   26

commodification   29, 64, 105, 127-128, 170

commodity   65, 105, 127

communal life   61, 90

Confucius   35, 145, 206

constitutionalism   123

Copenhagen Criteria   27

Council of Europe   21, 24, 26, 74

CPT (European Committee for the Prevention of Torture)   21

Cyrus the Great   139

Darius   140

Darwinism   48

David   141

democracy   20, 26-28, 123, 147, 154-156, 160

democratic confederalism   30, 68

democratic modernity   60, 63

democratic nation   68, 199

Democratic society   68, 171

Democritus   45, 152, 199

Descartes   35-36, 44, 51, 66, 200

dialectics   34-35, 48, 56, 67, 153, 165, 174

Diocletian, Emperor   162

Dionysus   14, 91, 205

dogma   24, 33-35, 38, 47-48

dogmatic method   34-35, 38

domination   18, 36, 41, 66, 112, 115-117, 157, 160, 175, 177, 187

Dorian tribes   151

Durkheim, Émile   62, 83

Ecbatana   138-139

ecology   15, 43, 61-63, 67-68, 85, 92, 127-128, 169, 174

economic reductionism   62-63

economies   12, 27, 29, 32, 61-62, 83, 85, 94-96, 125, 163, 198, 202

egalitarian   14, 19-20, 33, 67, 197

Egypt,   57, 72, 74-77, 80, 105, 121, 130, 134-137, 139-144, 148-153, 156-157, 159, 161, 163-164, 166, 174, 177-178, 183, 191, 196, 202, 206

Egypt, Kingdoms of   135-136

El   141

El-Lisht   135

Elam   77, 139

emotional intelligence   41-42, 53, 54

England   51, 128, 163

Enki   99, 102-103, 136, 185, 206

Enlightenment   14, 35, 61, 65, 80, 139

Enlil   99

Enuma Elish   131

environment   29, 32, 35, 37, 39, 43, 58, 86, 89, 95, 146, 154, 173-174, 180, 200

erastes   116

Eridu   103

Eromenoi   116

European Union   23-27

Euphrates river   15, 74, 97, 105-106, 129-130, 133, 137, 161, 170, 206

European Court of Human Rights   25-26, 199

exploitation   14, 17, 25, 31, 34, 36, 40, 42-43, 59, 66, 69, 74, 84, 89, 99, 104, 110-112, 114, 117, 122, 153, 162, 168, 171, 174, 181-182, 197

fascism   58, 74

feminist   16, 43, 63

Fertile Crescent   15-17, 71-73, 77-83, 87-90, 109

Feyerabend, Paul   62

Foucault, Michel   12, 43, 60-61, 80, 118

Frankfurt School, the   60-61

freedom   8-9, 12, 25-27, 30-32, 37-39, 43-44, 53-55, 58, 61, 64-65, 68, 86-87, 89, 93, 96, 110-114, 116, 118, 125, 129, 149, 166-167, 173, 180, 184, 191, 195-196, 200-201

free life   29-30, 38-39, 41, 44, 90, 93, 111, 113, 128-129, 148, 167, 171-172, 174, 195

Geist   49

genocide   37, 67, 69, 90,111

Germans   60, 78, 143, 161, 197, 207

Gilgamesh   103, 122, 131

god   29, 34-37, 41-42, 46, 49-52, 57-59, 61, 64, 75, 78, 80, 83-84, 90-92, 98-101, 103, 105, 107-108, 113, 119-122, 126, 131, 134-135, 137, 139-141, 145-146,

151-152, 155, 157-158, 161, 164, 168,
174-176, 179, 185-186, 190-192, 195-
196, 203, 205-207

goddess   15, 18, 87, 91-92, 99, 102-104, 107,
109, 121, 131, 155, 168, 185, 203, 206

god-king   34, 80, 108, 140, 158

Gothic   143, 162

Goths   141, 143, 148, 161-162, 178, 183,
196, 207

Göbekli Tepe   133, 204

Gre Virike   133, 204

Greece   21-22, 24, 30, 35, 78, 116, 121-123,
126, 128, 131, 135, 138-142, 148, 150-
153, 155-159, 161,163-164, 179-180,
186, 196, 205-206

Gutians   138

Haldi   137

Hammurabi   123

Harappa   77, 105, 150

Harpagus   139

Harran   141

Hattians   134

Hattusa   134

Hattusili III   135

Hebrew   76, 136, 139, 141-143, 163,
177-178, 184, 190, 195, 205-206

Hegel, Georg W.F.   49, 111, 204

Hellenic   153, 157

Herodotus   138-139, 150

Himalayas   147

Hindu   146

Hittite   134,-136, 150-153, 155, 177, 205

Hobbes, Thomas   67

housewifization   67, 107, 109, 115-117,
180, 201

human rights   24, 27, 124

Huns   143, 148, 161-162, 196

Hurrians   29, 132-134, 137-139, 197

Hyksos   76, 135-136, 202

Ice Age   72, 80, 82, 132, 144

Ideology   13, 16, 17, 23-25, 66, 74, 94-95,
106, 114, 121, 153, 174

IMF   27

Imperialist   16, 25

Imrali   8, 21, 24-26, 31, 199

Inanimate   36, 38, 45, 47, 128

Inanna   99, 102-103, 131, 136, 155, 175,
185, 206

Indian   75, 78, 144, 146, 150

Indonesia   144-145

Industrialism   61, 93, 179

Ineb-Hedg   135

Inquisition   37

Intellectual   13, 18, 40, 43-44, 52-53, 56,
62, 69, 83, 107, 122, 139, 142, 152, 154

Ionian   140, 151-152

Iran   14, 23, 30, 73, 77, 80, 130, 134, 138,
143, 158, 160, 162, 183-184, 197, 205

Iraq   23, 27, 30, 74, 90, 103, 161

Iron Age   19, 138

Isis   136

Islam   25, 64-65, 76, 80, 89, 100, 120, 148,
156, 163, 181, 182, 184, 188-191, 193-
196, 207

Israel   21-24, 30, 131, 177, 190, 199

Itj-Tawi   135

Jesus   142, 178, 184-185, 189, 205, 207

Jews   30, 161, 189

Judaism   61, 142, 188, 191

Kabhur River   133

Kanesh   132

Karnak   136

Kaska   134

Kassites   131, 138

Kazane   133, 204

KCK (Union of Kurdish Communities)   30

KDP (Kurdistan Democratic Party)   22

Kenya   26

Khadijah   189

Kikkuli   133

Knowledge   8, 20, 31-32, 37, 43-46, 50, 53,
   55-57, 59-66, 73-74, 78, 80-81, 96, 102,
   111,118, 124, 129, 150, 153-154, 156,
   166, 172, 183, 199-200

Krishna   146

Kropotkin, Peter   117

Kültepe   132

Kurdistan   8, 16, 22-23, 30, 71, 198, 205

Kurds   7, 24, 25, 30, 69, 74, 75, 79, 132, 205

Lenin, V.I.   23, 117

Leviathan   37, 41, 89, 112, 145, 148

liberalism   23, 25, 29, 62-64, 66-67

libertarian   67

longue durée, la   61, 75, 82-83, 144, 192, 202

Luxor   135

Lydians   152

Macedonia   141, 153, 156, 159

Magi priests   139

Mani   41, 184

Marduk   131

Marmara   156

Marx, Karl   11-12, 23, 61, 95, 101, 126, 203

Marxist-Leninism   23

masculinity   99, 109, 116

material culture   140, 157

materialism   12-13, 40, 58-59, 67, 95, 126,
   128, 153, 200

matrilineal   107-108, 170

Mecca   189

Medes   132, 138-139, 150, 178, 205

Mediterranean   71, 132-133, 156, 159, 161,
   203, 205-206

Memphis   135-136

Mesopotamia   14, 76, 97, 105-106, 132-
   133, 138, 142, 157, 162, 164, 170, 202

metaphysics   17, 35, 40, 44-45, 48, 55-59,
   62-63, 66-68, 82, 84, 118, 119, 124-126,
   128, 146, 169, 172, 175, 190, 193, 197,
   201, 202

Middle Ages   34-35, 38, 165, 167, 186

militarism   61

Mitanni   132-134, 136, 205

Mithra   157

Moenjo-daro   77, 105

Mohammed   142, 178, 183, 188-191

money   23, 66, 142, 152, 195

Mongolian   89, 143, 147, 197

morals   35, 57, 59, 88, 110, 120, 123, 139-
   140, 145-146, 150, 164, 168, 172, 189

Moscow   23, 162

Moses   100, 137, 141, 177-178, 184, 189

Mossad   22, 205

Mosul   132

Musasir   139

mythological approach   32-33

mythology   32-33, 39, 52, 155-156, 163, 176

Nabis   142

Nairians   137

nation-state   21, 23-25, 29-30, 41, 59-60,
    64, 68, 81, 85, 93, 120-121, 148

national liberation movements   43, 63, 118

national question, the   24

nationalism   24, 28, 64, 74, 78, 120

Native American   144, 147

NATO   25

Neolithic   15-18, 24, 33, 72-73, 78-79, 81,
    84-85, 87-88, 97, 99-100, 102, 109-110,
    118, 121, 124, 126, 128, 130, 133, 135,
    139, 144, 145, 146-148, 150, 152-153,
    157-160, 165, 166-171, 176, 186-188,
    192-193, 195, 197, 202, 203, 204

Netherlands, the   51, 128

Nietzsche   43, 60, 91, 200

Nile   130, 135-136, 170

Nimrod   141, 177, 190

Nineveh   132

Nippur Lament   131

Nordics   148

Nur mountains   92, 203

objective approach   36 37

Odoacer, King   162

Odyssey   164, 206

Oghuz tribes   143

Orientalism   63-65

Osiris   136

Ottoman Empire   142-143

Palestine   141

Palmyra   161, 163

Paris Commune, the   112, 118

Parthians   14, 157, 160

patriarchy   108

Paul, Saint   41

Pax Romana   161, 163

pederasty   179-181

Pençav   140

Pergamum   153, 157, 163

Persepolis   139-140, 205

Persia   14, 75, 79, 131, 136, 138-142, 146,
    149-153, 156-157, 159, 161-162, 177-
    178, 183, 195, 199, 204-205

Pharaoh   57, 75-76, 103, 135, 137, 141,
    176-177, 184, 190

Pharisees   142

Phoenicians   76, 151, 155, 159

Phrygians   152

PKK (Kurdistan Workers' Party)   8, 22,
    24-25, 27, 31

plant kingdom   48-50

Plato   35, 41, 154, 196

political Islam   64, 191

Polytheism   119

positivism   13, 58-59, 62-63, 66, 80, 84, 86,
    90, 94-96, 99, 111

prophets   121, 139, 142, 176-178, 193, 195

Ptolemy   157

PUK (Patriotic Union of Kurdistan)   22

Pythagoras   151-152, 206

quantum physics   45

rabbi   142, 205
rajah   145-147, 183
Ramses II   135-136
rationality   57, 61
real socialism   117
Red Sea   133, 158
Reformation   35, 65, 80, 194
regime of truth   28, 32-69
religion   13, 15, 17, 39, 52, 56-57, 59, 64,
    66, 72-73, 75, 81-83, 85, 87-88, 95, 98-
    100, 103, 111-112, 118-125, 136-137,
    140, 142, 146, 150, 154, 158, 162, 168,
    172, 185-186, 189, 194-197, 207
religious method   32, 34-35
Renaissance   35, 65, 80, 122, 150
republicanism   123
resistance   8, 18, 24, 29, 31, 41, 43, 67, 92,
    112, 131-132, 138, 141-142, 156, 165-
    166, 175-178, 181, 183-184, 196, 201
revolutionary   8, 11-13, 15-17, 67, 72, 117,
    155, 158, 190, 192
Rome   23, 123, 136, 143, 155, 158-167,
    178-181

Sadducees   142
Samuel   141
Sarduri   137
Saul   141
scientific method   33, 35-38, 43, 94, 201
scientific socialism   37-38, 43, 62

scientism   28, 58-59, 90, 200
Scythians   138, 140, 142-143, 148, 161, 178
Seleucid empire   157
self-defence   49
Semitic   15, 72, 75-76, 82, 89, 106, 119,
    136, 141, 148, 159, 178, 202
Shapur I   161
slavery   15, 34, 55, 67-68. 91, 102, 182,
    191, 193
social science   11-12, 82, 200
socialism   37-38, 43, 62, 67, 74, 94, 103,
    113, 117-118, 144, 195
sociology   12, 29, 55, 56, 60, 62, 67, 74, 83,
    86-89, 95, 111, 114, 125, 129, 166, 167,
    171, 195-196, 206
Sociology of Freedom   12, 29, 86-89, 11,
    114, 125, 129, 166, 171, 195-196, 206
Socrates   116, 145, 153, 178, 180, 183, 206
Solomon   141
Solon   131, 151
Sparta   156
Spartacus   112
structural crisis   62, 67
subject-object distinction   67
Sudan   136, 148
Sufism   42, 195
Sumer   16, 38, 72, 74-77, 80-81, 89, 96-
    110, 113, 119, 121-124, 129-146, 149,
    152, 155, 157, 166, 176-177, 183, 186,
    191, 196, 203, 206
Suruç   141-142
Syria   21-23, 133, 137, 157, 161, 185, 199

Taoism   145

Index

Taurus   71, 90, 105, 131-132, 135, 161, 183, 187, 203, 205

technology   66, 68, 111, 201, 203

Telipinus   134

Tell Halaf   76-77, 96-97, 102, 124,

Teshup   137

Thales   151-152

Thebes   135-136

Thutmosis, I   133

Thutmosis, III   133

Tiamat   131

Tigris river   15, 74, 97, 105-106, 129-133, 162, 170

Titriş   133, 204

totalitarian   67

Troy   134, 151, 159, 205, 206

truth   28, 32-69, 117-118, 201

Turkey   7-9, 21-29, 142, 199, 206

Turkmenistan   77, 130

Tushpa   137, 139

Ubaid   106

übermensch   50

Ummah   64, 190, 207

unemployment   37, 67, 98

universe   33, 38, 44-51, 54. 56-57, 83, 86, 118, 128, 140, 145, 200

Ur   105, 108, 131, 144, 170

Ur-Nammu, Code of   123

Urartu   132, 137-140, 149-150, 152, 162, 204

Urfa   75, 133, 141-142, 163, 206

Uruk   103, 105-106, 108, 130, 144, 147, 150-151, 155, 160, 165

USA   21-24, 26-27, 30, 130, 148

USSR   22, 27, 57, 62

utopia   23, 31, 68, 172, 177, 191, 193-194, 196

Van   137, 205

Veda   145

Wallerstein, Immanuel   60-62, 117, 194, 206

Waset   135

Washukanni   133, 205

Weber, Max   61-62, 103, 194

western Europe   35, 65, 79, 124, 202

wisdom   18, 30, 41-42, 62, 66, 116, 121

world system   34, 50, 61, 118, 148, 206

World Word II   21

Yahweh   141

Zagros mountains   14, 71, 75, 90, 92, 105, 131-132, 135, 137-138, 183, 187

Zenobia   161

Zeugma   162

Zeytinlibahçe   133, 204

Ziggurat   19, 97-105, 113, 134, 136, 174, 183, 185

Zoroaster   35, 139, 145, 178, 183, 206

Zoroastrianism   35

CPSIA information can be obtained
at www.ICGtesting.com
Printed in the USA
BVHW042114240920
589595BV00005B/11/J

9 788293 0643